Facts About the Chinchilla

By Lisa Strattin

© 2019 Lisa Strattin

Revised 2022 © Lisa Strattin

FREE BOOK

FREE FOR ALL SUBSCRIBERS

LisaStrattin.com/Subscribe-Here

BOX SET

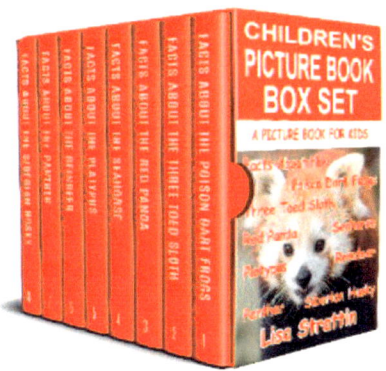

- **FACTS ABOUT THE POISON DART FROGS**
- **FACTS ABOUT THE THREE TOED SLOTH**
  - **FACTS ABOUT THE RED PANDA**
  - **FACTS ABOUT THE SEAHORSE**
  - **FACTS ABOUT THE PLATYPUS**
  - **FACTS ABOUT THE REINDEER**
  - **FACTS ABOUT THE PANTHER**
- **FACTS ABOUT THE SIBERIAN HUSKY**

LisaStrattin.com/BookBundle

Facts for Kids Picture Books by Lisa Strattin

Little Blue Penguin, Vol 92

Chipmunk, Vol 5

Frilled Lizard, Vol 39

Blue and Gold Macaw, Vol 13

Poison Dart Frogs, Vol 50

Blue Tarantula, Vol 115

African Elephants, Vol 8

Amur Leopard, Vol 89

Sabre Tooth Tiger, Vol 167

Baboon, Vol 174

Sign Up for New Release Emails Here

LisaStrattin.com/subscribe-here

All rights reserved. No part of this book may be reproduced by any means whatsoever without the written permission from the author, except brief portions quoted for purpose of review.

All information in this book has been carefully researched and checked for factual accuracy. However, the author and publisher makes no warranty, express or implied, that the information contained herein is appropriate for every individual, situation or purpose and assume no responsibility for errors or omissions. The reader assumes the risk and full responsibility for all actions, and the author will not be held responsible for any loss or damage, whether consequential, incidental, special or otherwise, that may result from the information presented in this book.

All images are free for use or purchased from stock photo sites or royalty free for commercial use.

Some coloring pages might be of the general species due to lack of available images.

I have relied on my own observations as well as many different sources for this book and I have done my best to check facts and give credit where it is due. In the event that any material is used without proper permission, please contact me so that the oversight can be corrected.

⋆⋆COVER IMAGE⋆⋆

https://www.flickr.com/photos/filipe-ramos/21692370861/

⋆⋆ADDITIONAL IMAGES⋆⋆

https://www.flickr.com/photos/tux0racer/8666546446/

https://www.flickr.com/photos/ilya_ktsn/7627361238/

https://www.flickr.com/photos/ilya_ktsn/6940300314/

https://www.flickr.com/photos/karmakitten/2251117206/

https://www.flickr.com/photos/qiv/9295937196/

https://www.flickr.com/photos/sakucae/3869401950/

https://www.flickr.com/photos/56832361@N00/358764695/

https://www.flickr.com/photos/filipe-ramos/21692370861/

https://www.flickr.com/photos/15016964@N02/5921986378/

https://www.flickr.com/photos/cuboulderalumni/31900076863/

Contents

INTRODUCTION 9

CHARACTERISTICS 11

APPEARANCE.. 13

LIFE STAGES... 15

LIFE SPAN.. 17

SIZE 19

HABITAT 21

DIET 23

ENEMIES.. 25

SUITABILITY AS PETS 27

INTRODUCTION

Chinchillas are medium-sized rodents native to the Andes mountains in South America. Chinchillas are named after the tribe that hunted the chinchillas for their dense fur, the Chinchas.

A chinchilla is a fairly rare animal in its natural habitat today since they were hunted so much in years gone by.

CHARACTERISTICS

It is estimated that chinchillas appeared on earth about 41 million years ago. The chinchilla's ancestors were some of the very first rodents (animals like rats and mice) to infest South America.

Chinchilla fur became popular in the 1700s, and the animals were hunted nearly to extinction by 1900. About that time, Argentina, Bolivia, Chile, and Peru banned the hunting of wild chinchillas in an effort to protect them.

They are solitary animals, living alone until they search for a mate during breeding season. Although they might stay together in large numbers in wild habitats, they are not really social with one another.

APPEARANCE

Chinchillas are related to guinea pigs and porcupines. With short forelimbs and long, muscular hind legs, they resemble rabbits, however their ears are much shorter and rounder.

They have large, black eyes and bushy tails. They have four toes on each foot, and the thin claws on each toe are surrounded by stiff bristles.

Chinchilla fur was originally mottled yellowish gray in the wild. Through selective breeding, other colors have become common, including silver, yellow-gray, bluish-gray, white, beige, and black. Each hair ends in a black tip, no matter what color the chinchillas are!

LIFE STAGES

Chinchillas are mammals, so their babies are born live, as opposed to in an egg, like birds. Once a female chinchilla becomes pregnant, she will carry her babies for about 111 days before giving birth. Females have babies twice a year.

Each time the female gives birth, she will have one to six babies. These groups of babies are called litters. Individual babies are called *kits*.

Newborn kits are born with hair and with their eyes open. They weigh only 1.2 ounces (35 grams) at birth. The babies nurse for six to eight weeks, and when they're about 8 months old, the babies are ready to have offspring of their own. So, they seem to have only two life stages, that of a kit and then an adult.

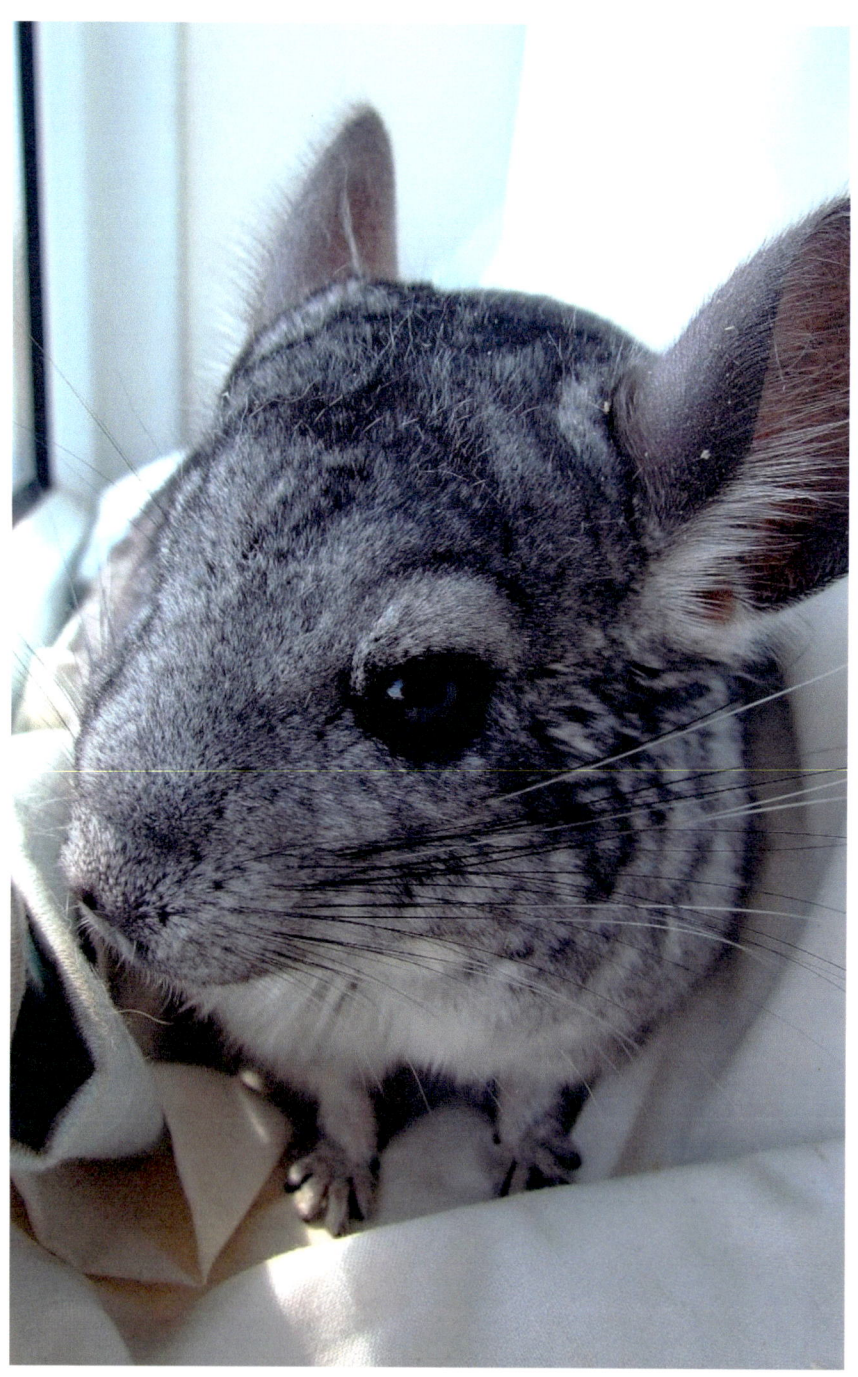

LIFE SPAN

Generally, chinchillas live eight to 10 years, though some have been known to live as long as 20 years.

SIZE

An adult chinchilla grows to be from 10 to 14 inches long, with the tail adding up to another 6 inches to their overall length and weighs just around 1 to 2 pounds.

HABITAT

Chinchillas, historically, preferred to live in dry and mountainous regions, however, they are endangered and there have not been many of them found living in the wild in recent years. Though, since these areas can be difficult to get to, it is unknown if there are populations of them in the wild that we have not identified.

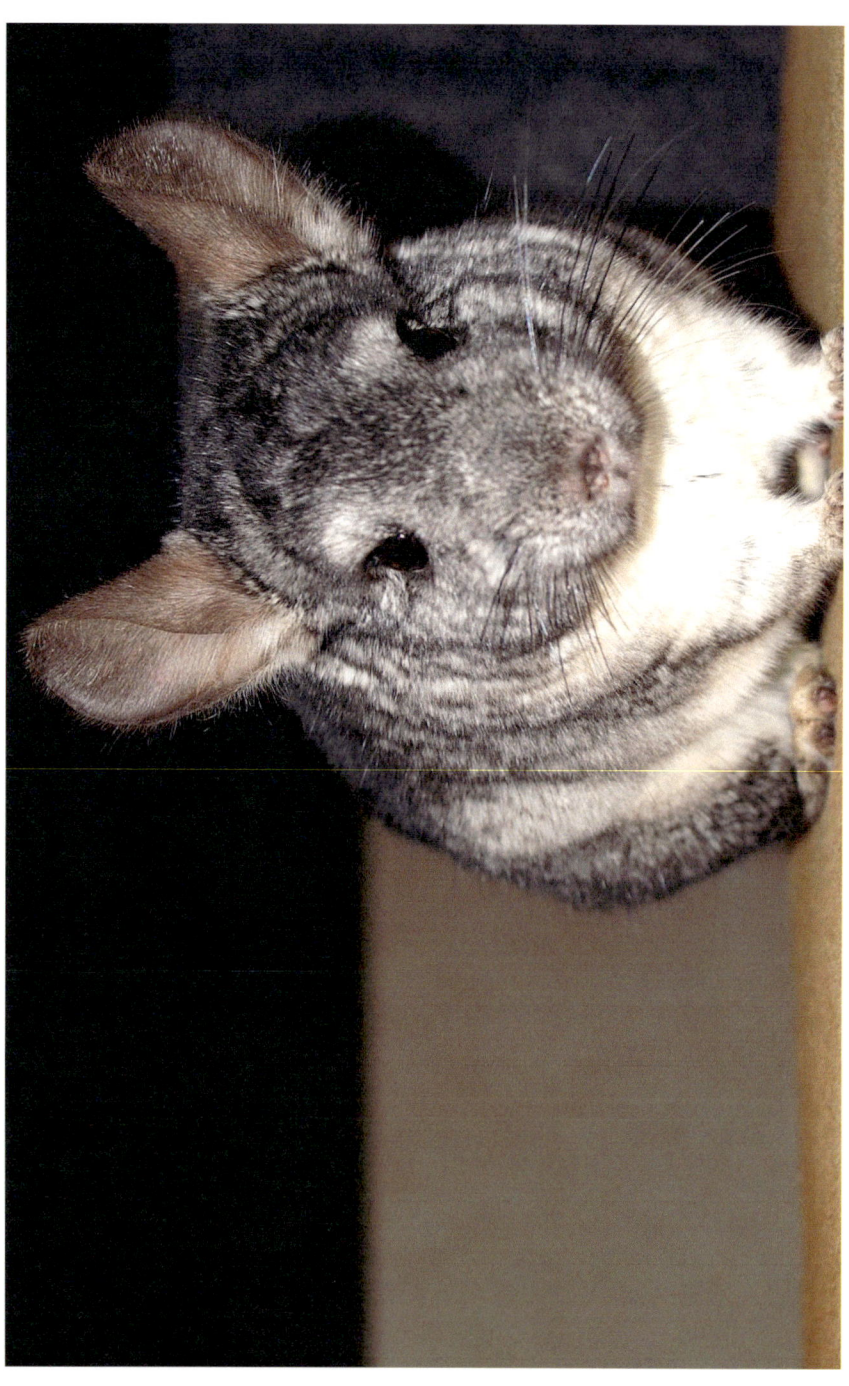

DIET

Chinchillas feed on nuts, seeds, and berries. They are reportedly classified as an herbivore, but they have been known to eat insects and bird eggs when they can find them.

ENEMIES

Owls, foxes, and cougars will all attack and kill the chinchillas for food. These are the animals most known in their native areas. However, it can be assumed that most meat-eating animals, and even birds of prey, will attack them since chinchillas are so small.

They can defend themselves by spraying urine and releasing their fur, like a porcupine releases quills, when they are under attack.

SUITABILITY AS PETS

In more recent years people have kept chinchillas as pets. Chinchilla domestication occurred in the 1920s when an engineer in Chile took a group of chinchillas to California. Since then, chinchillas have been bred as pets and sold all around the world.

When handling chinchillas, it is important to not pick them up from underneath like a rat or hamster, because they have a feature called "floating ribs." Their ribs are not fully attached to their spine and if pressure is applied upwards, the ribs could puncture vital organs and kill the chinchilla.

Pet chinchillas require frequent attention as well as a supply of dust for "dust baths." A good quality pet food is available in many pet stores.

If you want to have a pet chinchilla, you should be sure to read up on the things you must do to help them stay healthy and happy as your pet.

COLOR ME

COLOR ME

COLOR ME

COLOR ME

COLOR ME

COLOR ME

COLOR ME

COLOR ME

COLOR ME

COLOR ME

Please leave me a review here:

LisaStrattin.com/Review-Vol-185

For more Kindle Downloads Visit Lisa Strattin Author Page on Amazon Author Central

amazon.com/author/lisastrattin

To see upcoming titles, visit my website at LisaStrattin.com– most books available on Kindle!

LisaStrattin.com

FREE BOOK

FOR ALL SUBSCRIBERS – SIGN UP NOW

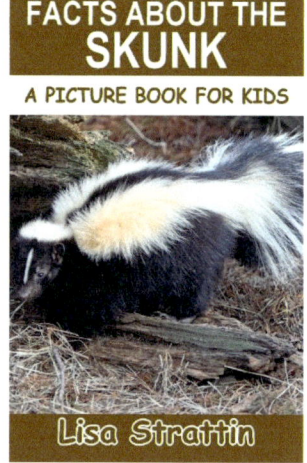

LisaStrattin.com/Subscribe-Here

LisaStrattin.com/Facebook

LisaStrattin.com/Youtube

Made in United States
Cleveland, OH
11 February 2025

14254629R00026

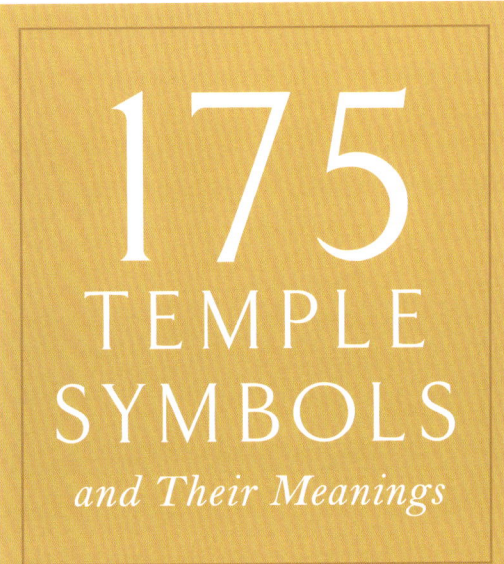

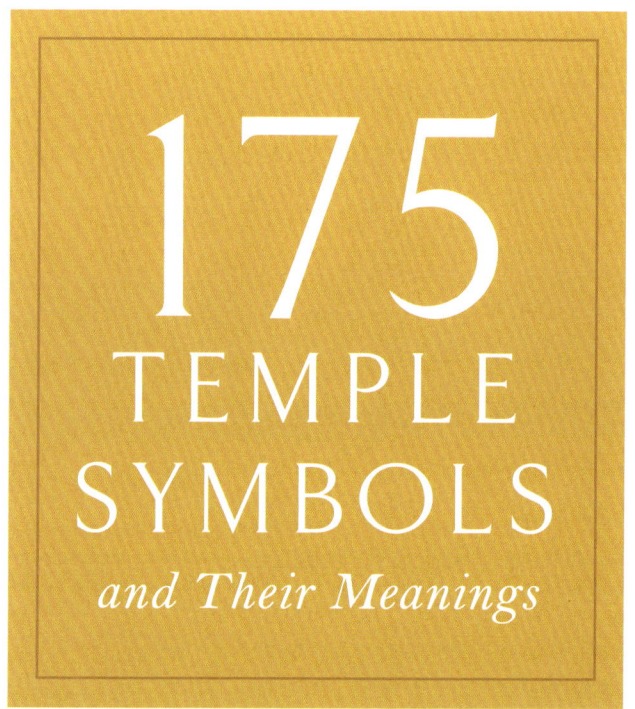

175 TEMPLE SYMBOLS
and Their Meanings

DONALD W. PARRY

DESERET BOOK

Salt Lake City, Utah

© 2020 Donald W. Parry

All rights reserved. No part of this book may be reproduced in any form or by any means without permission in writing from the publisher, Deseret Book Company, at permissions@deseretbook.com or PO Box 30178, Salt Lake City, Utah 84130. This work is not an official publication of The Church of Jesus Christ of Latter-day Saints. The views expressed herein are the responsibility of the author and do not necessarily represent the position of the Church or of Deseret Book Company.

DESERET BOOK is a registered trademark of Deseret Book Company.

Visit us at deseretbook.com

Library of Congress Cataloging-in-Publication Data

Names: Parry, Donald W., author.
Title: 175 temple symbols and their meanings / Donald W. Parry.
Other titles: One hundred seventy-five temple symbols and their meanings
Description: Salt Lake City : Deseret Book, [2020] | Includes bibliographical references and index. | Summary: "An explanation of 175 symbols used in or on the temples of The Church of Jesus Christ of Latter-day Saints by noted Latter-day Saint author Donald W. Parry"—Provided by publisher.
Identifiers: LCCN 2020005926 | ISBN 9781629727523 (hardback)
Subjects: LCSH: Church of Jesus Christ of Latter-day Saints—Doctrines. | Mormon temples. | Christian art and symbolism. | Mormon Church—Doctrines.
Classification: LCC BX8643.T4 P37 2020 | DDC 246/.9589332—dc23
LC record available at https://lccn.loc.gov/2020005926

Printed in China through Four Colour Print Group, Louisville, Kentucky

10 9 8 7 6 5 4 3 2 1

CONTENTS

Introduction | 1

Symbols of the Temple, Ancient and Modern | 31

Adam and Eve | 33

Alpha and Omega | 33

Altars | 34

Ancient Order of Things (Antiquity of Temple Ordinances) | 37

Angelic Weather Vane | 39

Angels, Communication with | 39

Animals, Female (Sacrificial Offerings) | 40

Anointing (with Olive Oil) | 42

Apron | 44

Architectural Features, Various Temples | 45

Architectural Safeguards | 53

Ark of the Covenant | 56

Ascension | 58

Atonement Money and Redemption Money | 59

Atonement of Jesus Christ, Temple Focuses on | 60

Baptism for the Dead | 62

Baptismal Font | 63

Beehives | 64

Bells of Gold | 64

Big Dipper (Ursa Major) | 65

Blemishes, Priests and High Priests with | 67

Blemishes, Sacrificial Animals with | 68

Blood, Meaning of | 68

Bodily Conditions and the Temple | 70

Cardinal Directions | 71

Celestial Bodies (Sun, Moon, Stars, etc.) Depicted on Temples | 73

Celestial Room, God's Living Room | 75

Center Place, Temple as the | 75

Center of the Map, the Temple | 78

Cherubim (Guardians of Sacred Space) | 80

Circle | 83

Clouds and Cloudstones | 84

Colors—Blue, Gold, Silver, Scarlet, Crimson, Red, White | 86

Cornerstones | 91

Covenants, Signs, and Tokens | 92

Creation Narrative in the Temple | 94

Day of Atonement | 97

Dedication of the Temple | 98

Dome | 99

Drama, Ritual | 100

Ear, Thumb, and Toe | 101

Earthstones | 102

Endowment/Endowed with Power | 102

Endowment House | 105

Eve, Life, and Life-Giver | 106

Eye, All-Seeing | 111

Fig Leaves | 111

Fire/Pillar of Fire | 112

Firstborn, Male | 113

Firstfruits | 113

Flaying the Burnt Offering | 114

Flowers | 115

Fortress, Temple as a | 117

Foundation, Temple | 118

Garden of Eden, Temple Symbolism in | 118

Garments | 121

Gate of Heaven | 123

Gate, the Tabernacle | 124

Gathering of Israel | 125

Geometry, Sacred | 126

Gestures of Approach | 127

Gethsemane, Temple Symbolism in | 130

Gradations of Holiness (Less Holy to Most Holy) | 132

Guards, Temple (Sentinels and Angels) | 136

Hands and Covenants | 138

Hand, Filling the Priest's | 140

Hand, Raised in Oath | 141

Hands, Clasped | 142

Hands, Laying on of | 144

Hands, Laying on of, on Sacrificial Animals | 145

Hands—Prayer with "Uplifted Hands" | 146

Hannah, Anna, and Mary | 147

Heifer, Red | 150

High Priest, Death of, and the Cities of Refuge | 150

Holiness to the Lord | 152

Holy of Holies | 152

Horns of the Two Altars (Sacrifice and Incense) | 155

Hosanna Shout | 157

House of Life, the Temple Is a | 158

House of Prayer | 158

House of the Lord | 160

Hyssop | 160

Incense at the Golden Altar | 161

Jacob's Ladder ("Flight of Steps") | 162

Jesus Christ–Focused, Temple Is | 162

Jesus Christ, Symbols of, in the Tabernacle of Moses | 162

Joseph Smith: Restorer of the Ancient Temple | 163

Keys | 166

Kings, Queens, Coronation, and Enthronement | 167

Lampstand, Golden (Menorah or Candlestick) | 169

Laver of Brass | 170

Law of Moses | 171

Leper | 172

Levites | 173

Light, Quintessential place of | 175

Linen | 177

Mercy Seat (Throne of Atonement) | 177

Mirrors | 178

Moonstones | 179

Moroni, Angel | 180

Mountain as "Temple" and Temple as "Mountain" | 182

Mount of Transfiguration | 184

Mount Sinai—Temple Symbolism | 185

Music—Praising the Lord in His Temple | 187

Names | 187

Olive Oil | 189

Ordinances, Understanding | 190

Oval | 193

Oxen, Twelve | 194

Pathway of Progression | 195

Passover | 196

Pillars of Temples | 198

Plagues, and the Atonement | 198

Pomegranate | 199

Prayer Circle (Ancient and Modern) | 200

Prayer, Directional (Praying toward the Temple) | 201

Prayer Roll | 202

Priestesses | 203

Priests and High Priests | 206

Prison-Temple | 207

Pulpits | 207

Recommend, Temple | 208

Refuge, Temple Is a Place of | 210

Revelation in the Temple | 211

Ritual (Sacred Ceremony) | 213

Sacred Triangle | 214

Sacrifices—Symbols of Jesus's Atoning Sacrifice | 215

Sacrifices under the Law of Moses—Six Acts | 216

Sacrificial Meals, Partaking of | 217

Scapegoat | 218

Sea, Molten (Bronze) | 218

Sealing Ordinance | 219

Seeing the Lord in the Temple | 220

Seven Promises "to Him That Overcometh" | 221

Shewbread (Bread of God's Presence) | 222

Shoes, Removing | 224

Sins, Intentional and Unintentional, and the Atonement | 224

Solemn Assembly | 225

Spires and Steeples | 226

Squares and the Squared Circle | 227

Stairs/Staircases | 228

Stars/Starstones | 228

Sunstones/Sun Images | 230

Symbols, Diverse | 231

Tabernacle (Portable Temple), Symbolism of | 232

Temple, Design of, Revealed by God | 233

Temple in Heaven | 235

Temples, Categories of | 237

"Temples Everywhere" | 238

Temples, Future | 239

Temples, God's People Always Commanded to Build | 240

Temple Texts—Representative Examples | 242

Three Times a Year | 246

Throne | 247

Towers | 248

Trumpets and Trumpet Stones | 250

University of the Lord | 250

Veil of the Temple | 250

Vessels | 253

Vestments, Sacred | 254

Vestments, Sacred, Anticipate the Resurrection | 256

Vestments, Sacred, Point to Jesus Christ and His Atonement | 257

Vestments, Sacred, Symbolism of | 260

Vestments, Sacred, Worn by God, Angels, and Redeemed Souls | 265

Vicarious Work for the Dead | 266

Violating Sacred Space | 269

Washing with Water, for Sacrificial Animals | 270

Washing with Water | 271

Water | 273

Women and the Ancient Temple | 274

Women Then, Women Now | 275

Bibliography | 279

Index | 295

Image Credits | 309

ACKNOWLEDGMENTS

I extend appreciation to many individuals who have contributed in a variety of ways to this volume. Lisa Roper, Deseret Book product director, has exerted masterful skills as she has helped me advance the book through its various stages. I am extremely grateful to Tracy Keck, editor at Deseret Book, for her significant skills and expertise; her proficient work has greatly improved the manuscript! Four individuals—Richard O. Cowan, Debra Theobald McClendon, Rebecca Poulter, and Zachery Poulter—have provided me with several remarkable insights and comments! Professor Richard O. Cowan is a well-known Latter-day Saint scholar who specializes in temple studies. I thank the anonymous individuals who reviewed the manuscript to determine that the content of this volume was appropriately presented, owing to the extremely sensitive and sacred nature of the temple. I also appreciate the efforts of BYU's editorial team: Suzy Bills, director, and Scarlett Lindsay, managing editor. I am also grateful to my student researchers Michael A. Goodman and Bethany Davis for source checking the hundreds of footnotes and scriptural passages.

INTRODUCTION

Regarding the symbolism of the temples of The Church of Jesus Christ of Latter-day Saints, President Russell M. Nelson taught us that "each temple is a house of learning. There we are taught in the Master's way. His way differs from modes of others. *His way is ancient and rich with symbolism. We can learn much by pondering the reality for which each symbol stands.* Teachings of the temple are beautifully simple and simply beautiful. They are understood by the humble, yet they can excite the intellect of the brightest minds."[1]

This volume constitutes an introduction to the temple and its symbols; it is no more and no less than a beginner's guide toward understanding various components associated with the temple. As a beginner's guide, the volume is not designed to provide advanced understanding of the temple and its symbols. Those who want advanced understanding must attend the temple often and receive instruction from the Holy Ghost. *The temple itself, together with divine instruction from the Holy Ghost, encompasses the quintessential and ultimate learning experience regarding the temple.*

This volume sets forth 175 entries, which provide notes or explanations of various symbols and insights regarding ancient and modern temples. Many of these insights constitute my own ideas and should *not* be regarded as doctrine or teachings of The Church of Jesus Christ of

---
1. Nelson, "Personal Preparation for Temple Blessings," 33; emphasis added.

Latter-day Saints. Stated differently, many of the proposed symbols in this book are simply that: proposals, suggestions, or items that may be considered. Listed in alphabetical order, the entries deal with a broad range of categories—rituals and ordinances, gestures of approach, sacred vestments, sacrificial offerings, geometric symbols, colors, heavenly bodies (sun, moon, stars), prayer and revelation, sacred names, furnishings and appurtenances, animals, religious festivals, and sacred spaces. When appropriate, I have identified symbols and concepts that deal with Jesus Christ and His atoning sacrifice. In point of fact, Jesus Christ is prominent throughout the temple—ancient and modern—and a significant portion of the 175 entries pertain to Him.

This book is topical but not encyclopedic in nature. It is not at all comprehensive and does not deal with every possible topic of the temple. A comprehensive work on the temple would fill multiple volumes. One may say, borrowing a line from Words of Mormon 1:5, I did not "write the hundredth part of the things" of the temple. Rather, by careful selection and choice, the book is at best representative, and it therefore contains typical examples of various aspects and components of the temple. And each of the 175 entries is briefly presented, to put it mildly; in fact, many of the entries provide no more than a glimpse of what could be written about that particular topic.

Importantly, restraint and caution should always be used when referring to temples and sacred topics. For this reason, I have not dealt with topics that are inappropriate to discuss outside of the temple; in fact, I have erred on the side of caution as I deal with the topics in this volume. I hold strictly to Elder David A. Bednar's two guidelines regarding what we may say regarding temples of The Church of Jesus Christ of Latter-day Saints. Guideline #1: "We should not disclose or describe the special symbols associated with the covenants we receive in sacred temple ceremonies. Neither should we discuss the holy information that we specifically promise in the temple not to reveal." And Guideline #2: "We may discuss the basic purposes of and the doctrine and principles associated with temple ordinances and covenants."[1]

Symbols—God's "Favorite Way of Teaching"

It is a certainty that symbols penetrate the whole of the temple and its ordinances. In point of fact, "God teaches with symbols," wrote Elder Orson F. Whitney. "It is his favorite method of teaching."[2] Symbols embrace the following temple components (belonging to ancient and/or modern temples): verbal-ceremonial communications, sacred vestments, ceremonial movements and gestures, sacred architecture, covenant making, the actual words of the covenants, various material items (anointing oil, ablutionary water, blood, shewbread, sacrificial animals, incense, and more), officiants (having proper authority), and the ordinances themselves.

By way of example, a number of symbols are attached to the ordinance of baptism. These include some of the baptismal words that are uttered by the baptizer, a ceremonial gesture (right arm to the square), two ceremonial movements (the acts of immersion and coming forth out of the waters—both acts involve the baptizer and the baptismal candidate), the mass of water in the font, white clothing, and the baptismal font itself.

Others have instructed us concerning the centrality of symbols in the setting of the temple. For example, President Boyd K. Packer stated, "Much of the teaching relating to the deeper spiritual things in the Church, particularly in the temple, is symbolic."[3] On another occasion he wrote, "Before going to the temple for the first time, or even after many times, it may help you to realize that the teaching of the temples is done in symbolic fashion. . . . If you will go to the temple and remember that the teaching is symbolic you will never go in the proper spirit without coming away with your vision extended, feeling a little more exalted, with your

---

1. Bednar, "Prepared to Obtain Every Needful Thing," 103.
2. Whitney, "Latter-day Saint Ideals and Institutions," 861.
3. Packer, *The Holy Temple,* 82.

knowledge increased as to things that are spiritual. The teaching plan is superb. It is inspired."[1]

Every Stone Is a Sermon

Regarding the Salt Lake Temple, J. Golden Kimball expressed, "Every stone in it is a sermon to me. It tells of suffering, it tells of sacrifice, it preaches—every rock in it, preaches a discourse. When it was dedicated, it seemed to me that it was the greatest sermon that has ever been preached since the Sermon on the Mount. . . . Every window, every steeple, everything about the Temple speaks of the things of God, and gives evidence of the faith of the people who built it."[2] Elder Kimball's statement regarding the Salt Lake Temple may be applied to each and every temple of the Lord—every stone, every glass window, and every steeple testifies of Jesus Christ's divinity, the power of His Atonement, and His redemptive work among the nations in the present era, in previous generations, and forever.

The Temple Provides a Lifetime of Learning

Elder Richard C. Scott observed that "the temple ordinances are so imbued with symbolic meaning as to provide a lifetime of productive contemplation and learning."[3] This statement reminds us of President David O. McKay's words to President Boyd K. Packer. After completing an endowment session, President McKay remarked, "I think I am beginning to understand it."[4] This is a remarkable statement by a prophet—even after decades of faithful temple attendance, he was still gaining knowledge and understanding of the temple and its ordinances.

---

1. Packer, *The Holy Temple*, 38, 41.
2. Kimball, in Conference Report, April 1915, 79.
3. Scott, "Receive the Temple Blessings," 27.
4. Woodger, "Recollections of David O. McKay's Educational Practices," 26.

Why Symbols? "To Teach Profound Truths"

Inasmuch as symbols have a prominent standing in both ancient and modern temples and symbols penetrate the whole of the temple and its ordinances, the questions may be asked, "Why are symbols so prominent, and why are they used?" President Russell M. Nelson provides the answer: "Anciently, symbols were used to teach profound truths, and this method of instruction is used in the temple today. *It is necessary, therefore, that we ponder the symbols presented in the temple and see the mighty realities for which each symbol stands.*"[5]

Why symbols? They are "used to teach profound truths," explains President Nelson. As a matter of fact, symbols constitute quintessential teaching devices—that is precisely why Jesus Christ employed symbols in His teachings, the prophets put forth symbols in their writings, and symbols are such a large part of each and all of the ordinances, including those belonging to the temple. How are symbols teaching devices? "Symbols are the most articulate of all languages. Indeed, symbols are the universal tongue. . . . Symbols bring color and strength to language, while deepening and enriching our understandings. Symbols enable us to give conceptual form to ideas and emotions that may otherwise defy the power of words. They take us beyond words and grant us eloquence in the expression of feelings. Symbolic language conceals certain doctrinal truths from the wicked and thereby protects sacred things from possible ridicule. At the same time, symbols reveal truth to the spiritually alert."[6]

How Can We Comprehend the Meaning of the Temple and Its Symbols?

Joseph Smith's prayer at the Kirtland Temple dedication sums up the idea of the temple as a place of learning: "That all those who shall worship

---

5. Nelson, "Prepare for Blessings of the Temple," 20; emphasis added.
6. McConkie and Parry, *Guide to Scriptural Symbols*, 1.

in this house . . . may seek learning *even by study, and also by faith*" (D&C 109:14; emphasis added). Hugh Nibley, a well-known temple scholar, cites a verse from the same dedicatory prayer (D&C 109:7) and then states, "They [men and women] are to bring their brains with them [to the temple]. . . . The temple is to be a place of study and learning, a school of real mental discipline. . . . [The temple] is a house of learning. Is this a surprise? If we are supposed to be studying and teaching diligently, thinking deeply, we must have something to think about, as well as something to show for our mental effort. That is called learning."[1]

There are several keys that assist us in gaining a better comprehension of the temple.

(1) The greatest and most powerful teacher is the Holy Ghost. As a member of the Godhead, He comprehends all things, including all truths pertaining to the house of the Lord. If we properly and appropriately seek for knowledge regarding God's temple—especially as we *study, pray,* and *fast*—the Holy Ghost will reveal truths to us, line upon line, as we are prepared to receive them. Inasmuch as each of us is "natural," we cannot comprehend the things of God; rather the things of God are "spiritually discerned" by the power of the Holy Ghost. As Paul explained, "The natural man receiveth not the things of the Spirit of God: for they are foolishness unto him: neither can he know them, because they are spiritually discerned" (1 Cor. 2:13–14).

(2) Read the words of the prophets and apostles. Beyond the power of the Holy Ghost, the best and chief sources for understanding the temple are the scriptures and our living prophets and apostles. Both ancient and modern prophets and apostles have revealed much about the temple. Elder David A. Bednar informs us, "Across the generations, from the Prophet Joseph Smith to President Russell M. Nelson, the doctrinal purposes of temple ordinances and covenants have been *taught extensively* by Church

---

1. Nibley, "A House of Glory," 31–33.

leaders. A rich reservoir of resources exists in print, audio, video, and other formats to help us learn about initiatory ordinances, endowments, marriages, and other sealing ordinances."[2] Why has so much been revealed regarding the temple? The Lord, through His prophets, desires for us to seek and to obtain great and significant knowledge about the temple and its ordinances.

President Russell M. Nelson emphasized the importance of scriptural study to better understand the temple: "Spiritual preparation is enhanced by study. I like to recommend that members going to the temple for the first time read short explanatory paragraphs in the Bible Dictionary, listed under seven topics: 'Anoint,' 'Atonement,' 'Christ,' 'Covenant,' 'Fall of Adam,' 'Sacrifices,' and 'Temple.' Doing so will provide a firm foundation.

"One may also read in the Old Testament and the books of Moses and Abraham in the Pearl of Great Price. Such a review of ancient scripture is even more enlightening *after* one is familiar with the temple endowment. Those books underscore the antiquity of temple work."[3]

Here are two brief examples of how our prophets have provided straightforward understandings of the temple. Doctrine and Covenants 128:13 explains the symbolism of the baptismal font: "The baptismal font was instituted as a similitude of the grave." And a second example: Elder Jeffrey R. Holland teaches regarding the symbolism of the temple priests; each righteous priest was no less than "a type and shadow of Christ."[4] President Russell M. Nelson has directed us to study the scriptures in order to come to a better understanding of the temple. This present volume cites literally hundreds of scriptures and writings from our modern prophets and apostles.

The study of scriptural symbols, when properly conducted, provides provable and verifiable results. Comprehending symbols is not a haphazard

---

2. Bednar, "Prepared to Obtain Every Needful Thing," 103; emphasis added.
3. Nelson, "Personal Preparation for Temple Blessings," 33–34.
4. Holland, *Christ and the New Covenant*, 116.

procedure; therefore, this book uses the scriptures and the teachings of God's prophets to interpret numerous symbols and vital understandings of the temple and its meaning. God did not provide us with magnificent temples and significant ordinances only for us to dwell in the dark, without giving us comprehension! All worthy women and men can thus enter the Lord's house and learn the meaning of sacred symbols.

(3) "My ways are higher than your ways," saith the Lord. If we have difficulty comprehending the temple, perhaps we should remember that God's "thoughts" and "ways" are not like ours. Isaiah 55:8–9 states, "For my thoughts are not your thoughts, neither are your ways my ways, saith the Lord. For as the heavens are higher than the earth, so are my ways higher than your ways, and my thoughts than your thoughts." God knows all and comprehends all things; He knows what is best for us and He comprehends the optimal way to instruct us concerning sacred things. Many of us cannot even understand ourselves or our immediate environment, let alone the sacred things of God, such as His temple. So we must rely on God and His way of teaching.

(4) "Lean not unto thine own understanding." With regard to the temple and its sacred symbols (and with all things), we must heed the counsel to "trust in the Lord with all thine heart; and *lean not unto thine own understanding*" (Prov. 3:5; emphasis added). Many of us attempt to make sense of the temple by leaning on our own understanding; this approach fails us because our understanding is minuscule, at best.

We are reminded that some of Jesus Christ's mortal contemporaries erroneously thought that He was John the Baptist, Elijah, Jeremiah, or another of the prophets (see Matt. 16:13–17). This is because they relied on "flesh and blood" for their knowledge. Peter, however, knew that Jesus was "the Christ, the Son of the living God" because "Father which is in heaven" revealed it to him (Matt. 16:13–17). We cannot rely on *flesh and blood*, or other mortals, for sacred knowledge about the temple; rather, we must learn from God Himself, or from His prophets and apostles, to whom God reveals so many significant, sacred truths.

(5) Do not superimpose our cultural understandings on the temple and its sacred rituals. The temple and its sacred ordinances are ancient, hearkening back to Adam and Eve. Because ancient practices and cultures are difficult for us to understand (including the ancient temple and its ordinances), it may be tempting for us to superimpose our modern cultural understandings on the temple and its sacred rituals. This is called *presentism*, which is "the tendency to interpret past events in terms of modern values and concepts."[1] Our culture is exorbitantly different and greatly detached from God's ancient order of temple truths and rituals. Many of the components that make up our culture—mass media, cinema, cuisine, fashion and dress, sports, social habits, arts, music, languages and dialects, governments and politics, automobiles and commuting, commercialism, literature, architecture, and technology—can easily misdirect us or even disconnect us from comprehending ancient temple rituals.

That is not to say that our modern cultural components are bad or evil. They are not. In fact, many of these things (modern transportation systems, technology, etc.) are God-given in order for us to build His kingdom in marvelous ways. But these components provide a dilemma—on the one hand, we can use them to build God's kingdom; but on the other hand, they are so much a part of us that we may try to understand God's ancient temple ceremonies through the lens of prominent aspects of our culture, thus resulting in a lack of understanding regarding the meaning of the temple. In sum, our own presuppositions and cultural environment may hinder us as we seek to comprehend God's temples and rituals.

(6) Attend the temple often. Temple attendees learn line upon line, through study, experience, and the power of the Holy Ghost. For men and women who attend the temple often, line-upon-line learning is accelerated.

---

1. Apple Dictionary Version 2.2.1 (143.1).

Here are two extraordinary and powerful examples of frequent temple attenders:

My niece Maylyn attended the temple on a weekly basis from twelve years old to the time that she graduated from high school. She writes,

> When I was twelve years old, I set a goal to go to the temple every week to do baptisms for the dead. We were blessed to have a temple in the city next to ours, and my parents drove me whenever they could. I was usually able to find a ride *to* the temple, but sometimes I would go without knowing how I would get home. Once I got out of the temple, I would call an older sibling or a neighbor to drive me home. I was able to go every week from the time I was twelve until I graduated from high school.
>
> Five things I learned in the temple:
> - There were times I could have made a bad decision, but I thought about my temple recommend and found the strength to make a better choice.
> - As a teenager it was easy to just think about my current day at school, my friends, or the upcoming weekend. Sitting in the reverence of the temple, I was able to think of my future and the things of eternity.
> - It helped me grow closer to Christ and feel His love for me. In a world where Satan is trying to conquer the hearts of men, this is a precious gift.
> - The temple helped me to know that I could make a goal and keep it. It took discipline for me to arrange my busy schedule to include the temple, but although some people might consider it as a sacrifice of time, I never felt that my visits to the temple took away from the other areas in my life.
> - Often I would go at times of the day where I was the only patron in the baptistry. Being able to sit in the

quiet, peaceful temple helped me disengage from the chaos of the world, and I was able to keep that peace with me when I left.

I am now happily married in the temple and I have two beautiful little boys. I look forward to teaching them about the blessings of the temple!

My nephew Alan frequently attends the temple. By the time he was twenty-six years old, he had participated in 551 endowments! This is not a typo. Owing to his frequent attendance, his comprehension and testimony of the temple is remarkable. In fact, his testimony of the gospel of Jesus Christ is unshakable. Inasmuch as Alan often attends the temple, he has gained great understanding concerning the meaning of the temple and its symbols.

In the end, even after much diligent study and application of these keys, we lack knowledge as to the meanings of some of the symbols associated with the temple; their meaning either escapes us or has not yet been revealed. Further complicating matters, many items that are associated with temples, especially architectural components, are decorative and have no direct symbolism attached to them.

Proper Understanding "Will Immeasurably Help"

"Parents should teach the importance of the temple from a child's earliest days," President Russell M. Nelson stated.[1] Sarah Dunkley Benson did exactly that—taught her son Ezra Taft the importance of the temple. President Ezra Taft Benson recalled, as a young boy in Whitney, Idaho, watching his mother iron her temple clothes. "I can still see her in my mind's eye bending over the ironing board with newspapers on the floor, ironing long strips of white cloth, with beads of perspiration on her

---

1. Nelson, "Prepare for Blessings of the Temple," 17.

forehead. When I asked her what she was doing, she said, 'These are temple robes, my son. Your father and I are going to the temple at Logan.'

"Then she put the old flatiron on the stove, drew a chair close to mine, and told me about temple work—how important it is to be able to go to the temple and participate in the sacred ordinances performed there. She also expressed her fervent hope that some day her children and grandchildren and great-grandchildren would have the opportunity to enjoy these priceless blessings."

President Benson then explained that, owing to the sacred nature of the temple, "We are sometimes reluctant to say anything about the temple to our children and grandchildren." Consequently, many people "do not develop a real desire to go to the temple, or when they go there, they do so without much background to prepare them for the obligations and covenants they enter into." President Benson then provided us with these important words: "I believe a proper understanding or background will immeasurably help prepare our youth for the temple. This understanding, I believe, will foster within them a desire to seek their priesthood blessings just as Abraham sought his."[1]

"Mighty Realities for Which the Symbols Stand"

As important as symbols are, they should never overwhelm us and detract from the power of the actual ordinance itself. Nor should we allow the symbols to replace the power of the Holy Spirit that we feel as we worship the Lord! And symbols should not supersede our manifold revelatory experiences as we seek the Lord's blessings in His holy house. For example, the essential ordinance of baptism (and baptism for the dead) is associated with several symbols, but these symbols should not distract us from the power of Jesus Christ's Atonement to remit our sins and to cleanse us from all categories of filth.

---

1. Benson, "What I Hope You Will Teach Your Children about the Temple," 8.

Another example: the statue of the angel Moroni is an imposing symbol that stands on numerous temples. Over many years and decades, millions of persons have viewed one or more of these statues. How many, for instance, have viewed the Moroni statue on the Salt Lake Temple? And how many freeway drivers on Interstate 495 have viewed the Moroni statue on the Washington D.C. Temple as they have commuted and traveled on that passageway? And yet, as visible as the statue of Moroni is in many lands and territories throughout the world, it is far less significant than the actual man Moroni who appeared to Joseph Smith and revealed many truths and doctrines, including the magnificent Book of Mormon.

Elder John A. Widtsoe articulated, "We live in a world of symbols. No man or woman can come out of the temple endowed as he should be, unless he has seen, beyond the symbol, the mighty realities for which the symbols stand."[2] Stated differently, the temple ordinances themselves are more consequential than are the symbols that are attached to the ordinances. So, too, the power of the Spirit and the blessings of prayer and revelation in the Lord's temples are spiritually powerful, while symbols are designed to serve as instructional devices.

The Temple Is of Paramount Importance

When God's prophets make statements like the following, we become aware of how vital the temple and its ordinances are to us:

- "Each holy temple stands as a symbol of our membership in the Church, as a sign of our faith in life after death, and as a sacred step toward eternal glory for us and our families"[3] (Russell M. Nelson).
- "The all-important and crowning blessings of membership in the Church are those blessings which we receive in the temples of God"[4] (Thomas S. Monson).

---

2. Widtsoe, "Temple Worship," 62.
3. Nelson, "Personal Preparation for Temple Blessings," 32.
4. Monson, "The Holy Temple—a Beacon to the World," 93.

- Church members are invited "to look to the temple of the Lord as the great symbol of [our] membership"[1] (Howard W. Hunter).
- "We feel when we go into these temples that we enjoy the Spirit of the Lord more fully than in any other place"[2] (Lorenzo Snow).
- The Lord's "most important work is carried on within [the] walls"[3] of the temple (Lorenzo Snow).
- "We need the temple more than anything else"[4] (Joseph Smith).

So essential are temples that God has "always commanded" His covenant people to build them (D&C 124:39); this means that each and every dispensation of the gospel has had temples, or the equivalent of temples, which includes mountains and mountaintops. And as a reminder of the great import of temples, in our own dispensation, the Saints built two temples (Kirtland and Nauvoo) and planned a third (Salt Lake City) before the first chapels were constructed.

At the Buenos Aires Argentina Temple dedication, then-Elder Boyd K. Packer spoke of the paramount import of the temple: "If the outside knew about what was happening here, the cars would stop, planes would not take off, and people would gather to see what the Lord hath wrought. This work we have a part in; it is cause for great rejoicing."[5] Another Apostle, Elder George Q. Cannon, stated that to the early Latter-day Saints, the temple and its sacred blessings "were valued beyond price." He then explained that an individual "that could go in and get his [or her] endowments was looked upon as though he [or she] had received some extraordinary blessing—something akin to that which the angels received—and it was estimated and valued in that way."[6]

Brigham Young underscored the temple's importance when he

---

1. *The Teachings of Howard W. Hunter*, 238.
2. *Teachings of Presidents of the Church: Lorenzo Snow*, 143.
3. *Teachings of Presidents of the Church: Lorenzo Snow*, 144.
4. *Teachings of Presidents of the Church: Joseph Smith*, 416.
5. Packer, "Temples Received with Thanks," 6.
6. Cannon, *Gospel Truth*, 1:228.

declared, "We never began to build a temple without the bells of hell beginning to ring." Regarding both the Kirtland and Nauvoo Temples, Brigham asked, "Did not the bells of hell toll all the time we were building them?" He then responded, "They did, every week and every day." And when the Saints were building the Salt Lake Temple, Brigham Young predicted, "All the tribes of hell will be on the move, if we uncover the walls of this [the Salt Lake] temple." During this same discourse, Brigham added these words: "I want to hear them [the bells of hell] ring again."[7]

Not only did Brigham Young speak concerning the importance of the temple, but his very actions served as a testimony of the temple's spiritual prominence. As the Saints were preparing, under great duress and persecution, to leave Nauvoo for their journey west, President Brigham Young labored night and day in the temple in order to provide the Saints with the blessings of the temple. On one certain day he wrote, "One hundred and forty-three persons received their endowments in the Temple. . . . Such has been the anxiety manifested by the saints to receive the ordinances [of the Temple], and such the anxiety on our part to administer to them, that I have given myself up entirely to the work of the Lord in the Temple night and day, not taking more than four hours sleep, upon an average, per day, and going home but once a week."[8]

Just days after the pioneer Saints arrived in the Salt Lake Valley in 1847, Brigham Young announced that a temple would be built in what would later be known as Salt Lake City. This despite the fact that the pioneers were exhausted and in need of food, shelter, and long-term sustenance; and this notwithstanding the truth that the Saints had built two temples (Kirtland and Nauvoo) during the past decade or so and had been required to abandon both as they fled from abusers and persecutors.

In the coming decades, the Saints would build and dedicate four temples in Utah—St. George (dedicated 1877), Logan (dedicated 1884),

---
7. All citations from this paragraph are from *Discourses of Brigham Young*, 410.
8. *Teachings of Presidents of the Church: Brigham Young*, 299.

Manti (dedicated 1888), and Salt Lake (dedicated 1893). Brigham Young would live to see one of them built; on January 1, 1877, Brigham Young, in the presence of a congregation of Saints, presided over the dedication of the St. George Temple; however, before the dedication, his legs were "so weak that he had to be carried into the room in a chair." Then, when addressing the congregation, he expressed, "We enjoy privileges that are enjoyed by no one else on the face of the earth.... When I think upon this subject, I want the tongue of seven thunders to wake up the people."[1]

And so the building of temples has continued, decade after decade, and now there are hundreds of temples on the face of the earth. In point of fact, "This is the greatest era of temple building in all the history of the world."[2] Each and every temple stands as a testimony that God's work will continue upon the earth; moreover, "Every foundation stone that is laid for a Temple, and every Temple completed," states George Q. Cannon, "lessens the power of Satan on the earth, and increases the power of God and Godliness."[3]

Seven Doctrines Focused on Jesus Christ

Jesus commanded us, "Look unto me in every thought" (D&C 6:36), and that is what we must do. Also, "We talk of Christ, we rejoice in Christ, we preach of Christ, we prophesy of Christ, and we write according to our prophecies, that our children may know to what source they may look for a remission of their sins" (2 Ne. 25:26). The following seven essential doctrines, all of which pertain to Jesus Christ, help us to build a foundation that will assist us in gaining a better comprehension of the temple and its symbols. The first item is from the prophet of the Restoration of the gospel, Joseph Smith, and the second is from our present prophet and seer, Russell M. Nelson.

---

1. *Teachings of Presidents of the Church: Brigham Young*, 299.
2. Hinckley, *Teachings of Gordon B. Hinckley*, 629.
3. Cannon, "Logan Temple," 743.

(1) Jesus Christ is the focal point of our religion. Joseph Smith taught this important truth: "The fundamental principles of our religion are the testimony of the Apostles and Prophets, concerning Jesus Christ, that He died, was buried, and rose again the third day, and ascended into heaven; and all other things which pertain to our religion are only appendages to it."[4]

(2) The temple is Jesus Christ–focused. President Russell M. Nelson summarized, "The basis for every temple ordinance and covenant—the heart of the plan of salvation—is the Atonement of Jesus Christ. Every activity, every lesson, all we do in the Church, point to the Lord and His holy house. Our efforts to proclaim the gospel, perfect the Saints, and redeem the dead all lead to the temple."[5]

(3) All ordinances, including those of the temple, testify of Jesus Christ. The "ordinances were given after this manner, that thereby the people might *look forward* on the Son of God, it being a type of his order, or it being his order, and this that they might *look forward* to him for a remission of their sins" (Alma 13:16; emphasis added). Elder Jeffrey R. Holland wrote, "The temple is His house, and He should be uppermost in our minds and hearts—the majestic doctrine of Christ pervading our very being *just as it pervades the temple ordinances*—from the time we read the inscription over the front door to the very last moment we spend in the building. Amid all the wonder we encounter, we are to see, above all else, the meaning of Jesus in the temple."[6]

(4) All prophets—ancient and modern—testify of Christ. All of the Lord's prophets—past and present—have testified of Jesus Christ; Jacob testified, "None of the prophets have written, nor prophesied, save they have spoken concerning this Christ" (Jacob 7:11). Another ancient witness adds support to Jacob's testimony: "To him [Christ] give all the prophets

---

4. *Teachings of Presidents of the Church: Joseph Smith*, 49.
5. Nelson, "Personal Preparation for Temple Blessings," 32.
6. Holland, "The Message, the Meaning, and the Multitude," 7; emphasis added.

witness" (Acts 10:43; see also Jacob 4:4; Mosiah 13:33–35; Hel. 8:14, 16, 19, 22; 3 Ne. 11:9–10; Luke 24:27).

(5) **"All things bear record" of Jesus Christ.** *"All things* have their likeness, and *all things* are created and made to bear record of me" (Moses 6:63; emphasis added). To this passage we add 2 Nephi 11:4: *"All things* which have been given of God from the beginning of the world, unto man, are the typifying of him [Christ]" (see also Alma 34:14). Elder Bruce R. McConkie expressed, "It is wholesome and proper to look for similitudes of Christ everywhere and to use them repeatedly in keeping him and his laws uppermost in our minds."[1] These words also pertain to the temple.

(6) **The law of Moses (including the laws pertaining to the temple) testify of Jesus Christ.** All components and every aspect of the law of Moses testified of Jesus Christ (see Gal. 3:24; Jacob 4:5; Mosiah 13:31; Alma 34:13–14; Jarom 1:11), including its regulations, directives, ordinances, temple rituals, system of sacrifices, feasts, and festivals. The law of Moses encouraged Israelites to "look forward to the coming of Christ, considering that the law of Moses was a type of his coming" (Alma 25:15).

(7) **There are numerous symbols, types, and shadows of Jesus Christ!** John Taylor explained that there are "so many types, shadows and forms of which [Jesus] was the great prototype."[2]

Vital Truths Regarding Women and the Temple

The Old Testament sometimes focuses attention on the role of males in ancient Israelite temples, especially high priests, priests, and Levites. This focus sometimes creates misunderstandings, in our day, regarding the status of females in ancient temples; and too, occasionally we lack a clear comprehension regarding women in our modern temples. In recent years, however, a number of individuals have clarified many sacred truths

---

1. McConkie, *The Promised Messiah*, 453.
2. Taylor, *Mediation and Atonement*, 124.

regarding the elevated and significant position of women in Latter-day Saint temples. "All worthy members who have received their endowment and keep the covenants they have made in the temple have priesthood power," wrote Barbara Gardner, an associate professor of Church History and Doctrine, Brigham Young University. "Thus, women, married or single, can have priesthood power in their homes regardless of a visit from a priesthood holder."[3]

Sheri Dew, a former Counselor in the Relief Society General Presidency and author of *Women and the Priesthood*, wrote, "What does it mean to have access to priesthood power for our own lives? It means that we can receive revelation, be blessed and aided by the ministering of angels, learn to part the veil that separates us from our Heavenly Father, be strengthened to resist temptation, be protected, and be enlightened and made smarter than we are—all without any mortal intermediary."[4]

The temple endowment provides powerful teachings regarding the ennobled position of women. Temple patrons learn about these truths, line upon line, as they take heed over the years and decades, and more significantly, as they receive instruction from the Holy Ghost, who confirms in our hearts and minds the honored standing of women in God's kingdom.

During a devotional address, President M. Russell Ballard provided several foundational truths that aid us in comprehending the significant status of women: "When men and women go to the temple, *they are both endowed with the same power, which by definition is priesthood power.* While the authority of the priesthood is directed through priesthood keys, and priesthood keys are held only by worthy men, access to the power and blessings of the priesthood is available to all of God's children....

"The endowment is literally a gift of power. *All who enter the house of the Lord officiate in the ordinances of the priesthood. This applies to men and women alike.*

---

3. Gardner, "Connecting Daughters of God with His Priesthood Power," 33.
4. Dew, *Women and the Priesthood,* 125.

"Our Father in Heaven is generous with His power. All men and all women have access to this power for help in our own lives. All who have made sacred covenants with the Lord and who honor those covenants are eligible to receive personal revelation, to be blessed by the ministering of angels, to commune with God, to receive the fulness of the gospel, and, ultimately, to become heirs alongside Jesus Christ of all our Father has."[1]

During general conference in April 2014, President Dallin H. Oaks added greatly to our understanding of women and the priesthood: "We are not accustomed to speaking of women having the authority of the priesthood in their Church callings, but what other authority can it be? When a woman—young or old—is set apart to preach the gospel as a full-time missionary, she is given priesthood authority to perform a priesthood function. The same is true when a woman is set apart to function as an officer or teacher in a Church organization under the direction of one who holds the keys of the priesthood. Whoever functions in an office or calling received from one who holds priesthood keys exercises priesthood authority in performing her or his assigned duties."[2]

Beyond these teachings regarding women, there are several visual, but unspoken, particulars in the temple that also make us aware of the equality of God's daughters and sons. Some of these have been identified by President Nelson: "In the temple, all are dressed in spotless white.... Through a democracy of dress, temple attendance reminds us that 'God is no respecter of persons.'"

President Nelson continues, "Age, nationality, language—even position in the Church—are of secondary significance." No preference is given to individuals from specific nations, no priority awarded to particular languages. Age does not matter! Young and old alike are equal. President Nelson's next point is yet another remarkable insight: "I have attended

---

1. Ballard, "Let Us Think Straight," speeches.byu.edu; emphasis added. Portions of this speech were published in Ballard, "Men and Women and Priesthood Power," 32.
2. Oaks, "Keys and Authority of the Priesthood," 51.

many endowment sessions when the President of the Church participated. Every man in the room was accorded the same high regard that was extended to the President." Men and women, regardless of their ecclesiastical status, all receive the same instructions during the endowment and are equal in the Lord's house.

President Nelson then writes: "All sit side by side and are considered equal in the eyes of the Lord."[3] During the endowment, there are no hierarchical seating arrangements and there is no podium for ecclesiastical leaders. Females and males are fully equal. And then, at the conclusion of the endowment, males and females have equal access to the celestial room, which signifies the celestial kingdom.

The Temple Constitutes Evidence that Joseph Smith Was God's Prophet and Seer

There exists a number of evidences that Joseph Smith was a prophet of God; these include the coming forth of the Book of Mormon and other scriptures, the restoration of various ordinances (including baptism and the sacrament), the building of God's temples, and much more. When Joseph Smith restored the doctrines of the temple, he reinstituted more than two dozen prominent features that also belonged to ancient temples. These will be set forth in the entry "Joseph Smith: Restorer of the Ancient Temple."

Beyond these various evidences, we can join President James E. Faust, who made this important claim: "Each temple that stands today is a vindication of Joseph and Hyrum Smith and a triumph for them and all of our people who suffered the destruction, the beatings, and the murders at the hands of the cruel tyrants in the mobs who drove our people west."[4]

---

3. Nelson, "Prepare for Blessings of the Temple," 45.
4. Faust, "Who Shall Ascend into the Hill of the Lord?" 2.

Why Study Ancient Temples?

The 175 entries in this volume pertain to both ancient and modern temples. Why does this volume deal with ancient temples, when we live in the age of modern temples? Because there are many close correspondences between ancient and modern temples, and virtually all aspects of ancient temples enhance our understanding of modern temples. As women and men seek to comprehend their own temple experience, they can glean scores of truths about the temple from the Old and New Testaments and other ancient scriptures. Both ancient and modern temples, therefore, are relevant to each of us.

I have been closely involved with two separate, full-sized replicas of the tabernacle of Moses. Each of these replicas (erected and assembled in various cities throughout the United States) have positively impacted thousands of individuals who received a guided tour and witnessed explanations of the tabernacle, its various components, and its powerful symbolism and meanings. I refer to these two replicas in order to demonstrate how the ancient temple impacts our understanding of modern temples. Furthermore, the following two examples (both of which are associated with the tabernacle replicas) serve to reveal the importance of studying ancient temples:

Example #1: In 2016, Jason Kotter (then the Young Men president of a stake in Meridian, Idaho) led a team of sisters and brothers who built a full-size replica of the tabernacle of Moses in New Meadows, Idaho, which included the courtyard curtains and gate, the tabernacle structure with its two veils, the altars of sacrifice and incense, the menorah, the table of shewbread, and the ark of the covenant. (I personally toured this tabernacle multiple times, and it is an extremely impressive replica! In fact, the entire tabernacle experience has greatly impacted me in numerous ways.) In August of that year, the replica tabernacle and its components became a massive object lesson for the youth of that stake! The youth stood around the altar of sacrifice (a life-sized replica) and learned the six actions that belonged to every sacrifice under the law of Moses; they stood in the holy place and viewed life-size replicas of the menorah, table of shewbread, and altar of incense. They passed through the beautiful veil of the tabernacle into the Holy of Holies and saw the ark of the covenant. Most importantly, the youth learned the many ways that the ancient tabernacle was a Jesus Christ–focused institution.

Fast forward a couple of weeks, when the same tabernacle was erected in Meridian, Idaho. Now the youth were taking their parents and other adults through the tabernacle, and now they were the instructors. Jason Kotter wrote to me concerning this event: "On Saturday we witnessed a miracle as eight young men took 1,550 people through the tabernacle. It was powerful to see these young men as they testified of Jesus Christ, His role as the Redeemer, and the tender feelings they have developed over the past month. . . . I can't begin to tell you how many parents approached me with tears in their eyes expressing gratitude for [the tabernacle experience]. Many of them shared stories about their young men and how they have changed. We had all the young men giving/attending tours in white shirts and ties. It was so powerful to see these young men as they took the stake through the tabernacle. Every group that met with us after the tour made the same comment, they couldn't believe the way the youth had taught and testified."[1]

I have had several other follow-up communications with Brother Kotter concerning this tabernacle experience. He is now the stake president of that same stake, and he informs me that this experience served to prepare his youth for their own endowments, as they entered our latter-day temples, and also that the tabernacle experience strengthened the understanding of seasoned, mature temple patrons.

Example #2: In 2016, President Rick Johnson directed his stake (the

---

1. Jason Kotter, Personal Correspondence, September 3, 2015.

Huntington Beach Stake in Southern California) as they also created a life-size replica of the tabernacle of Moses. Similar to the one in Idaho, this tabernacle in California also included the tabernacle structure with all of its appurtenances; and like the tabernacle in Idaho, this tabernacle was extraordinary in its scope and appearance. Furthermore, Sister Julie Carr had recreated life-size sacred vestments of the high priest, according to the description in Exodus 28 and elsewhere. In a private communication, President Johnson explained to me that his stake had created the replica of the tabernacle of Moses "to help our youth better understand the priesthood, temple, and to help them develop a great sense of the sacred. After the event we found they learned much, much more. The symbolism and parallels to our modern-day temples is very instructive and insightful." President Johnson also wrote, "Prior to our youth's tabernacle experience it was not uncommon for me to have youth going through the temple for the first time feel overwhelmed and unsure." But after the tabernacle experience, President Johnson states, "I often ask the members who are going through the temple for the first time what one thing helped prepare you the most for the temple. The answer is always the 'tabernacle experience.'"

President Johnson referred to one particular experience he'd had with a husband and wife: "I was interviewing a couple who hadn't had a temple recommend for years. As I sat down with them individually I asked why they hadn't been attending the temple. They reported that their first temple experience overwhelmed them because they didn't understand the experience. When I asked what changed, they reported that the tabernacle tour changed their thinking. They had spent time during the tour reviewing the sacred clothing [of the ancient high priest, as presented on a mannequin]. As they learned the history and the 'why' for sacred clothing, they understood their own temple experience and the importance of the sacred clothing. The experience at the tour caused them to rethink their experience and they wanted to get back to the temple to enjoy the blessings of the temple." President Johnson concluded with this reflection: "I will always be grateful for the many known and unknown blessings from the tabernacle experience. The Old Testament now means much more to me and our members as they understand the tabernacle, which was an Aaronic Priesthood temple. . . . I am now sending members to the temple better prepared for their experience and they are able to understand what is happening and why. Instead of being distracted by the clothing, they can focus on the covenants they make, and the clothing supports and reinforces those covenants."[1]

Some Personal Items

It is my testimony that by carefully studying scriptural texts, we heighten and magnify our understanding of the temple and its powerful symbols. Many years ago, I was a young missionary receiving instruction in Salt Lake City before departing to my assigned mission. On June 12, I arose at 5:00 a.m. and arrived at the Salt Lake Temple for a 6:00 endowment session. After the session, a large group of us met in the assembly room of the temple. There was a total of 295 of us, all inexperienced and spiritually unseasoned. We sat together, still dressed in white clothing. It was our rare opportunity and privilege to hear from President Harold B. Lee; after speaking to us, he invited us to ask questions. I do not remember any specific question, but I vividly recall that he answered most of the questions from the scriptures. After receiving a question from a missionary, he would respond by saying something like, "The answer to that question is found in [such and such book of scripture]." He would turn to that passage and read it, and then make some comments. This teaching procedure went on for a period of time. I concluded at that time that most of the questions that we ask about the temple and the endowment are found in the scriptures.

---

1. Rick Johnson, Personal Correspondence, June 1, 2018.

During this same sacred occasion, I recall one elder asking something like, "How often does Christ visit the temple?"

President Lee responded, "How do we know He is not here right now?" Everyone was completely quiet. Then he continued, "There are 295 missionaries here to preach the gospel [suggesting that the Lord is very interested in His missionaries and their sacred work]. When He comes to the earth, He comes to this temple." Even then, in my ignorance, I knew that President Lee's response was highly significant and consequential!

Now, decades later, I teach a three-credit course at Brigham Young University that deals with Ancient Near Eastern "Texts and Temples." The main objective of this course is to gain an understanding and appreciation of ancient temples with regard to their significance in the religious landscapes of the Ancient Near East and world of the Bible. We deal, of course, with only topics that are appropriate to discuss.

For this course, we spend about forty hours in the classroom and then the students spend dozens more hours outside of the classroom as they conduct research and write papers. Because of this class and because of other opportunities to teach about ancient temples, I am regularly asked, "What is the best book that will help me to understand the temple?" My response is simple and to the point: "The scriptures."

Temple architect Truman O. Angell related a very important item to John Taylor regarding how President Brigham Young selected some of the symbols that belong to the Salt Lake Temple. Angell's words were brief: Brigham Young chose many of the temple's symbols "after [an] intense study of scripture, particularly [the] Old Testament."[1] This accords with President Russell M. Nelson's statement, cited previously, that we should search the Old Testament and other scriptures to enhance our understanding of the temple.[2]

---

1. Letter from Truman O. Angell, Sr., to President John Taylor. John Taylor Letter File, LDS Church Archives, 29 April 1886.
2. Nelson, "Personal Preparation for Temple Blessings," 33–34.

God's Temple Ceremonies Are "Foolishness" to the World

Some individuals have considered God's ancient rituals and ceremonies to be perplexing or perhaps a little strange. How can such strange things be from God, they ask? For example, why would God command His prophet to sprinkle animals' blood on other people and on their clothing (see Ex. 29:21)? Some would consider this practice to be unconventional. Or why would God command His temple priests to dip a finger in animals' blood and then to sprinkle the blood seven times (see Lev. 4:6, 17), or to ceremonially lay their hands on the heads of animals (see Lev. 1:2, 4) before the animals are sacrificed in the temple precinct; or to dip a living bird in the blood of a sacrificed bird (see Lev. 14:6–7), or to sprinkle bird's blood on a leper that is to be cleansed (see Lev. 14:7)?

Other examples—a Nazarite shaved her/his head at the door of the tabernacle and then burned her/his hair in the sacrificial fire (see Num. 6:13–21); such a sacred practice may seem strange to those who do not know God's ways. Or what about killing animals in the name of religion in the temple precinct, day after day, year after year? How many of our modern animal rights groups would file formal complaints against such a practice? And yet all of these ancient temple rituals are from God! He *commanded* His covenant people to conduct these sacred ceremonies. Therefore, who would dare to designate them *strange* or *odd*?

Another very strange or peculiar ritual (according to some individuals) pertains to the extremely intimate and personal rite of circumcision. This requires a male (including adult males) to uncover himself while another person performs a ritual action that is not only exceptionally private but also very painful. And yet this was God's covenant, which He established with Abraham: "This is my covenant, which ye shall keep, between me and you and thy seed after thee; Every man child [Hebrew: "male"] among you shall be circumcised. . . . It shall be a token of the covenant betwixt me and you. . . . My covenant shall be in your flesh for an everlasting covenant"

(Gen. 17:10–11, 13). Some may question, why would God require such a practice and even call it a *covenant*?

Some of the things of God have always been foolishness to others, especially to those who lack understanding regarding spiritual things and to those who lack the power of the Holy Ghost. Paul wrote to the Corinthians, "For the preaching of the cross is to them that perish *foolishness*" (1 Cor. 1:18; emphasis added); also, "But we preach Christ crucified . . . unto the Greeks *foolishness*" (1 Cor. 1:23). In this same epistle, Paul explained how we can comprehend God's sacred things (which include ancient and modern temple ceremonies) so that we do not fall into the category of individuals who call God's teachings "foolishness." Paul gave us several key items:

"The things of God knoweth no man, but the Spirit of God" (1 Cor. 2:11); we cannot understand the things of God unless we have the Holy Ghost.

"Now we have received, not the spirit of the world, but the spirit which is of God; that we might know the things that are freely given to us of God" (1 Cor. 2:12); the world cannot give us knowledge regarding God; we can know of such things only through His Spirit.

"Which things also we speak, not in the words which man's wisdom teacheth, but which the Holy Ghost teacheth" (1 Cor. 2:13); the world's wisdom and learning cannot teach men and women regarding God and His sacred things; only the Holy Ghost can teach us such things.

"Comparing spiritual things with spiritual" (1 Cor. 2:13); we cannot compare temporal or worldly matters to spiritual things (and fully comprehend such things), rather we must compare "spiritual things with spiritual."

In sum, as long as we attempt to comprehend God's teachings, covenants, and temple rituals through our own learning and cultural norms, such teachings will remain foolishness to us. We need the Holy Ghost (and God's prophets, who teach by the Holy Ghost) to teach us, because such things are "spiritually discerned" (1 Cor. 2:14).

Special Note: The book's title, *175 Temple Symbols and Their Meanings*, suggests that each of the 175 entries presents a temple symbol together with its meaning. Although this is normally the case, there is an occasional entry that provides an important insight on or significance of the temple, but that entry does not necessarily introduce a symbol. For example, the entry "Angels, Communication with" contains powerful truths, but it is not directly related to a symbol. But note also that some entries contain multiple symbols, such as the entry "Baptism for the Dead," which identifies several symbolic elements that are associated with this sacred ordinance.

A number of photos in this volume portray a life-size copy of the tabernacle of Moses, together with its various components (altars, menorah, ark of the covenant, etc.). Both the tabernacle and the components are privately owned *replicas*, designed to serve as instructional aids. Regarding the priests and high priests in the photos—these are models, also designed to serve as instructional aids. The models are *not* actual priestly figures! And the "blood" in the images (as well as other similar items) is a simple prop (i.e., artificial blood).

SYMBOLS
of the
TEMPLE

Ancient and Modern

The Expulsion of Adam and Eve from Paradise, 1791, by Benjamin West, by Anglo-American painting, oil on canvas

ADAM AND EVE

The names *Adam* and *Eve* and their experiences in the Garden of Eden provide us with understanding regarding our own eternal roles and spiritual aspirations. Just as Adam (who is also called Michael) serves as the great archetype of all righteous men, so Eve is the prototype for upright women. And as Adam's role is reenacted and dramatized in our temple ceremony, so Eve is evoked in sacred drama—the story of Adam and Eve is our own. Each of us have lived, transgressed, fallen, and then received redemption through Jesus Christ's Atonement. In fact, Adam and Eve's experiences in the garden are ritualized in very special ways in our temple. Our temple clearly demonstrates how Eve and Adam serve as types and shadows of women and men.

Adam is a type for all people (see Rom. 5:12–21; 1 Cor. 15:21–22). Like Adam, each of us lives in a fallen world; and also, like Adam, each of us can rise above the fallen world as we return to the Garden of Eden through temple ritual.

ALPHA AND OMEGA

The words "I AM ALPHA AND OMEGA" (in capital letters) are set in gold lettering on a scroll that exists on the exterior of the Salt Lake Temple, above a representation of clasped hands. *Alpha* and *Omega,* the first and last letters of the Greek alphabet, are titles of Jesus Christ (see Rev. 1:8, 11; D&C 19:1; 35:1; 38:1). He is "Alpha and Omega, the beginning and the end, whose course is one eternal round, the same today as yesterday, and forever" (D&C 35:1).

Alpha and Omega, Salt Lake Temple.

ALTARS

The temple altar is a place of *sacrifice, prayer,* and *theophany* (a manifestation of God to a man or a woman). In the Old Testament, an altar was literally "a place of slaughter or sacrifice" (the Hebrew word for altar, *mizbach*, is derived from the Hebrew root *zbch*, "to sacrifice"). Anciently, from Adam to the time of Jesus Christ's Crucifixion, animal sacrifices were performed at altars. Those sacrifices pointed forward to Jesus Christ (Moses 5:5–7), the ultimate and infinite sacrifice.

High priest (model) offers incense at the altar of incense.

The altar was also a place of prayer. Abram built an altar and then "called upon the name of the Lord" (Gen. 12:8; see also Gen. 13:4). Solomon "stood before the altar of the Lord in the presence of all the congregation of Israel, and spread forth his hands toward heaven" and then prayed (see, especially, 1 Kgs. 8:22–23, 54; see also Rev. 8:3). As a result of prayer at the altar, the altar became the place of theophany: Jacob "built there an altar . . . there God appeared unto him" (Gen. 35:7). To a Church audience at general conference, President N. Eldon Tanner related praying at the altar of the Salt Lake Temple, together with other Church leaders.[1]

Two altars existed in ancient Israelite temples—the altar of sacrifice and the altar of incense.

(1) *The altar of incense:* The altar of incense was a beautiful, stunning, artistic object that existed in the tabernacle's holy place, in front of the veil that covered the Holy of Holies. Owing to this important location and its

---

1. See Tanner, "The Administration of the Church," 47.

Holy place, showing the altar of incense before the veil.
Note menorah on the left and table of shewbread on the right.

multiple purposes, this altar signified the place of prayer par excellence as well as a significant place of atonement.

The altar was made of acacia wood and overlaid with pure gold, which provided a shiny bearing, perhaps reflecting the light of the lampstand that also existed in the holy place. The altar's height was three feet and its width one and a half feet square (see Ex. 37:25–26). The four horns, all of the same size and appearance, existed at its four corners (see Ex. 30:2–3).

The book of Exodus states, "Aaron shall burn thereon sweet incense every morning," and again in the evening "he shall burn incense upon it" and this will be "a perpetual incense before the Lord throughout your generations" (Ex. 30:7–8). The requirements of the ritual had to be precisely according to the Lord's commands: "Ye shall offer no strange incense thereon, nor burnt sacrifice, nor meat offering; neither shall ye pour drink offering thereon" (Ex. 30:9).

In addition to burning incense, once a year on the Day of Atonement the high priest was required to approach the altar in order to "make an atonement for it." He would do so by taking the blood of both the goat

High priest (model) at the altar of incense.

and the bull and putting the blood on the altar's four horns; "He shall go out unto the altar that is before the Lord, and make an atonement for it; . . . he shall sprinkle of the blood upon it with his finger seven times" in order to "cleanse it, and hallow it from the uncleanness of the children of Israel" (Lev. 16:18–19; see also Ex. 30:10). For other symbols associated with the altar, see "Incense at the Golden Altar," "Horns of the Altar of Incense," and "Blood, Sprinkling of."

(2) *The altar of sacrifice.* This altar in the tabernacle and temple was a quintessential atonement-focused object, placed prominently in the courtyard. This altar was the most conspicuous item in the courtyard, located in its center and visible to all worshippers when they entered the temple precinct. Its blood-stained appearance reminded viewers of various blood sacrifices. Presumably, worshippers who approached the temple from a distance could see the altar's pillar of smoke.

The tabernacle altar of sacrifice was made of acacia wood and overlaid with bronze; it measured five by five cubits (about seven and a half feet) on four sides (square) and had a height of three cubits (about four and a half feet) (see Ex. 27:1).

The altar was the place of atonement: "For the life of the flesh is in the blood: and I have given it to you upon the altar to make an atonement for your souls: for it is the blood that maketh an atonement for the soul" (Lev. 17:11); also, "Moses took the blood [of the sacrifice], and put it upon the horns of the altar round about with his finger, and purified the altar, and poured the blood at the bottom of the altar, and sanctified it, to make reconciliation upon it" (Hebrew: "to make atonement on it") (Lev. 8:15).

Altar of sacrifice, with the tabernacle in the background.

ANCIENT ORDER OF THINGS (ANTIQUITY OF TEMPLE ORDINANCES)

"Temple patterns are as old as human life on earth. Actually, the plan for temples was established even *before* the foundation of the world," taught President Russell M. Nelson.[1] Moreover, he states, "Temple ordinances and covenants have been an integral part of the gospel since the days of Adam and Eve."[2] At the April 2019 general conference, President Nelson added this understanding: the couples "Adam and Eve, Noah and his wife, Abraham and Sarah, Lehi and Sariah," plus "all other devoted disciples of Jesus Christ—since the world was created—have made the *same* covenants with God. They have received the *same* ordinances that we as members of the Lord's restored Church today have made: those covenants that we receive at baptism and in the temple."[3]

---

1. Nelson, *Teachings of Russell M. Nelson*, 365; emphasis in the original.
2. Nelson, "Prepare for Blessings of the Temple, 20.
3. Nelson, "'Come, Follow Me,'" 89; emphasis in the original.

On May 4, 1842, Joseph Smith "instituted the Ancient order of things for the first time in these last days," referring to the endowment, and designating it the "order pertaining to the ancient of Days."[1] *Ancient of Days* is a title of Adam (see D&C 27:11; 116:1; 138:38), indicating that through this order Adam and Eve received the blessings of the endowment. During the course of the day, Joseph Smith "attend[ed] to washings, anointings, endowments and the communication of Keys pertaining to the Aaronic Priesthood, and so on to the highest order of Melchisedec Priesthood, setting forth the order pertaining to the ancient of Days, and all those plans and principles, by which any one is enabled to secure the fulness of those blessings, which have been prepared for the Church of the first born, and come up and abide in the presence of the Eloheim in the Eternal worlds."[2] Of course, Joseph Smith had spent more than a decade preparing the Saints for this ancient order, through a number of revelations and teachings.

Consistent with the topic of the "ancient order," Joseph Smith explained, "The order of the house of God has been, and ever will be, the same, even after Christ comes; and after the termination of the thousand years it will be the same; and we shall finally enter into the celestial Kingdom of God, and enjoy it forever."[3]

Why are these matters so important? President Nelson explains, "The *antiquity* and *modernity* of temple activity blend and bridge the gulf of time. Even the newest temples closely relate to ancient times."[4] President

---

1. "History, 1838–1856, volume C-1 [2 November 1838–31 July 1842]," p. 1328, The Joseph Smith Papers, accessed March 26, 2019, https://www.josephsmithpapers.org/paper-summary/history-1838-1856-volume-c-1-2-november-1838-31-july-1842/502.
2. "History, 1838–1856, volume C-1 [2 November 1838–31 July 1842]," p. 1328, The Joseph Smith Papers, accessed March 26, 2019, https://www.josephsmithpapers.org/paper-summary/history-1838-1856-volume-c-1-2-november-1838-31-july-1842/502.
3. *Teachings of Presidents of the Church: Joseph Smith*, 419.
4. Nelson, *Teachings of Russell M. Nelson*, 367; emphasis in the original.

Nelson sums up, "These sacred temple rites are ancient. To me that antiquity is thrilling and another evidence of their authenticity."[5]

ANGELIC WEATHER VANE

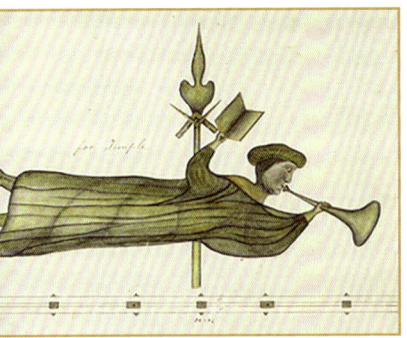

Nauvoo Temple Weathervane drawing.

On January 30, 1846, an angelic weather vane was installed on the octagonal tower of the Nauvoo Temple.[6] It is unknown whether or not the vane's angel represented Moroni. That vane is now lost to history, but it was considered to be similar to William Weeks's drawing, which depicts an angel, horizontally positioned, with a book in his left hand and a trumpet in his right hand. The angel is blowing the trumpet (see entry "Trumpets and Trumpet Stones").

ANGELS, COMMUNICATION WITH

The temple is the quintessential place of divine communication with God, angels, and spirits. During the initial building stages of the Salt Lake Temple, Parley P. Pratt stood on its northeast cornerstone and taught, "The Lord has ordained that all the most holy things pertaining to the salvation of the dead, and *all the most holy conversations and correspondence with God, angels, and spirits, shall be had only in the sanctuary of His holy Temple* on the earth, when prepared for that purpose by His Saints; and shall be received and administered by those who are ordained and sealed unto this power, to hold the keys of the sacred oracles of God."[7] There are numerous examples of such communications in the Lord's temples.

---

5. Nelson, "Becoming Exemplary Latter-day Saints," 114.
6. Smith, *HC* 7:577.
7. Pratt, "Spiritual Communication," *Journal of Discourses* (hereafter *JD*) 2:46; emphasis added.

During the Kirtland Temple period, especially during the first half of 1836, a number of holy angels appeared in the temple and ministered to the Saints. Joseph Smith recorded the following statements: "Angels ministered unto them, as well as myself."[1] Also, "The visions of heaven were opened to them . . . others were ministered unto by holy Angels . . . we all communed with the heavenly hosts."[2] And again, Joseph Smith wrote, "President F[rederick] G. Williams arose and testified that while President [Sidney] Rigdon was making his first prayer, an angel entered the window and took his seat between father Smith and himself and remained there during his prayer. President David Whitmer, also saw angels in the house."[3]

Joseph Smith also recorded, "I beheld the Temple was filled with angels, which fact I declared to the congregation."[4] Examples of angelic communications can be found in various temples throughout the history of the Church.

ANIMALS, FEMALE (SACRIFICIAL OFFERINGS)

Under the law of Moses, sacrificial animals consisted of both males and females. Depending on the offerer's economic status and the category of sin, these animals included a bull, red heifer, lamb (ram or ewe), goat

---

1. "History, 1838–1856, volume B-1 [1 September 1834–2 November 1838]," p. 696, The Joseph Smith Papers, accessed March 26, 2019, https://www.josephsmithpapers.org/paper-summary/history-1838-1856-volume-b-1-1-september-1834-2-november-1838/150.
2. "History, 1838–1856, volume B-1 [1 September 1834–2 November 1838]," p. 697, The Joseph Smith Papers, accessed March 26, 2019, https://www.josephsmithpapers.org/paper-summary/history-1838-1856-volume-b-1-1-september-1834-2-november-1838/151.
3. "History, 1838–1856, volume B-1 [1 September 1834–2 November 1838]," p. 723, The Joseph Smith Papers, accessed March 26, 2019, https://www.josephsmithpapers.org/paper-summary/history-1838-1856-volume-b-1-1-september-1834-2-november-1838/177. See also the account of William Draper, in Uchtdorf, "Hold on a Little Longer," 6–7.
4. "History, 1838–1856, volume B-1 [1 September 1834–2 November 1838] [addenda]," p. 3–4 [addenda], The Joseph Smith Papers, accessed March 26, 2019, https://www.josephsmithpapers.org/paper-summary/history-1838-1856-volume-b-1-1-september-1834-2-november-1838/306-307.

(billy or nanny), turtledove, or young pigeon. Ewe lambs (see Lev. 4:32; 14:10; Num. 6:14), nannies (see Lev. 4:28), and the red heifer (see Num. 19:2)—all "without blemish"—had significant positions in the work of the Atonement in the temple! For example: "He shall bring his trespass offering unto the Lord for his sin which he hath sinned, a *female from the flock,* a lamb or a kid of the goats, for a sin offering; and the priest shall make an atonement for him concerning his sin" (Lev. 5:6; emphasis added). Also, "a female [goat] without blemish, for his sin which he hath sinned" (Lev. 4:28; emphasis added). All sacrificial offerings pointed to Christ and His Atonement—the animal (male or female), the slaughter and death of the victim, the spilled blood, the victim without blemish, and so forth.

Why female animals? Female animals are the bearers of new life, and as such, they had specific life-giving qualities that pointed to Jesus Christ, who is the giver of immortality and eternal life. Such sacrificial animals,

Both female and male animals were sacrificed under the law of Moses.

then, served as important types and shadows of Jesus Christ. It is also important to bear in mind that female animals signified the greater sacrifice for the offerer because of the loss of potential offspring in the herd. Over the years and decades, the cumulative loss would have been significant. Notably, in a prophecy about Jesus, Isaiah used the image of a ewe lamb (Hebrew: *rachel*): "He was oppressed, and he was afflicted, yet he opened not his mouth . . . and as a [ewe lamb] before her shearers is dumb, so he openeth not his mouth" (Isa. 53:7).

ANOINTING (WITH OLIVE OIL)

Anciently, anointing with oil was a profoundly powerful, sacred gesture conducted in various settings to spiritually elevate the person or the thing that was anointed; both people and things were anointed. The anointing was so significant that it was forbidden for souls to speak out against the anointed of the Lord (see 1 Sam. 24:6, 10; 26:9, 11, 23; 2 Sam. 19:21). Repeatedly the oil is called *holy*. It shall be a "holy anointing oil. . . . It is holy, and it shall be holy unto you. . . . It shall be unto you most holy. . . . it shall be unto thee holy for the Lord" (Ex. 30:31–32, 36–37). Anointings also belong to modern temples, where both females and males are anointed. President Packer wrote, "Associated with the endowment are washings and anointings—mostly symbolic in nature, but promising definite, immediate blessings as well as future blessings."[1] Sacred anointings are mentioned in the Doctrine and Covenants: "Let the anointing of thy ministers be sealed upon them with power from on high" (D&C 109:35; see also 124:39).

Who and what was anointed? The Lord commanded Moses to anoint priests and high priests of the tabernacle: "Then shalt thou take the anointing oil, and pour it upon his head, and anoint him" (Ex. 29:7;

---

1. Packer, *The Holy Temple*, 154.

see also 28:41; 40:13; Lev. 8:12; 21:10). The Lord also commanded Moses to anoint vessels, appurtenances, and items that belonged to the tabernacle (see Ex. 30:26–33; 40:9–10; Num. 7:1), including the altar (see Ex. 29:36; 40:10). Although a mortal may conduct the anointing, it is as if God Himself has performed it: "Now he which stablisheth us with you in Christ, and hath anointed us, is God" (2 Cor. 1:21; see also Ps. 23:5; 1 John 2:20).

Anointing of priest (model) with olive oil.

What did the anointings symbolize? The anointing had powerful symbols attached to it. Referring to ancient temple anointings and the anointing of the king, Elder Oaks explained, "The Old Testament frequently mentions anointing with oil as part of a blessing conferred by priesthood authority. Anointings were declared to be for sanctification and perhaps can also be seen as symbolic of the blessings to be poured out from heaven as a result of this sacred act."[2]

The scriptures testify that the anointing rite served to sanctify an object or person for divine service: Moses "anointed the altar and all his vessels, both the laver and his foot, to sanctify them" (Lev. 8:11; see also Ex. 29:36; 40:10–11); Moses "poured of the anointing oil upon Aaron's head, and anointed him, to sanctify him" (Lev. 8:12; see also Ex. 28:40–41).

Significantly, anointed priests were types and shadows of Jesus Christ, who is the Anointed One. Their anointing echoed the anointing

---

2. Oaks, "Healing the Sick," 48. Elder Oaks references the following scriptures: Ex. 28:41; 1 Sam. 10:1; 16:13; 2 Sam. 5:3; Lev. 8:10–12.

of the Messiah. Certainly, the anointing ritual was Christ-centered. Metaphorically, Jesus is the "Horn of Salvation" (Luke 1:69), a reference to the horn of oil that is poured upon recipients of the anointing (see 1 Sam. 16:1; 1 Kgs. 1:39, 45). The anointing was part of a "gesture of approach" rite that qualified the anointed person to approach sacred space.

Associated with this, olive oil, the material utilized in the anointing ritual, could be interpreted to express the Holy Ghost (see Acts 10:38; D&C 45:56–57; see "Olive Oil"). Those who received the anointing were sanctified through the agency of the Holy Ghost, enabling them to enter the presence of God.

Jesus Christ received the sacred anointing, thus becoming the *Messiah* (Hebrew: "anointed one") and the *Christ* (Greek: "anointed one)." Both terms were employed by John when he wrote, "the Messias [Messiah], which is, being interpreted, the Christ" (John 1:41; see also 4:25). In Psalm 45, the Lord is represented as being anointed with oil by God: "Therefore God, thy God, hath anointed thee with the oil of gladness above thy fellows" (Ps. 45:7; see also Heb. 1:9). Two citations in the Acts of the Apostles indicate a divine anointing of Christ by God (see Acts 4:27; 10:38).

APRON

The high priest's vestments included an ephod (or "special apron," Ex. 39:2, note a), which was made of "gold, blue, and purple, and scarlet, and fine twined linen" (Ex. 39:2). Biblical scholar Menahem Haran states that the ephod "is a sort of apron encircling the body from the loins downward."[1] Based on his reading of Exodus 28:27 and 39:20, Haran explains, "We may assume that when the priest wishes to remove the apron from his waist, he . . . can untie the 'joining' at his back and take off the ephod frontwards."[2]

---

1. Haran, *Temples and Temple-Service in Ancient Israel*, 166.
2. Haran, *Temples and Temple-Service in Ancient Israel*, 167.

The ephod, together with the Urim and Thummim, was associated with prophetic powers. According to the ancient work the Testament of Levi 8:2–10, "I [Levi] saw seven men in white clothing, who were saying to me, 'Arise, put on the vestments of the priesthood, the crown of righteousness, the oracle of understanding, the robe of truth, the breastplate of faith, the miter for the head and the *apron for prophetic power*" (emphasis added). Beyond the high priest's special apron, Genesis 3:7 refers to Adam and Eve's aprons, made of fig leaves, which were worn in the garden of Eden (see entry "Fig Leaves").

ARCHITECTURAL FEATURES, VARIOUS TEMPLES

All temple worshippers who enter the temple are impacted by its various architectural elements. As they approach the temple from a distance, they view a perfectly majestic, monumental landmark. As they draw closer (depending on the temple), they look heavenward and see a steeple, great towers, or perhaps a large statue of Moroni, with its gold gleaming in the sunlight. Once they arrive on the temple grounds, worshippers set their eyes on battlements, crenellated towers, various stained-glass windows, sunstones, or carved friezes. Water features and beautifully landscaped gardens, which demonstrate fruitfulness, may serve to recall the garden of Eden itself. The words "Holiness to the Lord" and "House of the Lord" inscribed on the temple greatly impact the mind of worshippers—they are about to enter the Lord's own home.

Once they cross the threshold and move into the temple's interior, a number of architectural elements suggest holiness, impacting worshippers and preparing them for sacred ordinances. These elements include decorative motifs, flower designs, columns, arches, elegant light fixtures and chandeliers, railings, carpet sculptings, various panels or murals, floor-to-ceiling windows, marble floors and walls, grand staircases, and much more.

Below are representative examples of architectural features of specific temples that may have symbolic values. Unfortunately, because of space limitations, I cannot write concerning the features of all temples. Many of the features listed below, including starstones, sunstones, moonstones, the Big Dipper, North Star, etc., are treated individually elsewhere in this book. Some temples feature localized cultural themes (for example, the Rexburg Idaho Temple wheat stalk or the historical architectural influence in the Buenos Aires Argentina Temple), while other temples have symbols that are not associated with the local culture, such as sunstones and moonstones.

Albuquerque New Mexico Temple: Starstones, sunstones, moonstones, sun image in art glass on east side of temple.

Anchorage Alaska Temple: Representation in granite of Big Dipper and North Star on exterior wall. Huge seven-hundred-pound chandelier, with thousands of crystals, featured in celestial room.

Buenos Aires Argentina Temple: Reflects aspects of Argentine historical architecture of Buenos Aires and art glass with the colors of the Argentine flag.

Columbus Ohio Temple: Exterior consists of Imperial Danby White marble that was quarried in the greater vicinity of Sharon, Vermont, which was the birthplace of Joseph Smith.

Art glass, Albuquerque New Mexico Temple.

Concepción Chile Temple: Interior includes artwork that features Chilean landscape and themes.

Copenhagen Denmark Temple: A renovation of an older building, the Priorvej chapel, constructed in 1931 and dedicated by Elder John A. Widtsoe. Portions of the building's architecture recall this early chapel. Other renovated buildings that became temples include the Vernal Utah Temple and Provo City Center Temple.

Draper Utah Temple: Windows feature log cabin quilt patterns, reminiscent of pioneer quilting practices. Utah's state flower, the sego lily, is a theme in this temple.

Edmonton Alberta Temple: Representations of Alberta's wild rose are located on the temple front. Also, wheat shafts, recalling Alberta's farming community, are located there.

Fort Lauderdale Florida Temple: Features sun motifs and palm tree motifs. Temple and its steeple, columns, and arches are reminiscent of Neoclassical architecture.

Hartford Connecticut Temple: The architecture is New England style and reflects the famous First Church of Christ Congregational Church, which was built in Farmington, 1772.

Hong Kong China Temple: Features Hong Kong colonial-style architecture, with a single spire on the top of a gold dome.

Idaho Falls Idaho Temple: Architect John Fetzer Sr. was inspired to design the temple to reflect his idea of an ancient Nephite temple.

Kansas City Missouri Temple: Olive branches signify a dominant theme; they are represented on the exterior of the temple on panels and stained-glass and etched-glass windows; the interior of the temple features them in art glass, light fixtures, railings, carpet sculptings, walls and panels, and various other places in the temple.

Laie Hawaii Temple: Exterior consists of native lava rock and coral, which was crushed and incorporated into concrete. Sculptor Avard Fairbanks created friezes that exist at the top of the temple's four sides, depicting four historical eras: the Old Testament (west), the New Testament (south), the Book of Mormon (north), and the latter days (east).

Las Vegas Nevada Temple: The celestial room features floor-to-ceiling windows; when the natural light flows through the windows, beautiful rainbow-like colors appear in the celestial room.

Logan Utah Temple: This and other temples, including Salt Lake, Manti, San Diego, and Washington D.C., feature battlements, crenellated towers, and other castle-like architectural features, giving the appearance of a fortress.

Lubbock Texas Temple: Exterior windows feature stained glass, and granite walls include etchings.

Manhattan New York Temple: Many door handles bear the shape of the Statue of Liberty's torch.

Manti Utah Temple: Two renowned spiral staircases wind upward for five stories in the octagonal towers on the temple's west side. They are open-centered and self-supporting, with walnut hand railings. Considered to be a pioneer engineering marvel.

Meridian Idaho Temple: The syringa, Idaho's state flower, is a common motif throughout the temple. Also, large murals present Idaho's wilderness and mountains.

Mesa Arizona Temple: A grand staircase leads to the celestial room. Carved friezes depict gathering of Israel themes from Isaiah's writings. Each of the temple's four corners (exterior) features a sculptured frieze that illustrates the Saints' gathering from the earth's four corners. Eight friezes of Saints gathering to the Rocky Mountains, including Welsh, English, Dutch, German, Swiss, French, Native American, and Pacific Islander.

Mexico City Mexico Temple: Architect Emil B. Fetzer designed this temple to reflect Mayan culture and motifs; representations of ancient Maya are therefore presented on the temple's exterior.

Nauvoo Illinois Temple: A faithful reproduction of the earlier Nauvoo Temple. A statue of the Prophet Joseph Smith and his brother Hyrum,

Palmyra New York Temple, windows depicting the Sacred Grove.

both on horseback, is located near the temple. Both were martyred during the original temple's construction. In fact, this temple's dedication occurred on the anniversary—the exact day and hour—of their martyrdom.

Oakland California Temple: Two sculpted panels, each thirty-five feet in length, exist on the temple's north and south sides. One portrays Jesus Christ's appearance to the Nephites (south) and the other His teaching in the Holy Land (north).

Palmyra New York Temple: Built on a site having historical significance (compare the Nauvoo Illinois Temple and the Winter Quarters Nebraska Temple); the major theme is the Sacred Grove, which is depicted in multiple stained-glass windows; a stained glass also portrays the First Vision.

Paris France Temple: Art glass surrounding the temple doors features plants native to France and the flowers of Claude Monet's gardens.

Philadelphia Pennsylvania Temple: The granite building reflects classic designs and architecture of some of Philadelphia's significant historic buildings; for example, the temple's spires recall Independence Hall's clock tower, and the temple's walls are the same height as both the Philadelphia Free Library and the Philadelphia Family Court, which are located west of the temple. Also, the temple's furniture is reminiscent of the early period of Philadelphia.

Rexburg Idaho Temple: A central theme of the temple is the wheat stalk, depicted in art-glass windows, bringing to mind the agricultural setting of the region. Also, murals in the ordinance rooms depict landscapes and wildlife of the Snake River valley.

Rome Italy Temple: Interior walls, floors, and countertops feature Italian-quarried Perlato Svevo marble. Aspects of Michelangelo's Piazza del Campidoglio are featured in the floors of the temple's grand foyer and baptistry and also sculpted into the off-white carpets located in the sealing rooms and celestial room.

Salt Lake Temple: Several symbolic architectural features, including cloudstones, starstones, earthstones, moonstones, sunstones, the Big Dipper, an all-seeing eye, a handclasp, and others.[1]

San Salvador El Salvador Temple: The building recalls the area's Spanish colonial architecture, with conches, arches, and other styles and designs. El Salvador's national flower, the *flor de izote*, is depicted in motifs in art-glass windows and other places.

Santiago Chile Temple: Motifs and depictions of Chile's national flower, the *copíhue*, are featured in art-glass windows, on door handles, and in flooring designs. Chilean marble and lapis lazuli (a beautiful native blue stone) are also used in the temple.

---

1. See Oman, "Exterior Symbolism of the Salt Lake Temple," 6–68.

(left) Paris France Temple art glass.

Sapporo Japan Temple: The building is inspired by Asian architecture, and the grounds include plants and trees that are distinctively common to the area.

Seoul Korea Temple: Features a tiled roof similar to Korean "hundred-year" roof, silk wall hangings, and other elements common to Korea.

Snowflake Arizona Temple: Interior parts of the temple feature pioneer themes or Native American history and cultural traditions, including pottery, baskets, and handcrafted rugs. For example, some of the custom-built furniture includes Native American designs that are carved. The temple also presents stained-glass windows portraying Jesus Christ instructing women, men, and children.

Taipei Taiwan Temple: Architecture inspired by local architectural themes. For example, its blue tile roof brings to mind the neighboring National Chiang Kaishek Memorial Hall.

Tijuana Mexico Temple: Architecture recalls old Spanish mission structures, especially the San Xavier del Bac Mission in Tucson, Arizona.

Tijuana Mexico Temple.

Tucson Arizona Temple: A prominent dome-shaped cupola was inspired by the dome belonging to the famous Florence Cathedral in Italy.

Twin Falls Idaho Temple: The spectacular Shoshone Falls, located about five miles from the temple, inspired architects to include a waterfall theme in the temple's stained-glass windows, walls, and landscape. Also, Idaho's state flower, the syringa, is featured as a motif in many of the two hundred art-glass windows, which consist of some twelve thousand pieces of glass.

Washington D.C. Temple: "The seven floors represent the six days of

Winter Quarters Nebraska Temple artistic designs, front entrance.

creation and the day of rest."[1] The magnificent six spires recall the Salt Lake Temple's spires. The gates and doors feature eight bronze depictions, representing creation, mortality, and the degrees of glory. Also featured are the North Star, Big Dipper, the sun, stars, moon, planets, the earth, and "seven concentric pentagons," which perhaps recall the seven dispensations.[2] The temple's main lobby has huge, thirty-foot-long mural of Jesus Christ's Second Coming, with a representation of the temple found in the mural.

Winter Quarters Nebraska Temple: Three panes of glass in the baptistry are sculpted to depict an olive branch, a fig branch, and an almond branch. The temple's front doors also depict olive branches.

ARCHITECTURAL SAFEGUARDS

God has established several safeguards to protect His temples, ancient and modern; these protections discourage unqualified persons from approaching sacred areas or from seeing things that are beyond their authority or spiritual circumstances. He uses angels, sentinels, cherubim (with the flaming, revolving sword), temple recommend procedures, and more. Furthermore, He established various architectural safeguards to protect the holiness of His temples, including boundaries, thresholds, horizontal zones, vertical features, and walls, gates, doors, and veils.

---

1. England, "Washington D.C. Temple," 88.
2. England, "Washington D.C. Temple," 88.

Walls around the tabernacle demarcate secular space from holy space.

For example, walls are basic but vital architectural components in sacred dwellings. Each wall creates a frame around a designated spot, a pronounced border that all can see and that no one can misapprehend. Walls define horizontal spaces and serve to demarcate between zones of holiness and secular areas. Walls also present border configurations between different gradations of holiness, such as the tabernacle courtyard, holy place, and Holy of Holies; so, too, walls divide various rooms in present-day temples. In the end, the same walls that retain the sacred atmosphere inside the temple also bar the secular world on the outside.

Just as walls serve to arrest the approach of unclean individuals and to halt their movement, an opening in the wall exists that allows secular space to be transcended, or sacred space to be entered; such openings were generally represented by temple doors, gates, and veils, each of which allowed ingress and egress from profane to holy space, then to holier, and finally to the holiest space in the Lord's house. Not only did doors have a utilitarian function; many of them were decorated beautifully. The door leading from the holy place to the Holy of Holies in Solomon's temple had "carvings of cherubims and palm trees and open flowers" and the doors were "overlaid . . . with gold" (1 Kgs. 6:31–32).

Notwithstanding various safeguards, temple architecture provides secure passage for ritually qualified individuals (i.e., those who participate in the gestures of approach). The ancient high priest, for example, traversed through three chief horizontal zones—the courtyard(s), the holy place, and the Holy of Holies—and their respective walls and openings. And in modern temples, worthy women and men traverse various sacred areas of the temple, from its threshold to the celestial room.

Nibley summarizes the role of boundaries and openings: "All temples are marked by boundaries, stations, levels, doors, stairs, passages, gates, veils, etc.—they all denote rites of passage going from one condition or state to another, from lower to higher, from dark to light, a complete transition from one world, telestial or terrestrial, to another, ultimately the celestial. At certain crucial passages one must identify oneself by an exchange of names and tokens and show oneself qualified by an exchange of words. This was characteristic of all ancient temples."[1]

---

1. Nibley, *A House of Glory*, 37–38.

East doors of the Salt Lake Temple.

ARK OF THE COVENANT

The ark was an atonement-centered object that resided in the tabernacle, the temple of Solomon (see 1 Kgs. 8:1–8), and the temple in heaven (see Rev. 11:19). Anciently, the ark was the most holy piece of furniture. It was housed behind the veil (see Ex. 40:21; Num. 4:4–6) in the most holy space (Holy of Holies).

God commanded Moses to construct the ark, and He provided him with detailed instructions for its construction (Ex. 25:1, 10–22). It was made of acacia wood, which was overlaid with gold; its measurements were two and a half cubits long and one and a half cubits high and broad (length, 45"; width 27"; height 27") (see Ex. 37:1–2). The mercy seat and cherubs were made of pure gold (see Ex. 25:17–19). Two cherubs (guardians of sacred space) rested over the ark (see Ex. 25:19–20).

The ark was a formidable instrument; it brought blessings to believers (see Josh. 3–4; 1 Sam. 7:1; 2 Sam. 6:2–17) and cursings to unbelievers (see Josh. 6; 1 Sam. 5:1–7; 6:19–20). On one occasion, its presence blessed

Ark of the covenant with two cherubs.

Obed-edom and his family (see 2 Sam. 6:11–12); on another occasion, the powerful ark was deadly to those who trespassed God's commandments regarding it (see 1 Sam. 6:19). The ark was also a place of prayer and revelation, to both the Lord's prophets and His high priests (see Ex. 25:22; Num. 7:89; Jdg. 20:27–28; see also entry, "Mercy Seat [Throne of Atonement]").

The ark of the covenant housed three items: the rod of Aaron that budded with almond buds and blossoms, the golden container with manna, and the tablets of stone with the Ten Commandments (see Heb. 9:4); all three items are symbols of Jesus Christ.

Three items in the ark: Aaron's rod, tablets of the Ten Commandments, container of manna.

The rod of Aaron has two direct connections to the ancient temple: (1) Moses placed Aaron's rod in the Holy of Holies and there (overnight!) it miraculously budded, blossomed, and yielded almonds; (2) As a "token" (Num. 17:10) and powerful symbol, the rod of Aaron was stored in the ark of the covenant (see Heb. 9:4). The primary symbolism of the rod pointed to Jesus Christ—the Hebrew *sha-ked* (*almond, almond tree*) has a special meaning that suggests the Resurrection; *sha-ked* denotes "to wake up early," and the almond tree is "so called from its early waking out of winter's sleep."[1] In Israel, the almond tree buds and blossoms early in the season. As an almond tree, Aaron's rod calls to mind Jesus Christ, who was the first to awaken at the Resurrection.

Manna, or "bread from heaven" (Ex. 16:4), served as a type and shadow of Jesus Christ. In the context of the miraculous feeding of bread

---

1. *A Hebrew and English Lexicon of the Old Testament*, 1052.

and fish to five thousand people, Jesus taught, "I am the living bread which came down from heaven" (John 6:51).

The Lord gave Moses two stone tablets, on which were inscribed the Ten Commandments (see Ex. 31:18). The tablets call to mind Christ, who is the *Lawgiver* (Isa. 33:22; D&C 45:59), the *Word of God* (Rev. 19:13), and the *Stone* (Jacob 4:15; D&C 50:44).

ASCENSION

The concept of *ascension* is significant to both ancient and modern temples because worshippers, then and now, *ascend* to the Lord's house. The Hebrew term *alah* ("go up," "ascend") is a watchword utilized by biblical writers in connection with individuals who ascend unto God's sacred places. The Israelites were required to *"go up* to appear before the Lord" to worship in the temple three times a year (Ex. 34:24, emphasis added); when King Hezekiah needed divine help, he *"went up* into the house of the Lord" (2 Kgs. 19:14, emphasis added); King Josiah, too, *"went up* into the house of the Lord" (2 Kgs. 23:2, emphasis added; see also Jer. 26:10). Moses ascended Mount Sinai and received a temple experience: "Moses *went up* into the mount of God" (Ex. 24:13, emphasis added; see also 19:3). The Psalmist asked, "Who shall *ascend* into the hill [Hebrew: "mountain"] of the Lord?" (Ps. 24:3, emphasis added), a reference to the temple.

President David O. McKay spoke of the endowment as an ascension: "Seen for what it is, [the endowment] is the *step-by-step ascent* into the eternal Presence."[1] The step-by-step ascent may be literal, from one level or floor to the next, but the step-by-step ascent is *always* a spiritual ascent that each temple worshipper experiences when he or she worthily attends the temple.

Why ascend? Because God is elevated above mortals and the world.

---

1. Cited in J. Richard Clarke, "The Temple—What It Means to You," *New Era*, April 1993, 7; emphasis added.

He is "the most high God" (Gen. 14:20) and He sits "upon a throne, high and lifted up" (Isa. 6:1). Some prayers express God's elevated status: "O Lord . . . thou art exalted as head above all" (1 Chr. 29:11; see also 2 Sam. 22:47); "Be thou exalted, O God, above the heavens" (Ps. 57:5); "For thou, Lord, art high above all the earth: thou art exalted far above all gods" (Ps. 97:9). See entry "Stairs/Staircases."

ATONEMENT MONEY AND REDEMPTION MONEY

Under the law of Moses, adult Israelite males ("from twenty years old and above") were required to pay "atonement money" (or "atonement silver"). This money was used to support "the service of the tabernacle," to "make an atonement for [their] souls," and to assure the Israelites "that there be no plague among them" (Ex. 30:12, 14, 16). This act of paying atonement money could bring to mind our own commandment to pay tithing so that we are not burned at Jesus's coming (see D&C 64:23; see also "Plagues, and the Atonement").

Also, during the period of the law of Moses, Israelites who were not of the priestly family (of temple workers) were commanded to pay redemption money for their firstborn son. The commandment is called *pidyon haben,* or "the redemption of the first born" son. Numbers 18:15–16 states: "Every thing that openeth the [womb] in all flesh, which they bring unto the Lord, whether it be of men or beasts, shall be thine: nevertheless the firstborn of man shalt thou surely redeem, and the firstling of unclean beasts shalt thou redeem. And those that are to be redeemed from a month old shalt thou redeem, according to thine estimation, for the money of five shekels, after the shekel of the sanctuary, which is twenty gerahs" (see also Num. 3:45; 8:17).

ATONEMENT OF JESUS CHRIST, TEMPLE FOCUSES ON

Latter-day Saint temples focus on Jesus Christ and His Atonement. As President Russell M. Nelson testified, "Temple ordinances and covenants teach of the redeeming power of the Atonement."[1]

In several ways, both ancient and modern temples convey the meaning of Jesus Christ's Atonement to all of those who worship therein. In fact, temples dispense numerous teachings and symbols of the Atonement—the temple is indeed a sacred space where women and men make the Atonement a matter of significance in their lives. Demonstrating the connection between the Atonement and the ancient temple, the law of Moses uses the Hebrew word *kpr* (translated "to atone, atonement," etc.) about eighty times in association with the tabernacle and the temple (Exodus, 10 times; Leviticus, 49 times; Numbers, 18 times; and Deuteronomy, 3 times). This fact establishes that the temple was an Atonement-focused institution.

Multiple components that teach regarding Jesus Christ's Atonement in the ancient temple include the temple furniture (laver of brass, altars, horns of the altar, lampstand, ark of the covenant), priestly vestments, animal sacrifices, sacrificial blood, foods (portions of sacrificial offerings, shewbread), sacred objects (jar of manna, tablets of the law, rod of Aaron), and diverse parts of the temple, such as the veil. Leviticus 16:33 summarizes, the high priest "shall make an atonement for the holy sanctuary, and he shall make an atonement for the tabernacle of the congregation, and for the altar, and he shall make an atonement for the priests, and for all the people of the congregation."

---

1. Nelson, "Prepare for Blessings of the Temple," 22.

Jesus Praying in Gethsemane by Harry Anderson.

BAPTISM FOR THE DEAD

The ritual of baptism, both for the living and the dead, is Jesus Christ–centered: "Baptism is in similitude of the death, burial, and resurrection of Christ" (Romans 6, chapter heading). In fact, Jesus is symbolically associated with every element dealing with baptism—prayer, the font, white clothing, water, and the acts of immersion and emerging from the water. As to the antiquity of baptism for the dead, Joseph Smith taught, "The doctrine of Baptism for the dead is clearly shown in the new testament."[1] Paul's statement reads, "Else what shall they do which are baptized for the dead, if the dead rise not at all? why are they then baptized for the dead?" (1 Cor. 15:29). Joseph Smith also stated, regarding the ordinance of baptism for the dead, "God decreed before the foundation of the world that that ordinance should be administered in a font prepared for that purpose in the house of the Lord."[2] However, we note here that baptisms for the dead were started only after Jesus Christ preached to the spirits in prison.

Jesus Christ–focused items include the following:

Baptismal prayer: Three names of Jesus are found in the prayer, "Jesus Christ," "the Son," and "Amen" (Rev. 3:14).

Baptismal font: See entry "Baptismal Font."

Ritual immersion: Baptism is called a "burial" (JST, Gen. 17:5; D&C 76:51). In Romans 6:3–11, a discourse on baptism, Paul used many terms that pertain to death—*dead, buried, death,* and *died.* He also used terms that speak of the Resurrection—*raised up, newness of life, resurrection, live, raised from the dead, liveth,* and *alive.*

Emerging from the waters: The immersion (signifying the burial) in the waters is followed by the emerging from the waters, which signifies the Resurrection. When the recipient of baptism comes "forth out of the water

---

1. "Discourse, 11 June 1843–A, as Reported by Wilford Woodruff," p. [44], The Joseph Smith Papers, accessed March 27, 2019, https://www.josephsmithpapers.org/paper-summary/discourse-11-june-1843-a-as-reported-by-wilford-woodruff/3.
2. *Teachings of Presidents of the Church: Joseph Smith*, 417.

[it] is in the likeness of the resurrection of the dead in coming forth out of their graves" (D&C 128:12). In other words, the candidate becomes a new person or a "new creature" in Christ (2 Cor. 5:17; see also Eph. 4:20–24). Thus, both the immersion and emerging from the waters are symbolic, of the tomb and of the womb. In sum, immersion in baptism represents both our physical and spiritual death and our being made alive again in Christ.

"Born Again": The scriptures record that those who submit to baptism are "born again" and become like children. Moses 6:58–60 presents a juxtaposition of children born naturally of mothers and of persons born spiritually of Christ. When born of woman, three elements are present: water, the blood of our life-giver mother, and spirit. These three elements are present at our spiritual rebirth: the water of baptism, the blood of our Life-giver Jesus Christ, and the Spirit of God. And they are present, or represented, as we remember Christ and our covenant to Him when we partake of the sacrament. Those born again become "the children of Christ, his sons, and his daughters . . . spiritually begotten . . . born of him" (Mosiah 5:7).

White clothing: Denotes purity, which is possible only through the Atonement of Christ.

Water: Water is a vital component in the baptismal rite—"The ordinance of baptism by water . . . to be immersed in the water and come forth out of the water" (D&C 128:12). The water of life, or, the "fountain of living waters" (Jer. 2:13; 17:13) calls to mind Jesus Christ. The water symbolically washes and cleanses us from our sins: "Why tarriest thou? arise, and be baptized, and wash away thy sins" (Acts 22:16).

BAPTISMAL FONT

Our temples feature baptismal fonts, which are utilized for baptisms on behalf of the dead. These fonts are located below where the living are accustomed to gather, as per the scriptural instruction, "The baptismal font . . . was commanded to be in a place underneath where the living are wont to assemble" (D&C 128:13). Why below the ground level? Because "the baptismal font was instituted as a similitude of the grave" (D&C 128:13). Connected with this, baptism is called a "burial" (JST, Gen. 17:5; Rom. 6:3–4, 6; D&C 76:51) (see entry "Oxen, Twelve").

BEEHIVES

Beehive, center of door panel, Salt Lake Temple.

Images of beehives exist throughout the Salt Lake Temple, including on exterior doors (in the middle of two roundels), in etched pieces of glass, and on various interior doorknobs; above the beehive images of the doorknobs are the words "Holiness to the Lord." Other temples also feature representations or images of the beehive, including Manhattan New York, Manti Utah, St. George Utah,[1] and Logan Utah (the former steps leading to the baptismal font). The "honey bee and the hive" are "symbols of industry," wrote George Albert Smith.[2]

BELLS OF GOLD

The Lord instructed Moses to place bells of pure gold on the hem of the high priest's robe. The bells were alternated with beautiful representations of pomegranates made of three colors—blue, purple, and scarlet (see

---

1. Brinkerhoff, "Symbolism of the Beehive," 146.
2. Smith, *Sharing the Gospel with Others*, 134.

Bells of pure gold attached to the high priest's robe.

Ex. 28:33). The Lord revealed the bells' purpose: "It shall be upon Aaron to minister: and his sound [i.e., the sound of the bells] shall be heard when he goeth in unto the holy place before the Lord, and when he cometh out, that he die not" (Ex. 28:35). That is to say, during the very consequential time when the high priest ministered in the temple, Israelite worshippers (who were gathered in the temple courtyard) could hear the sound of the bells. They, the worshippers, knew exactly where the high priest was serving, because of the bells' unique, musical notes. Those who understood the impact of the high priest's sacred work must have been filled with joy at the sound.

BIG DIPPER (URSA MAJOR)

The Big Dipper (Ursa Major) is a prominent asterism that comprises seven stars. Together these stars present the view of a large, cup-shaped bowl with a handle (sort of like a ladle); four stars designate the bowl and three the handle. The two stars at the end of the bowl (named *Merak* and *Dubhe*) point to the North or Polar Star, which travelers and others have

Big Dipper, Salt Lake Temple.

used for celestial navigation for millennia. Thus the Big Dipper is an important guidepost created by God for our benefit.

At least four temples present representations of the Big Dipper—the Salt Lake, Washington D.C., Winter Quarters Nebraska, and Anchorage Alaska Temples. The representations of the Big Dipper on temples suggest multiple meanings: (1) Inasmuch as God is the Creator of all stars and constellations, it is appropriate that this prominent star cluster exists on several of His temples; (2) Just as the Big Dipper has guided navigators and travelers for millennia, the temple serves as a divine guide for us with regard to both temporal and spiritual matters. Through the temple, we can find our spiritual bearings as we navigate through mortality. Church

Big Dipper and North Star (featured in two squares, presented in a circle, which is found in a square), Washington D.C. Temple.

architect Truman O. Angell explained it this way: "Ursa Major (commonly called in this country The Dipper), with the Pointers ranging with the North Star. (Moral:—The lost may find their way by the aid of the Priesthood)";[1] (3) The Big Dipper points to the North Star, which is a symbolic representation of Jesus Christ.

BLEMISHES, PRIESTS AND HIGH PRIESTS WITH

Priests and high priests who possessed certain physical conditions were not permitted to participate in sacrificial offerings (could not "come nigh unto the altar") nor partake of the holy food (Lev. 21:16–23). The Lord revealed: "For whatsoever man he be that hath a blemish, he shall not approach: a blind man, or a lame, or he that hath a flat nose, or any thing superfluous, Or a man that is brokenfooted, or brokenhanded, Or crookbackt, or a dwarf, or that hath a blemish in his eye, or be scurvy, or scabbed, or hath his stones broken; No man that hath a blemish of the seed of Aaron the priest shall come nigh to offer the offerings of the Lord made by fire: he hath a blemish; he shall not come nigh to offer the bread of his God" (Lev. 21:18–21). Priests who violated these commandments were subject to excommunication or even death (see Lev. 22:1–9).

The physical conditions (or "blemish," which is used twice) identified in these verses may be symbolic of spiritual blemishes, or sins. Priests, who represent Jesus Christ, must be clean and spiritually unblemished in order to serve in the temple. These verses in Leviticus may be likened to each of us who serve in God's temples—we must strive to serve without spiritual blemishes.

---

1. Angell, "The Salt Lake City Temple," 274.

BLEMISHES, SACRIFICIAL ANIMALS WITH

In order to qualify as sacred sacrifices for the ancient temple, animals could not have physical blemishes. The law covered both male and female animals: "Whether it be a male or female, he shall offer it without blemish before the Lord" (Lev. 3:1, see also v. 6; Ex. 12:5; 29:1).

Deuteronomy 15:21 provides some clarification regarding the nature of the blemishes: "If there be any blemish therein, as if it be lame, or blind, or have any ill blemish, thou shalt not sacrifice it unto the Lord thy God" (see also Deut. 17:1). The unblemished sacrificial animals symbolized Jesus Christ, who was "as . . . a lamb without blemish and without spot" (1 Pet. 1:19).

BLOOD, MEANING OF

Sacrificed animals' blood was sprinkled on various persons (high priests, priests, cleansed lepers, Israelites) and a variety of objects (the mercy seat, altar's four horns, priestly garments, and the leper's house; see Ex. 29:16, 21; Lev. 4:6, 17; 5:9; 14:6–7, 51; 16:14). The sprinkling of the blood of a sacrificial animal was a Jesus Christ–focused procedure that had a direct connection to the Atonement. The sprinkled blood of the sacrificial animal foreshadows Jesus Christ's blood, which cleanses us and makes us holy. The following New Testament passages directly associate the sprinkled blood of the sacrificial victim to Jesus Christ and His atoning sacrifice: "Unto obedience and sprinkling of the blood of Jesus Christ" (1 Pet. 1:2); "to Jesus the mediator of the

The priest (model), dressed in sacred vestments, places blood (artificial) on the horn of the incense altar.

BLOOD, MEANING OF | 69

The high priest (model), dressed in sacred vestments, sprinkles bull's blood (artificial) on the ark of the covenant on the Day of Atonement.

new covenant, and to the blood of sprinkling" (Heb. 12:24); "by the blood of Jesus . . . having our hearts sprinkled from an evil conscience, and our bodies washed with pure water" (Heb. 10:19, 22); "For if the blood of bulls and of goats, and the ashes of an heifer sprinkling the unclean, sanctifieth to the purifying of the flesh: How much more shall the blood of Christ . . . purge your conscience from dead works to serve the living God?" (Heb. 9:13–14).

Why the emphasis on blood? The scriptures provide a number of points where blood focuses on Jesus Christ's blood:

Blood purges and provides remission: "Almost all things are by the law purged with blood; and without shedding of blood is no remission" (Heb. 9:22).

Blood makes an atonement: "It is the blood that maketh an atonement for the soul" (Lev. 17:11).

Christ's blood brings redemption: "There could be no redemption for mankind save it were through the death and sufferings of Christ, and the atonement of his blood" (Alma 21:9; see also 24:13; 1 Pet. 1:18–19).

BODILY CONDITIONS AND THE TEMPLE

The book of Leviticus contains a series of regulations and directives that pertain to bodily conditions (such as diseases, physical blemishes, running issues). These regulations belong to the temple, ritually *clean* or *unclean* individuals, and the placement of ritually unclean individuals outside of the temple's zones of holiness.

The regulations include: (1) *A male or female with a running issue* from the flesh was ritually unclean; such a person required an atonement (see Lev. 15:1–30); (2) *Lepers and those with certain skin diseases* were ritually unclean and were required to "dwell alone; without the camp [or city] shall his habitation be" (Lev. 13:46). When lepers were healed, then "the priest shall offer the sin offering... and the priest shall make an atonement for him, and he shall be clean" (Lev. 14:19–20); (3) *Priests with physical blemishes,* such as lameness, a hunched back, crippled feet or hands, or other deformities or disfigurements could not participate in certain temple rituals (see Lev. 21:16–23) (4) *A woman after childbirth* was considered ritually unclean after her issue of blood following childbirth, and the law required a period of purification followed by temple rituals, sacrifices, and atonement on her behalf (see Lev. 12:1–8). Noteworthy, Mary, after giving birth to Jesus, obeyed the law of a woman after childbirth, as articulated in Leviticus 12:2–8. Luke wrote that after "the days of her purification," she brought Jesus to the temple and offered two young pigeons as a sacrifice (Luke 2:22–24).

Additionally, mortals with such bodily conditions could convey ritual uncleanness to clothing or houses, so that there existed an (5) *atonement for clothing* that has mildew or that has been infected by a skin disease or plague, the priest's diagnosis of that clothing, his pronouncement of "clean" or "unclean," and the subsequent washing or burning the clothing (Lev. 13:47–59; 14:54–57); and an (6) *atonement for a house* that has been contaminated by leprosy or another skin disease requires purification through the Atonement (Lev. 14:33–57).

Sometimes diseases are metaphors for sin (see Ex. 15:26; Deut. 7:15; Ps. 103:3); and occasionally disobedient individuals were afflicted with leprosy (see Num. 12:1–15; 2 Chr. 26:16–21). Elder Dale G. Renlund taught, "Since God uses disease as a metaphor for sin throughout the scriptures, it is reasonable to ask, 'How does Jesus Christ react when faced with our metaphorical diseases—our sins?' After all, the Savior said that He 'cannot look upon sin with the least degree of allowance'; so how can He look at us, imperfect as we are, without recoiling in horror and disgust?"[1] Inasmuch as diseases sometimes represent sin, this explains the placement of ritually unclean individuals outside of the temple's zones of holiness and the ritual requirements of atonement for such individuals (according to Leviticus), which atonement repairs unclean persons so that they can return to the temple.

What is the relationship to certain bodily conditions and the temple? Biblical scholar Mary Douglas adds this insight—the mortal body is a microcosm of the tabernacle and temple: "The body is a theological microcosm: the blemished, bleeding, leaking, suppurating, torn body, now presented as a woman, now a man, now as garment, then a house, now as an imperfect priest, now an inadequate offering, and then climaxing as the sanctuary defiled, is an image of Israel in the horrible condition she would be in, if unsanctified."[2]

CARDINAL DIRECTIONS

East, south, north, and west are cardinal directions or points. "The temple is oriented toward the four world regions or cardinal directions,"[3]

---

1. Renlund, "Our Good Shepherd," 30.
2. Douglas, "Atonement in Leviticus," 123, 129.
3. Lundquist, "What is a Temple? A Preliminary Typology," 92.

wrote John Lundquist. Why are the cardinal directions significant, especially with regard to temples? The cardinal directions represent the totality of the earth and her inhabitants, and the temple has the capacity to impact all of earth's inhabitants; furthermore, the Lord's missionaries go forward in all directions to preach the gospel. Some scholars maintain that the axis—where the four directions meet in the center—designates where the temple is built.

The cardinal directions are affiliated with ancient and modern temples in the following ways: (1) The molten sea featured twelve oxen; three faced east, three faced west, three faced south, and three faced north (see 1 Kgs. 7:23, 25) (see entry "Oxen, Twelve"). (2) The order of encampment of the ancient Israelites around the tabernacle emphasized the cardinal directions (see Num. 2:1–31). (3) The Garden of Eden temple featured a river that "parted, and became . . . four heads," which were named Pison, Gihon, Hiddekel, and Euphrates (Gen. 2:10–14). The text seems to imply that the four heads were oriented to the four cardinal directions.

The cardinal direction *east* is especially emphasized in temple settings, including: (1) The statue of the angel Moroni, situated on several Latter-day Saint temples, is often oriented eastward. (2) The significant phrase "Holiness to the Lord" is located on the east side of most Latter-day Saint temples. (3) Both the tabernacle and Solomon's temple were oriented eastward, meaning the temple's arrangement—court, holy place, and Holy of Holies—were ordered from east to west. Similarly, when the magnificent temple described in Ezekiel is built (see Ezek. 40–46), God's glory will come from the east (see Ezek. 43:2, 4). (4) Three times *east* has significance in the Garden of Eden narrative (see Gen. 2:8, 10–14; 3:24; Alma 12:21). (5) For the import of the eastern towers of the Salt Lake, Logan, and Manti Temples, see entry "Tower(s)."

Richard Cowan explains the significance of east: "In ancient times, Israelite temples typically were built so that their main doorways opened toward the east. The rising of the sun announced the new day, symbolizing new beginnings and opportunities. . . . This eastward orientation symbolizes watching for the second coming of Christ, which has been likened to the dawning of a new day."[1]

CELESTIAL BODIES (SUN, MOON, STARS, ETC.) DEPICTED ON TEMPLES

Several temples feature images and representations of heavenly or celestial bodies, such as the sun, moon, and stars. For example, the Salt Lake Temple presents earthstones, moonstones, sunstones, stars, and the Big Dipper on its exterior.[2] There are representations of one or more stars on the following temples: Albuquerque New Mexico, St. George Utah, Washington D.C., Nauvoo Illinois, Portland Oregon, Las Vegas Nevada, St. Louis Missouri, Winter Quarters Nebraska, and others. Furthermore, many of the temples feature other heavenly bodies on their exterior or interior parts, including representations of a sunstone, a moonstone, an image of a sun with its rays, the Big Dipper, and so forth (see the entries "Sunstones," "Moonstones," "Big Dipper"). These representations have multiple possible meanings:

Images of heavenly bodies, blue heavens, sun, large star, phase of moon.

(1) On July 31, 1854, George A. Smith described the earthstones, moonstones, and sunstones of the Salt Lake Temple, and then wrote, "Every stone has its moral lesson, and all point

---

1. Cowan, "Latter-day Saint Temples as Symbols," 6–7.
2. For a discussion of celestial features on the Salt Lake Temple, see Oman, "Exterior Symbolism of the Salt Lake Temple," 6–68.

Sunstones, starstones, and star images, Nauvoo Illinois Temple.

to the celestial world."[1] Associated with this, the Salt Lake Temple's earthstones, moonstones, and sunstones, Richard Holzapfel suggests that they "represent the 'three degrees of glory,' the telestial, terrestrial, and celestial kingdoms of heaven."[2]

(2) They serve as reminders to us that God is the Creator of the magnificent heavens and the earth.

(3) Poetically, the great heavenly bodies join with others of God's creations to declare that God lives and that He has set forth great wonders: "Let the sun, moon, and the morning stars sing together, and let all the sons of God shout for joy! And let the eternal creations declare his

---

1. Smith, "Description of the Temple," 636.
2. Holzapfel, "Every Window, Every Spire 'Speaks of the Things of God,'" 16; see also Cowan, "Latter-day Saint Temples as Symbols," 7.

name forever and ever!" (D&C 128:23). The Psalmist wrote: "Praise ye the Lord. . . . Praise ye him, sun and moon: praise him, all ye stars of light. . . . Let them praise the name of the Lord: for his name alone is excellent; his glory is above the earth and heaven" (Ps. 148:1, 3, 13).

(4) The representations of the heavenly bodies on the temples could remind us that "all things denote there is a God; yea, even the earth, and all things that are upon the face of it, yea, and its motion, yea, and also all the planets which move in their regular form do witness that there is a Supreme Creator" (Alma 30:44).

CELESTIAL ROOM, GOD'S LIVING ROOM

Each of our temples gives prominence to a celestial room, which temple worshippers enter at the culmination of the endowment ceremony, at the end of the spiritual path. President Gordon B. Hinckley stated that "this room was created to represent the celestial kingdom" and, as such, "it well might be" described as "God's living room." He also taught that "it is our privilege, unique and exclusive, while dressed in white, to sit at the conclusion of our ordinance work in the beautiful celestial room and ponder, meditate, and silently pray."[3]

CENTER PLACE, TEMPLE AS THE

Both ancient and modern sources disclose that the temple was the center place of the earth and her inhabitants; even if the temple is not the actual geographical center, it is always the spiritual core and religious center of God's covenant people.

The tabernacle, for example, was the actual, geographical center of the Israelite tribes. The order of encampment of the ancient Israelites positioned the tabernacle in the center (see Num. 2:1–31). The Levites and

---
3. Hinckley, "Closing Remarks," 105.

Mosaic tabernacle was the geographical center of the Israelite tribes.

the priestly family (e.g., Moses, Aaron, and priests) encamped adjacent to the tabernacle, and the encampment of other Israelite tribes surrounded the Levites.

Similarly, the entire schematic map of Ezekiel 48 sets Jerusalem at the center of the twelve tribes. Certainly, the notion of the centrality of Jerusalem and the temple is well attested in the period of late antiquity. Scriptural passages present the temple of Jerusalem to be the focus of the nations in the last days (see Isa. 2:1–4; Zech. 8:20–23). "It shall come to pass . . . all nations shall flow" to it, wrote Isaiah (Isa. 2:2). This passage may also apply to all of the Lord's temples.

Modern geographical arrangements also emphasize the centrality of the temple. Joseph Smith's 1833 plat of the city of Zion[1] positions the temple in the center, with the Saints' residences built around the temple.

---

1. The Church of Jesus Christ of Latter-day Saints, Historical Department, Salt Lake City, Utah.

Compare also the 1833 plat for Kirtland, Ohio, and the circa 1838 plat for Far West, Missouri.[2]

Remarkably, the Lord revealed to Joseph Smith that Independence, with its temple, constitutes the center place: "Behold, the place which is now called Independence is the center place; and a spot for the temple is lying westward" (D&C 57:3; see also D&C 84:2–4).

Furthermore, the Salt Lake Temple serves as the center point of the road infrastructure for the city, so that the roads labeled North Temple, South Temple, East Temple (now Main Street), and West Temple frame the temple and Temple Square; and from there the Salt Lake City road system moves outward in the four cardinal directions. This road system emphasizes that the Salt Lake Temple is the focal point of the valley. Nibley, noting the etymological relationship of *template* and *temple,* wrote: "Everyone knows what a template is that you put over a map. It's as if we put a template over the temple in Salt Lake City; most every street in the city, and every city in the state, is measured east, west, north, and south from that arbitrary point."[3]

The Salt Lake City road system emphasizes that the Salt Lake Temple is the focal point of the valley.

Associated with the temple as the center place is the ancient idea that the temple is the "navel of the earth." The concept is found in many literatures, both Jewish[4] and non-Jewish, as biblical scholar Mircea Eliade and

---

2. See Hamilton, *Nineteenth-Century Mormon Architecture*, Illustrations, 1–4.
3. Nibley, *Temple and Cosmos,* 141.
4. For ancient Jewish sources that deal with this idea, see Jubilees 8:19; Babylonian Talmud Yoma 54b; Sanhedrin 37a; *Zohar,* 1:72a; 2:231a; 4:157a; 4:222a; 4:222b; 5:161b; *Midrash Tanhuma, Qedoshim* 10; and Josephus, *Jewish War,* III, 52. See also Terrien, "The Omphalos Myth and Hebrew Religion," 315–38; and for Jerusalem as the navel of the earth, see Patai, *Man and Temple in Ancient Jewish Myth and Ritual,* 85, 132, 155.

others have shown.[1] An ancient Jewish homiletic statement outlines the idea of the temple as a navel: "Just as the navel is found at the center of a human being, so the land of Israel is found at the center of the world ... Jerusalem is at the center of the land of Israel. The Temple is at the center of Jerusalem. The Holy of Holies is at the center of the Temple" (*Midrash Tanhuma, Qedoshim* 10). The author of these words compares a human's navel to Israel, Jerusalem, and the temple. The five-fold repetition of the word "center" emphasizes the important theme of centrality—each area of sacred space is found within the heart of the former.

The Israelite temple as the earth's navel denotes both a geometric position (i.e., the localization of the sanctuary at the center of civilization) and a spiritual meaning. The concept of *navel* suggests a center of nourishment, a place from which temporal and spiritual blessings emanate throughout the land of Israel. Just as a mother nourishes her baby through the umbilical cord, the Lord provides spiritual nourishment to His daughters and sons in the temple! A passage from the Jewish Zohar states that from the temple comes an "abundance of nourishment and all good things ... and there is no place in this inhabited world that is not nourished and sustained" by the temple (Zohar 4:157a; see also 5:161b). The *navel* comparison to the Jerusalem temple is not a doctrine, of course, but the idea serves to demonstrate the temple's power and influence in the thought of the Jews in ages past.

CENTER OF THE MAP, THE TEMPLE

So great has been the impact of the temple of Jerusalem on certain religious groups that some medieval cartographers who mapped the Holy Land or Jerusalem depicted the city of Jerusalem as having a geometric circular plan, or they mapped Jerusalem in the center of the world.

---

1. See especially Eliade, "Symbolism, the Sacred, and the Arts," 105–29.

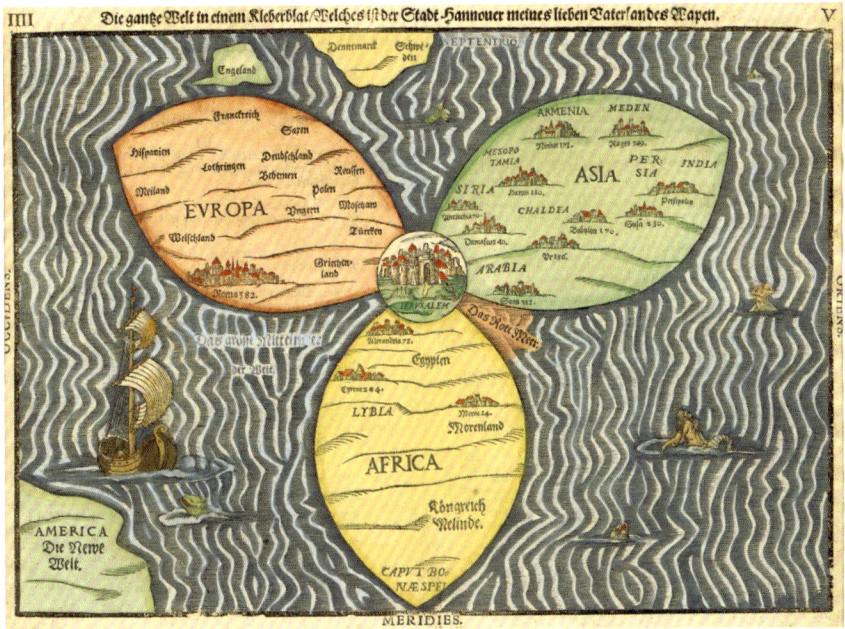

Bünting's world map depicts three continental land masses, with Jerusalem featured at the center.

Heinrich Bünting's map of the world depicts three continental land masses roughly in the form of a three-leaf clover. Published in *Itinerarium Sacrae Scripturae* in 1581, the continents are identified as Africa, Europe, and Asia. Set dead center where the three continents connect is the city of Jerusalem.[2] Why the emphasis on Jerusalem? Because it is the holy city that housed the temple of Solomon. This temple continued to greatly impact individuals and communities for millennia after its destruction.

Additional cartographers of the same general period delineate the Holy City in circular form. In 1493, the historian H. Schedel depicted a drawing of Jerusalem in his *Liber Chronicarum*, published in

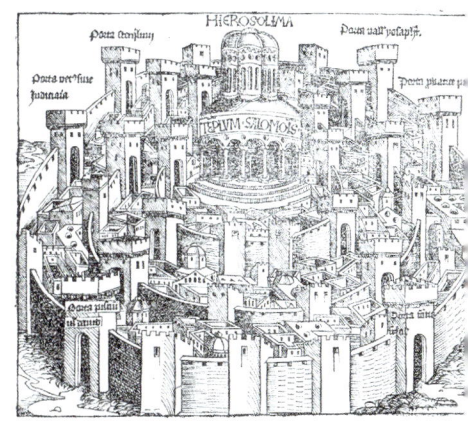

Schedel's drawing of Jerusalem, with four concentric circles.

---

2. Rubin, *Jerusalem through Maps and Views*, 50.

Nürnberg. The picture portrays the city as architecturally possessing four concentric circles. Each concentric circle is delimited by a high wall. Standing in the center of the city, and possessing the loftiest site in the area, stands the temple of Solomon. The temple, following other circular patterns found throughout the map, has a spherical dome, circular stairs, and other circular features.[1]

Other medieval cartographers place Jerusalem in the map's geometrical center,[2] thus emphasizing the great significance of Jerusalem's temple and its religious impact upon the world, even many centuries after its destruction.

CHERUBIM (GUARDIANS OF SACRED SPACE)

Cherubim (a Hebrew plural noun; the equivalent in English is *cherubs*) functioned as guardians[3] or sentinels of sacred places, preventing the trespass of unauthorized persons. "There is no doubt that these were heavenly beings, or angels."[4] Some scholars maintain that one of the cherubim was female and the other was male, suggesting wife and husband: "One of the Cherubim in the Temple represented a male, the other a female figure.... When Philo made his pilgrimage to the Temple, he saw the Cherubim 'entwined' like man and wife."[5] Rashi, a Jewish biblical scholar from the eleventh century, wrote that "the Cherubim were joined together, and were clinging to, and embracing, each other, like a male who embraces the female."[6] Therefore, according to these and other statements, both females

---

1. See Rubin, *Jerusalem through Maps and Views*, 60.
2. See Rubin, *Jerusalem through Maps and Views*, 17, 18.
3. See Parry, "Cherubim, the Flaming Sword, the Path, and the Tree of Life," 1–24.
4. Smith, *Answers to Gospel Questions*, 2:96 (see also 97); see also Widtsoe, *Gospel Interpretations*, 27; and Cannon, "The Angels Who Visit Us," 53–54.
5. Patai, *The Hebrew Goddess*, 115.
6. Patai, *The Hebrew Goddess,*, 123.

and males are represented in the temples' most sacred spaces—the Holy of Holies and the holy place!

Cherubim are found in the following temples:

(1) *Garden of Eden*: The cherubim in the Garden of Eden had a sword that whirled or zigzagged while blazing with fire (see Gen. 3:24; Alma 42:2–3). This portrayed a frightening image to those who were not qualified to approach sacred space or the tree of life.

Two cherubim on tabernacle veil covering the Holy of Holies.

(2) *Tabernacle*: Cherubim were represented in the tabernacle's Holy of Holies, on either side of the ark of the covenant (see Ex. 25:18–20), and images of cherubim were embroidered into the veil that separated the holy place of the Holy of Holies (see Ex. 26:31–33).

(3) *Solomon's temple*: This edifice featured very large cherubim ("each ten cubits high") made of olive wood and overlaid with gold (1 Kgs. 6:23–28), which were situated in the Holy of Holies. In addition, artisans carved images of cherubim on the temple walls and on the two olive wood doors that led to the Holy of Holies (see 1 Kgs. 6:29–32).

Two cherubs on the lid of the ark of the covenant.

(4) *Future temple:* Ezekiel refers to cherubim in his description of Jerusalem's temple that is yet to be built (Ezek. 41:18–25).

(5) *Temple in heaven*: Rather than representations (images) of cherubim, which are found in the tabernacle and Solomon's temple, actual living creatures are located in the temple in heaven. These are located around God's throne (see Rev. 4:6). The creatures worship God, and, as sentinels, they protect God's holiness from the unauthorized trespass of unworthy or unclean things and individuals.[1]

CIRCLE

A circle, which has no beginning and no ending, calls to mind eternity. Joseph Smith once referred to the ring he wore and taught that it had no beginning and no ending; he then spoke of "one eternal round."[2] *One eternal round* is also a scriptural phrase that refers to the Lord's divine course; "Wherefore, the course of the Lord is one eternal round" (1 Ne. 10:19; see also Alma 7:20; 37:12; D&C 3:2; 35:1).

Many temples feature circles in symbolic settings—in sacred ceremony, architectural designs and structures, appurtenances, including circular designs on exterior and interior walls, floors, steeples, furniture, or in garden spaces, windows, and more. Many of these circles are designed to remind worshippers of eternal things—things without beginning and without end, like Joseph Smith's ring.

Examples of the use of circles in our temples include:

Baptismal font: The font itself, which rests upon the backs of twelve oxen, sometimes forms a circle. The twelve oxen face outward to the four cardinal directions—east, south, west, and north—which form a square; thus the circle exists upon the square.

Prayer circle: Several things come together in this sacred setting—men

---
1. See Parry and Parry, *Understanding the Book of Revelation*, 55–56.
2. *Teachings of Presidents of the Church: Joseph Smith*, 210.

(left) Stained-glass window with geometric symbols, including prominently placed circles, Albuquerque New Mexico Temple.

and women worshipping together form a circle, in a holy space, gathered around an altar, praying together (see "Prayer Circle, Ancient and Modern").

Holy of Holies, Salt Lake Temple: Elder James E. Talmage described the Holy of Holies: "The room is of circular outline, 18 feet in diameter.... The ceiling is a dome in which are set circular and semi-circular windows of jeweled glass."[1] Thus, the holiest space in the Salt Lake Temple comprises a circle; it also has a circular dome, and several round windows exist in the dome.

Temple architecture: Dozens of temples feature circles on both interior and exterior parts. The Washington D.C. Temple has a five-pointed star set within a larger, ten-pointed star, with rays of light, all set within a circle, which is also set within a square. The Nauvoo Illinois Temple depicts a five-pointed star (with a deep crimson middle and deep blue color surrounding the star), which is set in a circle. The Albuquerque New Mexico Temple presents a stained-glass window with a thirty-two-pointed star, which is set in concentric circles. And the St. Louis Missouri Temple presents a stained-glass window with a six-pointed star. Phases of the moon are set in each of the six points; the star itself is set in concentric circles. A circle exists in the center of the star, with a square inside of the circle. And there are vertical and horizontal lines through the square that create four equal quadrants within the circle.

CLOUDS AND CLOUDSTONES

Clouds have a significant part in both temple settings and various sacred theophanies (manifestations of God to a woman or a man). Clouds are associated with God's presence, and they could be interpreted to symbolize His glory (see D&C 84:2–5; see also 1 Kgs. 8:11; Isa. 4:5–6; Ezek.

---

1. Talmage, *The House of the Lord*, 210.

Two cloudstones, Salt Lake Temple.

10:4); indeed, *cloud* and *glory* are occasionally juxtaposed together in the scriptures, as many of the following examples indicate:

Mount Sinai: "Moses went up into the mount, and a cloud covered the mount. And the glory of the Lord abode upon mount Sinai" (Ex. 24:15–16).

Solomon's temple: "The cloud filled the house of the Lord, So that the priests could not stand to minister because of the cloud: for the glory of the Lord had filled the house of the Lord" (1 Kgs. 8:10–11).

Kirtland Temple: Oliver Cowdery "saw the glory of God, like a great cloud, come down and rest upon the house, and fill the same like a mighty rushing wind."[2]

Other scriptural passages associate a cloud with God's presence:

Moses: "As Moses entered into the tabernacle, the cloudy pillar descended, and stood at the door of the tabernacle, and the Lord talked with Moses. . . . The Lord spake unto Moses face to face, as a man speaketh

---

2. Arrington, "Oliver Cowdery's Kirtland, Ohio, 'Sketch Book,'" 426.

Pillar of light (representing the pillar of fire), tabernacle of Moses.

unto his friend" (Ex. 33:9, 11); "The Lord said unto Moses, Lo, I come unto thee in a thick cloud" (Ex. 19:9); "The Lord descended in the cloud.... And Moses... bowed his head toward the earth, and worshipped" (Ex. 34:5, 8).

Peter, James, and John: "Behold, a bright cloud overshadowed them: and behold a voice out of the cloud, which said, This is my beloved Son, in whom I am well pleased; hear ye him" (Matt. 17:5).

The brother of Jared: "The Lord came down and talked with the brother of Jared; and he was in a cloud" (Ether 2:4; see also v. 14).

In association with the subject of clouds, two cloudstones are located on the Salt Lake Temple's east, central tower, with the sun's rays showing through clouds. The rays are evidence of God's heavenly light pouring down upon earth's inhabitants, blessing them through the restored gospel.

COLORS—BLUE, GOLD, SILVER, SCARLET, CRIMSON, RED, WHITE

Blue: The color blue was prominently featured on the high priest's vestments (sash, robe's hem, ephod, breastplate) and elsewhere in the tabernacle, including the courtyard gate's hanging and the two veils of the tabernacle (see Ex. 26:1, 31, 36; 27:16; 28:33; 36:8, 35, 37; 39:2, 8, 29). Also, the priests covered the table of shewbread with a blue cloth (see Num. 4:7). Blue is also used on interior and exterior features of several temples. For example, Elder James E. Talmage writes that the Holy of Holies of the Salt

Lake Temple "is decorated in blue and gold."[1] Blue could be interpreted to symbolize heaven, or the realm where God dwells.

Gold: Several sacred spaces and precincts feature gold, including the tabernacle, the temple of Solomon, and the celestial kingdom. Two chief points regarding gold: (1) Gold belongs to God ("the gold is mine, saith the Lord of hosts" [Hag. 2:8; see also Joel 3:5]); (2) Gold is precious, beautiful, incorruptible, and lustrously brilliant.

Artist rendition of Solomon's temple: "The floor of the house he overlaid with gold, within and without" (1 Kgs. 6:30).

The tabernacle featured a number of objects that were fashioned out of gold, including the ark of the covenant (see Ex. 25:11–13), the jar that held manna, the two cherubim (see 2 Chr. 3:10), various vessels (see Ex. 25:26, 29, 38–39; 37:16), the lampstand (see Ex. 25:31–38; 37:17–24), the mercy seat, the golden censer, and the high priest's head plate that read "Holiness to the Lord." Additionally, the altar of incense (see Ex. 30:1–3; 1 Kgs. 7:48), the table of shewbread, the tabernacle's nine pillars (from whence hung the two veils), and the tabernacle walls were overlaid with gold (see Ex. 26:18–25; 36:34, 38),[2] making the rooms both precious and beautiful.

---

1. Talmage, *The House of the Lord*, 210.
2. Brown, *The Tabernacle*, 12–23.

Gold chain of the high priest's breastplate.

King David prepared great quantities of gold and silver for Solomon's temple: "I have prepared for the house of the Lord an hundred thousand talents of gold, and a thousand thousand talents of silver; and of brass and iron without weight; for it is in abundance" (1 Chr. 22:14; see also 1 Chr. 29:3–4). The Bible Dictionary states that a talent weighs about 75.6 pounds.[1] "Solomon overlaid the [temple] within with pure gold" (1 Kgs. 6:21); also, "The floor of the house he overlaid with gold, within and without" (1 Kgs. 6:30).

Of the celestial kingdom, John recorded, "The city was pure gold, like unto clear glass. . . . The street of the city was pure gold, as it were transparent glass" (Rev 21:18, 21). Joseph Smith shared this vision: "I beheld the celestial kingdom of God. . . . I saw the beautiful streets of that kingdom, which had the appearance of being paved with gold" (D&C 137:1, 4).

Also, when Jesus Christ appears to certain mortals in a divine theophany, He sometimes stands on a platform of gold or a precious stone: "He stood right here, about three feet above the floor. It looked as though He stood on a plate of solid gold" (Lorenzo Snow).[2] And, "We saw the Lord standing upon the breastwork of the pulpit, before us; and under his feet was a paved work of pure gold, in color like amber" (D&C 110:2; see also Ex. 24:9–11).

Green: See "Fig Leaves."

Silver: The structure of the tabernacle of Moses had a "silver foundation,"[3] consisting of one hundred sockets made of the precious metal silver (Ex. 26:19–25; 38:27). Each socket weighed a talent (see Ex. 38:27). The

---

1. Bible Dictionary, 742.
2. Snow, "A Visit from the Savior," 80.
3. Brown, *The Tabernacle*, 4–9.

sockets held up the posts that surrounded the holy place and the Holy of Holies. The tabernacle's silver foundation reminded worshippers that the tabernacle was precious, exceptional, and unique.

Scarlet, Crimson, and Red: Scarlet is a brilliant red color and crimson is a rich, deep red color. Red, crimson, and scarlet are sometimes interpreted to signify Jesus Christ's blood and His infinite Atonement.

The tabernacle of Moses, the focal point of sacrifice and atonement during its existence, had a number of red (or scarlet or crimson) components. This was not simply by coincidence or chance, but by divine design. Worshippers who entered the tabernacle may have experienced visual magnificence as they viewed the colors of the various appurtenances. The courtyard gate's hanging, which served as the door of the tent, the curtains of the tabernacle, and the veil that separated the Holy of Holies from the holy place were all made of finely twisted linen and embroidery in colors of blue, purple, and scarlet (see Ex. 26:1, 31, 36; 27:16; see also 36:8, 35, 37). Further, the Lord commanded Moses, "Thou shalt make a covering for the tent of rams' skins dyed red" (Ex. 26:14).

The high priest's ephod, too, was an elaborate and beautiful sacred vestment that featured scarlet and other colors: "He made the ephod

The ceremonial cleansing of the leper included the use of cedar wood, hyssop, and blood.

of gold, blue, and purple, and scarlet, and fine twined linen" (Ex. 39:2). Similarly, the ephod's girdle, the breastplate, and the hems of the robe each featured gold, blue, purple, and scarlet yarn together with fine linen (Ex. 39:5, 8, 24).

The colors red and scarlet figure prominently in the ceremony of the sacrifice of the red heifer. The law required the heifer to be red, the sacrifice of the heifer produced red blood, and the slaughtered beast was burned, together with hyssop, cedar wood, and scarlet wool (see Num. 19:6, 18).

White: The color white is associated with the clothing of the high priests and the Levites in the ancient temple (see Ex. 28:2–3; 2 Chr. 5:12); and of our modern temples, Elder Quentin L. Cook wrote, "We are all equal before God. Everyone is dressed in white to signify we are a pure and righteous people. All sit side by side with a desire in their hearts to be worthy sons and daughters of a loving Heavenly Father."[1]

Further, John the Revelator "beheld . . . a great multitude, which no man could number, of all nations, and kindreds, and people, and tongues . . . arrayed in white robes" standing before God's throne. These are Saints—both females and males—who "have washed their robes, and made them white in the blood of the Lamb" (Rev. 7:9, 13, 14).

White clothing symbolizes purity. President Russell M. Nelson explains, "Within the temple, all are dressed in spotless white to remind us that God is to have a pure people."[2] Becoming white is possible only through the Atonement of Christ. "For there can no man be saved except his garments are washed white; yea, his garments must be purified until they are cleansed from all stain, through the blood of him of whom it has been spoken by our fathers, who should come to redeem his people from their sins" (Alma 5:21).

---

1. Cook, "See Yourself in the Temple," 99.
2. Nelson, "Personal Preparation for Temple Blessings," 33; see also Widtsoe, "Looking toward the Temple," 710.

CORNERSTONES

In ancient times, many monumental buildings were built on four cornerstones, which formed the base of these structures. Cornerstones are vital to a building's integrity, strength, and stability. Owing to the import of cornerstones, several of the prophets spoke of cornerstones, often in connection with the temple (see Ps. 118:22). Referring to the "holy temple" (Eph. 2:21), Paul explained that the chief cornerstone is none other than the Lord: "Jesus Christ himself being the chief corner stone" (Eph. 2:20). Concerning Jesus, the chief cornerstone, President Gordon B. Hinckley stated, "Thanks be to God for the gift of his Beloved Son, who gave his life that we might live, and who is the chief, immovable cornerstone of our faith and his church."[3]

In our dispensation, the earlier temples had great cornerstones that formed the base of several temples, including Nauvoo, Salt Lake, Manti, Logan, and St. George. A sacred ceremony accompanies the laying of the cornerstones, and great symbolic significance is attached to this ceremony.

For example, on April 6, 1853, President Brigham Young presided over the laying of the cornerstones of the Salt Lake Temple, which was conducted in the following order: the First Presidency laid the southeast cornerstone, the presiding bishop the southwest, high priests and elders the northwest, and the Twelve Apostles the northeast.[4] Why was the southeast cornerstone laid first? Because, as Brigham Young explained, "We commence by laying the stone on the south-*east corner,* because *there* is the most *light*."[5] Angels attended this grand event. The day after the

---

3. Hinckley, "The Cornerstones of Our Faith," 52.
4. Young, "The Temple Corner Stones—The Apostleship, &c." *JD* 1:135–36. For the laying of the Nauvoo Temple's cornerstones, see "Celebration of the Anniversary of the Church," *Times and Seasons,* 15 Apr. 1841, 2:375. https://www.josephsmithpapers.org/event/nauvoo-temple-cornerstones-laid?highlight=nauvoo%20temple%20cornerstone. For the Logan Temple cornerstones, see Wells, "Logan Temple," 355.
5. Young, "The Temple Corner Stones—The Apostleship, &c." *JD* 1:133; emphasis in the original.

cornerstone ceremony, Parley P. Pratt informed the Saints, "It appeared to me that Joseph Smith, and his associate spirits . . . hovered above us on the brink of that foundation, and with them all the angels and spirits from the other world, that might be permitted, or that were not too busy elsewhere."[1]

Another example of a cornerstone-laying ceremony occurred at the Manti Utah Temple. Under the direction of President John Taylor, the four cornerstones were laid, first the southeast, then the southwest, then the northwest, and finally the northeast. President Lorenzo Snow stated that the southeast was "the chief corner stone of the building."[2] After the other three cornerstones were laid, a dedicatory prayer was offered.

In modern days, our temples are constructed with concrete footings and foundations rather than large cornerstones. The cornerstone ceremony, however, continues, with men and women, girls and boys in attendance. This ceremony no longer marks the beginning of the temple's construction, but takes place after it has been built. After the dedicatory prayer of the new edifice, Church leaders conduct a symbolic ceremony where they apply mortar to the "cornerstone" plaque.

COVENANTS, SIGNS, AND TOKENS

President Russell M. Nelson spoke of a significant scriptural pattern that pertains to the temple, wherein the Lord instructs us with "covenants, signs, and tokens." He explained, "In the temple, we learn something of the unique pattern by which the Lord teaches His children. Here we make sacred covenants; in turn, the Lord emphasizes the importance of those covenants by giving us special signs and tokens. This pattern . . . is equally evident in many scriptural examples. Coupling a covenant with a sign or a token is an instructional model often employed by the Master Teacher.

---

1. Pratt, "Spiritual Communication," *JD* 1:14.
2. Rasmussen, *The Manti Temple*, 12.

"Recognition of a pattern among creators is expected. They all have their individual styles. A person familiar with the music of Beethoven, for example, can easily recognize his pattern of composition. One acquainted with the art of Van Gogh can readily identify his style of painting. So it is with this instructional model of the Lord.

"In the temple He uses covenants, signs, and tokens. The same pattern is evident in holy writ."[3]

The temple is indeed "a house of covenants."[4] God is the author of all of the covenants of the gospel, including those of the temple, and "He is the only one who has authority and power to guarantee their validity beyond the grave."[5] Anciently, temples and sacred spaces served as sites for making covenants—covenants between the Lord and His people (see Ex. 24:6–8; Jer. 34:15) and also between a king and his subjects (see 2 Kgs. 11:4; 2 Chr. 23:3). Different types of covenants existed (see Ex. 24:7–8; Num. 18:19; 25:12–13), and the most holy piece of temple furniture was "the ark of the covenant" (Num. 10:33).

The English expression "to make a covenant" or variants of it appear some eighty times in the Old Testament. The Hebrew behind the English literally reads "to cut a covenant" (Hebrew: *karat berit*), which may have reference to the cutting of a sacrificial animal as part of the covenantal process. In a certain covenantal setting, Moses read from "the book of the covenant," sprinkled sacrificial blood on the people, and then said, "Behold the blood of the covenant, which the Lord hath [cut] with you concerning all these words" (Ex. 24:7–8). And Psalm 50:5, "Gather my saints together unto me; those that have made a covenant with me by sacrifice." Two significant Old Testament passages—Genesis 15:7–18 and Jeremiah 34:18—pertain to the cutting of animals in a covenantal setting.

In the latter days, several Church authorities have made instructive

---

3. Nelson, *Teachings of Russell M. Nelson*, 368–69.
4. *The Teachings of Ezra Taft Benson*, 250.
5. Neuenschwander, "Ordinances and Covenants," 24.

statements regarding the temple covenants. President Nelson explained, "We should understand . . . the importance of keeping sacred covenants. Each temple ordinance 'is not just a ritual to go through, it is an act of solemn promising.'"[1]

President Gordon B. Hinckley taught: "We are a covenant people. I have had the feeling that if we could just encourage our people to live by three or four covenants everything else would take care of itself. . . . The first of these is the covenant of the sacrament. . . . Second, the covenant of tithing. . . . Three, the covenants of the temple: Sacrifice, the willingness to sacrifice for this the Lord's work—and inherent in that law of sacrifice is the very essence of the Atonement. . . . Consecration, which is associated with it, a willingness to give everything, if need be, to help in the on-rolling of this great work. And a covenant of love and loyalty one to another in the bonds of marriage, fidelity, chastity, morality."[2]

CREATION NARRATIVE IN THE TEMPLE

Latter-day Saint scholar Stephen Ricks has provided evidence that the Creation narrative (see Gen. 1) was recited or belonged to the ancient temple service of Israel during the Second Temple Period.[3] What's more, the Creation narrative is an important part of the temple endowment in our own day. Elder Talmage wrote that the temple endowment "includes a recital of the most prominent events of the creative period."[4]

Latter-day Saints hold sacred four Creation narratives; three are

---

1. Nelson, "Personal Preparation for Temple Blessings," 33, quoting *Teachings of Gordon B. Hinckley*, 638.
2. Hinckley, *Teachings of Gordon B. Hinckley*, 146–47.
3. See Ricks, "Liturgy and Cosmogony," 118–25; Note also Nibley's words, "All ancient temples rehearsed the story of the creation, and the establishment of mankind and the royal government of God upon this earth. Then they moved into the heavenly sphere and the theology associated with the worlds beyond," Nibley, "The Circle and the Square," in *Temple and Cosmos*, 149.
4. Talmage, *The House of the Lord*, 83.

Our earth, a divine creation.

written texts (Genesis, Moses, Abraham), and the fourth is that which belongs to the temple. The fact that there are four (instead of just one) underscores their import. All four are ritual texts that belong to the temple setting. The following truths about the earth and its creation provide us with a sense of why the Creation account holds a role in the endowment:

(1) *Jesus Christ is the Creator:* "Behold, I am Jesus Christ the Son of God. I created the heavens and the earth, and all things that in them are" (3 Ne. 9:15; see also Hel. 14:12).

(2) *Jesus Christ's creations are without number to mortals*: "And were it possible that man could number the particles of the earth, yea, millions of earths like this, it would not be a beginning to the number of thy creations; and thy curtains are stretched out still" (Moses 7:30).

(3) *Our earth will die and through Jesus Christ's Atonement will be resurrected:* The earth "shall die, it shall be quickened again, and shall abide the power by which it is quickened" (D&C 88:26). "The earth, as a living body, will have to die and be resurrected, for it, too, has been redeemed by the blood of Jesus Christ."[5]

---

5. Smith, *Doctrines of Salvation* 1:74.

(4) *Jesus Christ's Atonement extends to inhabitants of other earths*: President Russell M. Nelson taught, "The mercy of the Atonement extends not only to an infinite number of people, but also to an infinite number of worlds created by Him."[1]

(5) *"We have brothers and sisters on other earths,"* wrote Joseph Fielding Smith. "They look like us because they, too, are the children of God and were created in his image, for they are also his offspring. His great work is to create earths and people them with his children who are called upon to pass through the mortal probation like unto this we are now in."[2]

(6) *Our earth is obedient to God's laws*: "The earth abideth the law of a celestial kingdom" (D&C 88:25); it is governed by and moves in its times and seasons through God's law (see D&C 88:42–43). The earth will fill "the measure of its creation" (D&C 88:19, 25).

(7) *Our earth will "be sanctified" (D&C 88:26)* and it will "be crowned with glory," which is "the presence of God the Father" (D&C 88:19).

(8) *The earth was created for us, and the righteous will inherit this earth*: The "righteous" or "the poor and the meek of the earth shall inherit it" (D&C 88:17, 26); in fact, the earth was "made and created" so that celestial souls could inherit it, and they will "possess [the earth] forever and ever" (D&C 88:20).

(9) *The earth's creation is one of the three pillars of eternity*: Elder Bruce R. McConkie explained, "The three pillars of eternity, the three events, preeminent and transcendent above all others, are the creation, the fall, and the atonement. These three are the foundations upon which all things rest. Without any one of them all things would lose their purpose and meaning, and the plans and designs of Deity would come to naught."[3]

---

1. Nelson, "The Atonement," 35.
2. Smith, *Doctrines of Salvation* 1:62; emphasis in the original.
3. McConkie, "Three Pillars of Eternity," 27.

DAY OF ATONEMENT

The Day of Atonement (Hebrew: *Yom Kippur*) was an exceptionally hallowed ancient Israelite festival. It focused on a number of symbols and rituals that pertained to the Atonement, such as the sacrifice of a bull and a goat, the confession of sins on the head of a second goat (the scapegoat), the sprinkling of blood on the altar, and the high priest's entrance into the temple's Holy of Holies. The directive regarding the scapegoat was straightforward: "Aaron shall lay both his hands upon the head of the live goat, and confess over him all the iniquities of the children of Israel, and all their transgressions in all their sins, putting them upon the head of the goat. . . . And the goat shall bear upon him all their iniquities unto a land not inhabited" (Lev. 16:21–22). It was during the Day of Atonement that the high priest made atonement for the tabernacle and the altar, for the priests, and for men and women. "This shall be an everlasting statute unto you, to make an atonement for the children of Israel for all their sins once a year" (Lev. 16:34).

Confession of iniquities on the head of the goat.

Several symbols belonging to the Day of Atonement pointed to Jesus Christ's Atonement. For example, the high priest sacrificed animals to make atonement for Israel's uncleanness, transgressions, and sins (see Lev. 16:6, 11, 15–20); this anticipated Jesus offering Himself as a sacrifice for the sins of the world (see Heb. 7:27; Alma 34:8); His sacrifice was "neither by the blood of goats and calves, but by his own blood" (Heb. 9:12). Elder Bruce R. McConkie summarized, "The chief symbolisms, the most perfect similitudes, the types and shadows without peer, were displayed before all the people once each year, on the Day of Atonement."[1]

DEDICATION OF THE TEMPLE

The dedication of the Salt Lake Temple constitutes "the greatest and most significant event in the history of the Latter-day Saints in the Salt Lake Valley,"[2] wrote President Gordon B. Hinckley. And J. Golden Kimball declared that when the Salt Lake Temple "was dedicated . . . it was the greatest sermon that has ever been preached since the Sermon on the Mount."[3] Indeed, all temple dedications are of extraordinary consequence in the history of the world. 1 Kings 8 records Solomon's temple dedicatory prayer: "Solomon stood before the altar of the Lord in the presence of all the congregation of Israel, and spread forth his hands toward heaven: And he said, Lord God of Israel" (1 Kgs. 8:22–23; see the entire prayer, vv. 23–53).

Correspondingly, in the latter days, God's prophets or apostles dedicate temples to the Lord, beginning with the Kirtland Temple, dedicated by the Prophet Joseph Smith on March 27, 1836. And the pattern continues, temple by temple, in this last dispensation. Temple dedications serve multiple purposes, including the following (emphasis is added in quotations below):

(1) To ceremonially assign that particular temple to the Lord God: "Thanks be to thy name, O Lord God of Israel" (D&C 109:1; Kirtland Temple); "O God, the Eternal Father, the Creator of heaven and earth" (Joseph Fielding Smith, Provo Utah Temple); "Almighty God, we come unto Thee in solemn and reverent prayer" (Gordon B. Hinckley, Nauvoo Illinois Temple).

---

1. McConkie, *The Promised Messiah*, 435.
2. Hinckley, "Salt Lake Temple," 2.
3. Kimball, Conference Report (April 1915), 79.

(2) To respectfully ask God to accept the temple: "We ask thee, O Lord, to *accept* of this house" (D&C 109:4); "We pray that Thou wilt *accept* of this our offering" (Gordon B. Hinckley, Nauvoo Illinois Temple); "Design to *accept* this the fourth temple" (Wilford Woodruff, Salt Lake Temple); "We . . . pray that Thou wilt *accept* it" (John Taylor, Logan Utah Temple); "Father, we consecrate and dedicate this building unto Thee and ask Thee to *accept* it" (Spencer W. Kimball, St. George Utah Temple rededication).

(3) To set the temple apart and sanctify it from the profane and unclean world: "That it may be *sanctified* and *consecrated* to be holy" (D&C 109:12); "*Sanctify* it and make it holy" (Lorenzo Snow, Manti Utah Temple); "*Sanctify* it" (Gordon B. Hinckley, Manti Utah Temple rededication); "Accept of it and to *sanctify* it, and to *consecrate* it" (Heber J. Grant, Laie Hawaii Temple); "We pray Thee to *sanctify* this . . . we pray that no *unclean thing or persons* may ever enter the portals of this building" (Spencer W. Kimball, Laie Hawaii Temple rededication).

(4) To provide a place that is set apart for women and men to worship and to participate in sacred ordinances, prayer, solemn assemblies, and many other holy proceedings (see D&C 109:8–10).

DOME

Several temples exhibit a magnificent, imposing dome in one of the temple's principal spaces, such as the celestial room. For example, the Draper Utah Temple features a stunning and elegant dome, circular, with an eight-pointed star set in the center, serving as the dome's focal point. Shadows of the star, greater in size but with diminished brightness, gracefully fade out at the haunch. Other temples also give prominence to a beautiful, phenomenal dome, including the Boise Idaho, Apia Samoa, Brisbane Australia, Newport Beach California, Redlands California,

Sacramento California, San Antonio Texas, Sao Paulo Brazil, Snowflake Arizona, Provo Utah, and St. Louis Missouri Temples.

Beyond their aesthetic value, many of the domes have a fourfold symbolic significance: (1) The dome's rounded vault in the temple's ceiling could be interpreted to signify heaven. Various designs, patterns, or lighting schemes in the intrados reinforce the idea that the dome is none other than a celestial vault; (2) Most domes, but not all, form a circle. For a circle as a symbol of eternity, see entry "Circle"; (3) The points where the rounded vault's base encounter the square room below the dome may signify eternity coming into contact with the earth (see entry "Square"). Thus, this architectural representation (the dome and the room below) may represent the spot where heaven and earth meet, creating a visual that the temple serves as the meeting place between heaven and earth; (4) Many of the domes portray symbolic motifs within the rounded vault, such as trees, stars, various colors, or geometric designs.

DRAMA, RITUAL

Many scholars, including Hugh Nibley, have investigated the role of ritual drama in ancient temple settings; Nibley writes concerning the dramatization of the Creation story, the Council in Heaven, the Garden of Eden, and specifically of the "temple drama." He states, "The dramatic motifs of the temple and its ordinances are found throughout the world from the very earliest times."[1] His research has also demonstrated that various ancient communities—Egyptians, Babylonians, Romans, Greeks, and others—dramatized particular narratives in ritual settings.[2]

After exploring the concept of ritual drama, Latter-day Saint scholar John Lundquist concludes: "The mysteries of the temple take many forms, differing from culture to culture, and are in fact in many ways culture

---
1. Nibley, "Abraham's Temple Drama," 1–42.
2. See Nibley, "Meanings and Functions of Temples," 315–16.

specific, as we would expect. Two types of temple initiation, however, are particularly widespread, and these are the 'theatrical' staging of ritual performances based on the creation . . . and the initiation of the living into the knowledge and mysteries of the afterlife."[3]

Why dramatizations in temples, ancient and modern? Because sacred drama serves as a masterly teaching device that captures the attention of men and women who worship together, and provides them with a multitude of emotional, heartening, and spiritual impressions!

EAR, THUMB, AND TOE

The consecration of the high priests and priests was a multistage process, which included washings, anointings, putting on sacred vestments, and more (see Lev. 8). One of the stages included Moses applying a bullock's sacrificial blood to the right ear, to the thumb of the right hand, and to the largest toe of the right foot of Aaron and his sons (see Lev. 8:23–24; Ex. 29:20). This sacred act, together with the other rites of consecration of priests, had a sacred and symbolic significance. Perhaps the ear signifies *listening* to God's word; the thumb symbolizes *doing* His work (with our hands), and the toe denotes *walking* in God's commandments (the toe representing our feet).

Ceremonial application of sacrificial blood (artificial) to right thumb.

---

3. Lundquist, *The Temple: Meeting Place of Heaven and Earth*, 23.

Two earthstones, Salt Lake Temple.

EARTHSTONES

The Salt Lake Temple prominently features earthstones, located at the base of its buttresses (approximately at ground level). In 1893, Anderson explained, "There are fifty of these Earth Stones, representing different portions of the globe, but all combining to include its entire surface. Their name indicates their symbolism."[1] According to architect Truman O. Angell, the earthstones signify that "the Gospel has come for the whole earth,"[2] meaning, the gospel and the blessings of the temple are designed for all the kindreds and peoples of the earth.

ENDOWMENT/ENDOWED WITH POWER

President Russell M. Nelson instructed, "In the temple we receive an endowment, which is, literally speaking, a gift. In receiving this gift, we should understand its significance and the importance of keeping sacred

---

1. Anderson, "The Salt Lake Temple," 275.
2. Angell, "The Salt Lake City Temple," 275.

covenants."³ The endowment is of such great consequence that Joseph Smith was anxious that the Saints receive it: "'Hurry up the work, brethren,' he used to say,—'let us finish the temple; the Lord has a great endowment in store for you, and I am anxious that the brethren should have their endowments and receive the fullness of the priesthood. . . . Then,' said he, 'the Kingdom will be established.'"⁴ Although the Prophet was speaking to men at this moment in time, both women and men actually received their endowments and the fullness of the priesthood in Nauvoo.

Regarding the temple endowment, we may consider the following items:

(1) The endowment is connected to *power*; both ancient and modern scripture use the phrase, "Ye shall be endowed with power" (D&C 43:16; see also Luke 24:49). The dedicatory prayer of the Kirtland Temple three times connects the temple with power (see D&C 109:13, 22, 35).

(2) The endowment of power comes "from on high" (D&C 38:32, 38; 95:8), meaning, the power comes from God Himself, who lives on high. As a matter of fact, the endowment gives men and women power "to overcome all things."⁵ Women and men receive the same endowment and access to the same Godly power.

(3) The Lord labels the endowment a "great endowment" (D&C 105:12), and on three occasions the Lord makes it clear that the endowment is associated with "blessings" (D&C 105:11–12, 18). Note this verse: "The hearts of thousands and tens of thousands shall greatly rejoice in consequence of the blessings which shall be poured out, and the endowment with which my servants have been endowed in this house" (D&C 110:9).

(4) Regarding the endowment, President Brigham Young explained, "Let me give you a definition in brief. Your endowment is, to receive all

---

3. Nelson, "Personal Preparation for Temple Blessings," 33.
4. *Teachings of Presidents of the Church: Joseph Smith*, 507.
5. "History, 1834–1836," p. 127, The Joseph Smith Papers, accessed March 25, 2019, https://www.josephsmithpapers.org/paper-summary/history-1834-1836/131.

those ordinances in the house of the Lord, which are necessary for you, after you have departed this life, to enable you to walk back to the presence of the Father, passing the angels who stand as sentinels, being enabled to give them the key words, the signs and tokens, pertaining to the holy Priesthood, and gain your eternal exaltation in spite of earth and hell."[1]

(5) Jesus, too, has received His endowment. Wilford Woodruff taught, "He has had His endowments long ago; it is thousands and millions of years since He received His blessings, and if He had not received them, we could not give them to Him, for He is far in advance of us."[2] Also Heber C. Kimball: "Think of your holy endowments and what you have been anointed to become, and reflect upon the blessings which have been placed upon you, for they are the same in part that were placed upon Jesus; he was the one that inducted his Apostles into these ordinances."[3] And Joseph Smith: "If a man gets a fulness of the priesthood of God, he has to get it in the same way that Jesus Christ obtained it, and that was by keeping all the commandments and obeying all the ordinances of the house of the Lord."[4]

(6) The meaning of the word *endow*, as deduced from the Greek and Latin, also means to "clothe oneself in, put on, wear." In the temple setting, *endow* has the meaning of clothing oneself in sacred vestments, which is akin to clothing oneself with power. Greek scholar Roger Macfarlane wrote: "Luke 24:49 contains in the KJV the clause 'until ye be endued with power from on high.' . . . The operative verb is ἐνδύω [enduo] which in the middle voice means 'clothe oneself in, put on, wear' (Bauer, Gingrich,

---

1. Young, *Discourses of Brigham Young*, 416.
2. Woodruff, "Necessity of Obeying the Instructions and Revelations Given—The Importance of Obtaining the Holy Ghost—The Labours of the Saints Are for Their Own Salvation, and Not to Enrich the Lord," *JD* 4:192.
3. Kimball, "The Young Missionaries.—Increasing Unbelief of the People of the World—Teachings of Jesus and His Disciples, etc." *JD* 10:241.
4. *Teachings of Presidents of the Church: Joseph Smith*, 419.

Danker).... So, the Greek and Latin both mean 'to clothe' or 'to don upon oneself.'"[5]

The Endowment House on Temple Square before the Salt Lake Temple was built. Granite blocks from the Temple construction surround the Endowment House.

ENDOWMENT HOUSE

Less than a decade after their arrival in the Salt Lake Valley, the Latter-day Saints built a sacred structure on the northwest portion of the Temple Block in Salt Lake City. Completed on April 27, 1855, this building was called the "Endowment House" or the "House of the Lord."[6] On May 5, 1855, Heber C. Kimball, under the direction of Brigham Young, dedicated the building with a formal prayer.

The Endowment House served the Latter-day Saints until 1889, when it was disassembled. The temples built in Logan, St. George, Manti, and Salt Lake would supersede the Endowment House. The Endowment House's existence during these years stands as a testament to the import of temples to the Saints. Matthias F. Cowley wrote concerning the

---

5. Personal correspondence (May 18, 2016) from Roger Macfarlane, professor in classical studies, Brigham Young University.
6. Young, "The Necessity of the Saints Having the Spirit of Revelation—Faith and Works—The Power of God and of the Devil," *JD* 3:159.

Endowment House: "It would be difficult even to estimate the sacred influence which that building has exercised upon the lives of untold thousands who felt themselves within its sacred precincts in the presence of their God."[1]

EVE, LIFE, AND LIFE-GIVER

Eve is one of the most eminent and distinguished individuals in both mortal life and in eternity. She had a vital role in the Garden of Eden narrative, and that role is reenacted and dramatized in our temple ceremony. In fact, Eve serves as the great archetype of all women. Additionally, she is a life-giver, the progenitor of all living, and she saved humankind from mortal destruction and extinction. In fact, as a *help* (Hebrew: *'ezer*) she corresponds (as a close similarity, but not as an equal) to God Himself, who is also called *'ezer* ("help") because He sustains and maintains the life of His human creations and saves them from mortal destruction. Genesis 2–3 sets forth Eve's seven-fold uniqueness:

(1) *Built* versus *formed*. The Hebrew verb used to convey Adam's creation is the Hebrew *ytsr*, "to form" or "fashion."[2] "The Lord God formed (*ytsr*) man of the dust of the ground" (Gen. 2:7). The animals, too, were formed (*ytsr*) "out of the ground" (Gen. 2:19). However, a different verb (Hebrew: *bnh*, "to build") is used to describe God's creation of Eve. Some translations of Genesis 2:22 put it this way: "The Lord God built [*bnh*] the rib which he took from the man for the woman." *Bnh* is used in a variety of settings in the Hebrew Bible, with reference to building cities, diverse buildings, and much more; this includes sacred structures, including God's tabernacle and temples (see 2 Sam. 7:5, 13, 27; 1 Kgs. 3:1; 5:5; 6:1; 1 Chr. 22:19; 28:10) and altars (see Gen. 8:20; 12:7–8; 13:18; 22:9; 26:25; 35:7).[3]

---

1. Cowley, *Wilford Woodruff*, 372.
2. *The Hebrew and Aramaic Lexicon of the Old Testament*, 428.
3. *The Hebrew and Aramaic Lexicon of the Old Testament*, 139.

The construction of Eve, with the employment of *bnh*, recalls the building of temples and altars, making Eve a prototypical building and a sacred institution. Eve's creation is thus unique from all of God's other creations in Genesis 2, which were formed from the ground. Note also that two Old Testament passages also use *bnh* with regard to women bearing and delivering children, or, as the Hebrew specifically states, *building* children (Gen. 16:2; 30:3; see also Deut. 25:9).

(2) *Rib/side* versus *ground*. The second uniqueness of Eve's creation pertains to the fact that God used unique material or matter when He created Eve. He created Adam and the animals from inanimate substance, from *'adamah*, or the ground (see Gen. 2:7, 19), but He built Eve from a living creature, from a human. More specifically, she was built from a *tsela*, which scholars translate as *rib* or *side*.[4] But God did not build Eve from the rib alone; He also used flesh. One chief argument that *tsela* refers to flesh and bone comes from Adam's response when God brought the woman to him: "This is now bone of my bones, and flesh of my flesh: she shall be called Woman, because she was taken out of Man" (Gen. 2:23).

Just as *bnh* may nuance the temple, so too *tsela* is associated with building sacred structures. Of its thirty-one occurrences (I-*tsela*) in the Hebrew Bible, *tsela* refers three times to humans (see Gen. 2:21–22; Job 18:12; Jer. 20:10). In the great majority of the other occurrences, *tsela* refers to the construction of the tabernacle and its appurtenances, Solomon's temple, and Ezekiel's temple.[5] In sum, Eve was built from the rib and flesh, a refined substance, more refined than the elements found in the ground (*'adamah*), from whence Adam and the animals were created—Eve, then, was built like a temple.

(3) *Adam's deep sleep*. The third uniqueness of Eve's creation pertains

---

4. *The Hebrew and Aramaic Lexicon of the Old Testament*, 1030. Korsak, "... et GENETRIX," 28, translates *tsela* as "side" and not "rib." See also Korsak, *At the Start: Genesis Made New: A Translation of the Hebrew Text*, 7.
5. For a summary of the form I-*tsela* in the lexicon, see *The Hebrew and Aramaic Lexicon of the Old Testament*, 1030.

to the fact that God created Eve while Adam slept (see Gen. 2:21). We note that he is not asleep owing to his desire to slumber, but rather, God causes him to sleep a deep sleep (Hebrew: *tardemah*) while God creates Eve. The man, therefore, does not assist in her creation, nor is he a spectator, nor did God seek Adam's opinion on the matter. Nowhere else in the text, including the naming of the creatures, does the man sleep. In fact, he is awake in Genesis 2:15–20. And earlier, when God stated that He would make a help for the man, He asked not for Adam's view. God was the instigator, the grand planner; Adam was not a participant. "I [God] will make (*'asah*) him an help meet for him" (Gen. 2:18; see also v. 20). "I will make" shows that God is in charge and interested in making Eve.

(4) *Not good to be alone!* The fourth uniqueness of Eve's creation pertains to the expression, "It is not good that the man should be alone" (Gen. 2:18). These words are set in the context of a series of seven formulaic expressions that pertain to God's creative acts, wherein *good* is utilized: "God saw that it was good" (Gen. 1:4, 10, 12, 18, 21, 25, 31). *Good* refers to various forms of creation, signifying the exceptional quality of God's work. Note, however, that in Genesis 2:18 the formula changes: "It is not *good* that the man should be alone"; this is followed with "I will make him an help" (Gen. 2:18). Eve's absence from the Creation was "not good."

(5) *Eve is called Help.* The fifth uniqueness of Eve pertains to the fact that, of all of God's creative works, she singularly is called *'ezer* ("help"). Not only is Eve twice called *'ezer*, but on several occasions in scripture God is identified as *'ezer* (see Ex. 18:2–4; Deut. 33:7, 26, 29; Ps. 20:1–2; 33:19–20; 70:1–2, 5; 89:19; 115:9–11; 121:1–2; 124:8; Hosea 13:9). All passages that establish God as a help are connected, implicitly or explicitly, to His sustaining and maintaining the life of His human creations. He is a help because He protects His creative works, male and female, from mortal destruction, the sword, savage enemies, death, and the grave. He preserves them during periods of trouble and keeps them alive during famines. He crushes their foes and strikes down their adversaries. Unlike mortals "in

whom there is no help" (Ps. 146:3), the Lord is a help who preserves us in our time of need. Ultimately, the Lord is a help who ransoms His mortals "from the power of the grave" and "redeem[s] them from death" (Hos. 13:14).

Eve's role of life-giver and help echoes that of God, who is Life and who is Help. Eve, therefore is called *'ezer* because she is a life-giver, a life force, the progenitor of all living who saved humankind from mortal destruction and extinction.

Hebrew-English lexicons and biblical exegetes provide a wide range of meanings for *'ezer*; indeed, *'ezer* is a complex term, one that is difficult to translate. *'Ezer* may be translated "help," and the term may indicate one who is powerful, a savior, and one who saves humankind from mortal extinction.[1]

(6) *Eve is Life.* Genesis 3:20 contains two kingpin statements, both of which are of consequence to understanding the garden narrative. The first statement explicitly identifies Eve as *life*; *Eve* is a Hebrew word that means life.[2] In the passage under discussion, it appears that Adam is naming his wife, but Moses 4:26 provides evidence that the name *Eve* originated with God Himself: "Adam called his wife's name Eve, because she was the mother of all living; for thus have I, the Lord God, called the first of all women, which are many" (Moses 4:26). It is not likely that Adam originated the name; more likely God revealed it to him.

The word *because* serves to introduce the motive clause—why was she

---

1. Talmon notes that *'ezer* is used in multiple parallelisms with *'ysha* ("to save"), suggesting that *'ezer* and *'ysha* are synonymous; he cites as examples Deuteronomy 33:29; Joshua 10:6; Isaiah 49:8; and Psalm 37:46; Talmon, "Synonymous Readings in the Textual Traditions of the Old Testament," 381. For a summary of various theories regarding the meaning of *'ezer,* see Kvam, Schearing, and Ziegler, *Eve and Adam,* 28–29. See Freedman, "Woman, A Power Equal to Man," 56, 58. Freedman argues that the Hebrew *'ezer* "is a combination of two roots, *c-z-r* meaning 'to rescue,' 'to save,' and ... *g-z-r* meaning 'to be strong'" (ibid., 56). For a summary of meanings of the word *help,* see Parry, "Eve's Role as a 'Help' ('Ezer) Revisited," forthcoming.
2. *A Hebrew and English Lexicon of the Old Testament,* 295.

called Life? Because she was the mother of all living. Lest the audience lack knowledge of Hebrew, the author provides the explanatory statement, Eve means *life,* which signifies the mother (giver of life) of all *living*! With this explanation, the author of the scriptural account is emphasizing Eve's significance in the story. She is Life and she is Mother. While all mothers have exceptional significance, Eve is unlike all others—she is the Mother of *all* living.

Biblical scholar Isaac Kikawada, building on the work of others, argues that the tripartite Hebrew expression *'em kol hay* ("mother of all living") is an "honorific title" and that her name verifies "her role as a creatress of man."[1] Kikawada also writes that "Eve is exalted as the ancestress of all mankind."[2]

(7) *Eve is Mother.* The second kingpin statement in Genesis 3:20 is that Eve is "the mother of all living"; the term *mother* attested here (Hebrew: *'em*) is vital to the narrative. We recall that Eve received this designation *before* giving birth to her children—all women, regardless of whether or not they have birthed a child, can be *mothers.* Sheri Dew explains, "While *we* tend to equate motherhood solely with maternity, in the Lord's language, the word *mother* has layers of meaning." She explained to a large group of females, "*We are all mothers in Israel,* and our calling is to love and help lead the rising generation through the dangerous streets of mortality."[3]

Mothers are vital to society (this cannot be overstated!). Some cultures celebrate motherhood with special days of observance, such as Mother's Day and Mothering Sunday. Also, some religious communities employ honorific titles that include "mother," e.g., *Reverend Mother, Mother Superior, Mother of God, Mother Teresa*. But the first and greatest title is recorded in the garden narrative: Eve is *the Mother of All Living!*

---

1. Kikawada, "Two Notes on Eve," 33.
2. Kikawada, "Two Notes on Eve," 34.
3. Dew, "Are We Not All Mothers?" 96–97; emphasis in the original.

All-Seeing Eye, located on exterior of the Salt Lake Temple.

EYE, ALL-SEEING

There are representations of an all-seeing eye located on the Salt Lake Temple's east and west towers; each eye is surrounded by rays of light and immediately above the eye is a veil with folds; the entire image provides the impression that the eye is looking through a veil. The all-seeing eye represents God's eye, an emblem of His omniscience (God is "all knowing"). God "comprehendeth all things, and all things are before him" (D&C 88:41; see also D&C 93:11, 26). The scriptures also refer to God's eyes: "The eyes of the Lord are upon the righteous" (Ps. 34:15; see also Prov. 15:3); "Behold, the eye of the Lord is upon them that fear him, upon them that hope in his mercy" (Ps. 33:18; see also 2 Ne. 9:20; Mosiah 27:31; Alma 26:35; D&C 38:2; 88:7–13). Also, President Brigham Young referred to "the all-searching eye of the Great Jehovah."[4]

FIG LEAVES

In regard to Adam and Eve in the Garden of Eden, Genesis 3:7 states, "The eyes of them both were opened, and they knew that they were naked;

---

4. Brigham Young, "Necessity of Building Temples—The Endowment," *JD* 2:32. See also Orson Hyde, "The Marriage Relations," *JD* 2:84.

and they sewed fig leaves together, and made themselves aprons." Here the scriptural author skillfully uses two nuanced components that hint at sexual matters (and, by way of extension, procreation) with reference to fig leaves. The couple sewed these together to cover their nakedness; figs, which consist of an abundance of seeds, are suggestive of reproductive powers. So, too, the color green is sometimes associated with fertility, fruitfulness, and living things, speaking of both spiritual and physical things (see Job 15:32; Ps. 37:2; Jer. 11:16–17; Hosea 14:8; D&C 135:6).

FIRE/PILLAR OF FIRE

Fire, when associated with temples and theophanies, expresses the glory of God. When Moses ascended Mount Sinai, the Lord "called unto Moses out of the midst of the cloud. And the sight of the glory of the Lord was like devouring fire on the top of the mount in the eyes of the children of Israel" (Ex. 24:16–17; emphasis added; see also Num. 9:15). A passage about Solomon's temple also associates fire with glory: "When Solomon had made an end of praying, the fire came down from heaven, and consumed the burnt offering and the sacrifices; and the glory of the Lord filled the house" (2 Chr. 7:1; emphasis added).

For theophanies that include a pillar of fire, see Lehi's vision (1 Nephi 1:6–7), the account of Nephi and Lehi (Hel. 5:43), David's offerings (1 Chr. 21:26), plus others. Also, at the Second Coming, Jesus Christ will come "in a pillar of fire" (D&C 29:12).

Fire is also associated with the Kirtland Temple. During the period of the dedicatory services, some observers outside of the temple saw "a bright light like a piller of Fire resting upon the Temple."[1] The glorious celestial

---

1. "History, 1838–1856, volume B-1 [1 September 1834–2 November 1838] [addenda]," p. 4 [addenda], The Joseph Smith Papers, accessed March 26, 2019, https://www.josephsmithpapers.org/paper-summary/history-1838-1856-volume-b-1-1-september-1834-2-november-1838/307.

kingdom is associated with "flames of fire" and a "blazing throne" (D&C 137:2–3).

FIRSTBORN, MALE

Before the institution of the Mosaic law code, the nation Israel itself signified the Lord's firstborn: "Thus saith the Lord, Israel is my son, even my firstborn" (Ex. 4:22). Presumably, *Israel* here refers to both females and males. Once the law of Moses was in place, the tribe of Levi symbolically became the firstborn (see Num. 3:12, 40–45; 8:18). Firstborn males, both persons and animals, were dedicated to the Lord (see Ex. 13:2, 12; 22:29); such belonged to the Lord and were called "holy to the Lord" (Luke 2:23). The symbolism of firstborn males (beasts and humans) is clear—they bring to mind Jesus Christ, who was the Father's first spirit child (D&C 93:21).

President John Taylor explained the doctrine regarding Jesus Christ as the Firstborn: "If He was the *first born* and obedient to the laws of His Father, did He not inherit the position by right to be the representative of God, the Savior and Redeemer of the world? . . . And being Himself without sin (which no other mortal was), He took the position of Savior and Redeemer, which by right belonged to Him as the *first born*."[2]

FIRSTFRUITS

Ancient Israelites offered the firstfruits of the grain harvest unto the Lord at the temple: "The first of the firstfruits of thy land thou shalt bring into the house of the Lord thy God" (Ex. 23:19; see also Lev. 23:9–15). According to Rabbi Yisrael Ariel, women also brought the firstfruits to the temple and would ceremonially wave them together with the priest, "back and forth, up and down"; then they would bow down, facing the temple.[3]

---

2. Taylor, *Mediation and Atonement,* 136–37; emphasis added.
3. Ariel, *The Holy Temple in Jerusalem*, 211.

President M. Russell Ballard explained that "the firstfruits that were offered remind us that Christ was the firstfruits of the Resurrection."[1] 1 Corinthians 15:20 reads: "But now is Christ risen from the dead, and become the firstfruits of them that slept." Verse 23 straightforwardly declares "Christ the firstfruits."

FLAYING THE BURNT OFFERING

Leviticus refers to a practice that pertains to the flaying of the bullock for the burnt offerings: "He shall kill the bullock before the Lord. . . . And he shall flay the burnt offering" (Lev. 1:5–6). This task of flaying required much work, and the Levites sometimes assisted the priests: "The priests were too few, so that they could not flay all the burnt offerings: wherefore their brethren the Levites did help them, till the work was ended" (2 Chr. 29:34; see also 35:11). To flay here apparently means to skin the animal. After killing the sacrificial victim, the offerer or member of the priesthood would skin the animal. The Hebrew word *psht*, which the King James translators translated as "to flay," usually means "to strip off clothing" or "to strip naked" (see Gen. 37:23; 1 Sam. 19:24; Job 22:6; Ezek. 16:39; 26:16; 44:19; Hosea 2:3).

Perhaps flayed sacrificial victims were symbols of Jesus Christ. Jesus was unceremoniously stripped of clothing—His garments and "coat"—before His Crucifixion (John 19:23–24). President Spencer W. Kimball wrote, "How he must have suffered when [the soldiers] violated his privacy by stripping off his clothes and then putting on him the scarlet robe!"[2]

The flaying of the sacrificial victims may have also looked forward to the scourging of Jesus, when He was stripped of parts of His skin. During His trial, when He appeared before the Roman governor Pontius Pilate, He was scourged before His Crucifixion (see Matt. 27:26). Perhaps Peter

---

1. Ballard, "The Law of Sacrifice," 10.
2. Kimball, "Jesus of Nazareth," 6.

referred to this scourging when he wrote that Jesus "[bore] our sins in his own body" (1 Pet. 2:24). The Lord through Isaiah had prophesied of the scourging more than seven centuries earlier with these words, "I gave my back to the smiters" (Isa. 50:6).

FLOWERS

Anciently, Solomon's temple gave prominence to flowers on the brazen sea (see 1 Kgs. 7:19, 24, 26), the holy place (see 1 Kgs 6:17–18, 29, 32, 35), the two brass pillars, and the molten sea's brim (see 1 Kgs. 7:15, 22–26). Both worshippers and workers could view these decorations, which were likely elegantly beautiful, from various areas of the courtyard.

In the modern era, flowers belong to the decorative features of literally scores of temples, on both exterior and interior components—on walls and panels, decorations, doors, stained-glass windows, light fixtures, door hardware, railings, carpet sculptings, moldings and trim works, and elsewhere. Additionally, most temples feature flower beds and professionally appointed gardens. Flowers are conspicuously beautiful and vibrantly colorful, thus engaging the eyes to God's amazing creations.

Many temples feature flowers that are indigenous to the area. For example, the syringa, Idaho's state flower, decorates both the Twin Falls Idaho and Meridian Idaho Temples. The sunflower, Ukraine's national flower, decorates the Kyiv Ukraine Temple. The sego lily, Utah's state flower, adorns the Draper Utah Temple (note also that the sego lily's roots provided nourishment to the pioneers during their first winter in Utah); Alaska's state flower, the forget-me-not, graces the Anchorage Alaska Temple. The hibiscus, Hawaii's state flower, together with nuts and leaves from the kukui tree, decorate the Laie Hawaii Temple. And the Winter Quarters Nebraska Temple gives prominence to the state flowers of five states—Illinois, Iowa, Nebraska, Wyoming, and Utah—the five territories that the pioneers traveled through on their way to settle in Utah!

The San Diego California Temple has the appearance of a fortress.

Flowers have multiple symbolic values. The flowers' reproductive qualities remind us of God's beautiful creations; and so, too, the temple dedicates certain portions of the endowment to the Creation narrative.

FORTRESS, TEMPLE AS A

Many ancient castles, fortresses, and city walls have defensive architecture, which includes battlements, parapets, crenels, merlons, towers, great walls, and rectangular or square gaps used for discharging spears or arrows. Several of our temples, too, feature castle-like architectural components, including battlements, crenellated towers, turrets, and buttresses, including the Salt Lake, Logan, Manti, San Diego, and Washington D.C. temples. Additionally, some temples are surrounded by massive fences, elevated walls, or other safeguarding or shielding features. All of these castle-like features that belong to temples typify a separation from the outside world, from Babylon.

Just as these temples architecturally portray a fortress, they (and all of our temples) are spiritual fortresses; each temple serves as a protection from evil and from the world.

While each and every temple serves as a spiritual fortress, God Himself is our ultimate fortress! "The Lord is my rock, and my fortress . . . and my high tower" (Ps. 18:2); "O Lord. . . . Be thou my strong habitation, whereunto I may continually resort: thou hast given commandment to save me; for thou art my rock and my fortress" (Ps. 71:1, 3); "I have set thee [Lord] for a tower and

Logan Utah Temple, a fortress. Note the battlements and crenellated towers.

a fortress among my people" (Jer. 6:27; see also 16:19. See also Ps. 31:3; 91:2; 144:2). Inasmuch as God is our fortress (symbolically), we can obtain peace and safety in Him, because He has the power to save us from physical danger and spiritual harm.

FOUNDATION, TEMPLE

Writing to the Ephesians, Paul wrote of "an holy temple in the Lord" and explained that its foundation represents apostles and prophets. "Now therefore ye are no more strangers and foreigners, but fellowcitizens with the saints, and of the household of God; And are built upon the foundation of the apostles and prophets, Jesus Christ himself being the chief corner stone; In whom all the building fitly framed together groweth unto an holy temple in the Lord" (Eph. 2:19–21).

GARDEN OF EDEN, TEMPLE SYMBOLISM IN

"The Garden in Eden was the first sanctuary of earth," wrote Elder James E. Talmage.[1] Indeed, the Garden of Eden narrative, as set forth in Genesis 2–3 and elsewhere, contains several powerful symbols and features that prefigured subsequent Israelite temples, including the Mosaic tabernacle and the Jerusalem temple. These features included the tree of life, sacred waters, a representation of a sacred mountain, cherubim, sacred vestments, and others.[2] The Garden of Eden, then, served as the prototype, pattern, or originator of subsequent Israelite temples; it was "an archetypal sanctuary."[3] The garden was not a sanctuary of cedar or marble, for it is not necessary for a temple to be an edifice or structure; rather, it was a space made holy because it was created by Deity, and God's presence was found there.

---

1. Talmage, *The House of the Lord*, 15.
2. See Parry, "Garden of Eden: Prototype Sanctuary," 126–51.
3. Wenham, "Sanctuary Symbolism in the Garden of Eden Story," 19–25.

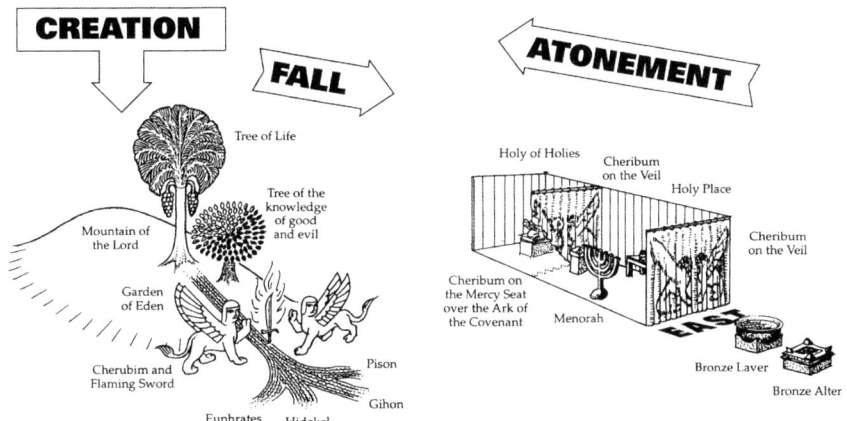

The temple signifies a return to the Garden of Eden, through the Atonement. Drawing sets forth the sacred topography of Eden and the temple.

Elder Talmage also associates the Garden of Eden narrative with modern temples: "The Temple Endowment, as administered in modern temples, comprises instruction relating to . . . the condition of our first parents in the Garden of Eden."[4] Elder John A. Widtsoe, too, taught that Adam, Noah, and other patriarchs had the equivalent of a temple.[5] Note also Abraham, Facsimile No. 2, figure 3: "represent[ed] also [are] the grand Key-words of the Holy Priesthood, as revealed to Adam in the Garden of Eden."

One of the chief purposes of temple rituals, both ancient and modern, is to reverse the negative effects of the Fall of Adam and to enable men and women to return to God's presence (i.e., in the celestial room and the Holy of Holies). The following diagram compares the Creation, Fall, and expulsion in the Garden of Eden to the return to God's presence (through the power of the Atonement of Jesus Christ) in the tabernacle of Moses. Correspondingly, our modern temples present powerful rituals that allow women and men to overcome the Fall's effects and to return to God's presence.

---

4. Talmage, *The House of the Lord*, 83.
5. Widtsoe, "Temple Worship," 52–53.

This chart sets forth eleven themes that belong to both the Garden of Eden and subsequent Israelite temples.

Eden	Theme	Israelite Temple(s)
God planted the tree of life in the middle of the garden (Gen. 2:9)	Tree of life	A menorah (lampstand fashioned into a seven-branched almond tree) was placed in the temple's holy place (1 Kgs. 7:49)
The direction east is part of the Garden of Eden narrative (Gen. 2:14; 3:24)	Eastward orientation	The temple had an eastward orientation (Ex. 27:9–18)
The garden was a mountain with rivers flowing downward (Gen. 2:10; see also Ezek. 28:13–14)	Mountain	The temple is referred to as "the mountain of the Lord's house . . . established in the top of the mountains" (Isa. 2:1–3)
The garden is connected to the ritual Creation drama (Gen. 1–3)	Earth's creation	The Creation sequence was reenacted in the temple
Cherubim guard the way back to the tree of life (Gen. 3:24)	Cherubim	Cherubim guarded the Holy of Holies (1 Kgs. 6:16–35)
God revealed many things to Adam and Eve in the garden (Moses 3:16–17; 4:22–29)	Revelation	The temple was a place of prayer and communion with God (Ps. 18:6; Acts 3:1)
Sacrifice was performed in the garden to make coats of skins (Gen. 3:21)	Sacrifice	Sacrifice was performed daily at the temple (Lev. 1–6; Num. 28:24)
Adam was commanded to keep and work the garden (Gen. 2:15)	Keep and work	Priests were to keep and work the temple (Num. 3:32; 8:24, 26)
God gave Adam and Eve sacred clothing (Moses 4:27–31)	Sacred clothing	God instructed the priests to wear sacred clothing (Ex. 28–29)
The garden was paradise, with every tree producing food (Gen. 1:29)	Abundance	The temple was viewed as a place of prosperity (Isa. 51:3)

GARMENTS

President Russell M. Nelson instructed, "Wearing the temple garment has deep symbolic significance. It represents a continuing commitment. Just as the Savior exemplified the need to endure to the end, we wear the garment faithfully as part of the enduring armor of God. Thus we demonstrate our faith in Him and in His eternal covenants with us."[1] President Boyd K. Packer explained, "Members who have received their temple ordinances thereafter wear the special garment or underclothing. . . . The garment represents sacred covenants. It fosters modesty and becomes a shield and protection to the wearer."[2]

The temple garment has an antecedent in the Old Testament. During the period of the law of Moses, both high priests and priests wore special linen breeches, which some scholars identify as undergarments.[3] "Thou shalt make them linen breeches to cover their nakedness; from the loins even unto the thighs they shall reach . . . it shall be a statute for ever unto him and his seed after him" (Ex. 28:42–43). These linen breeches, together with all other sacred vestments, were "holy garments" (Ex. 28:2; see also v. 40). According to Exodus 28, Aaron and his sons were required to wear the linen breeches when they entered the tabernacle lest they "bear . . . iniquity, and die" (v. 43).

Biblical scholar Deborah Rooke has written about the ancient priestly undergarments and compared them to our temple garments. She writes that "the obvious point of similarity between the ancient and the modern forms of underwear is that they are both invisible to the outward observer and yet both are a required part of correct sacred clothing in their

---

1. Nelson, "Personal Preparation for Temple Blessings," 33. See also Hales, "Blessings of the Priesthood," 32–34.
2. Packer, *The Holy Temple*, 75.
3. The linen breeches were "undergarments of plain linen." Durham, *Exodus*, 385.

respective contexts. It therefore seems reasonable to suggest that there may be some correspondence in function between the two."[1]

The undergarments of the high priest were distinctive because of their woven patterns (see Ex. 28:39); according to one Hebrew lexicon, the rare verb in Exodus 28:39 (Hebrew: *shibbatz*) means "to weave patterns."[2] Scholars can only guess at the design of the patterns. Elder Carlos E. Asay reveals also the distinctiveness of our temple garments: "Garments bear several simple marks of orientation toward the gospel principles of obedience, truth, life, and discipleship in Christ."[3]

On October 10, 1988, the First Presidency, Ezra Taft Benson, Gordon B. Hinckley, Thomas S. Monson, explained in a letter: "Church members who have been clothed with the garment in the temple have made a covenant to wear it throughout their lives.... The promise of protection and blessings is conditioned upon worthiness and faithfulness in keeping the covenant.... Endowed members of the Church wear the garment as a reminder of the sacred covenants they have made with the Lord and also as a protection against temptation and evil. *How it is worn is an outward expression of an inward commitment to follow the Savior.*"[4]

Spencer W. Kimball explains that the garment provides several categories of protection for us: "Temple garments afford protection.... Though generally I think our protection is a mental, spiritual, moral one, yet I am convinced that there could be and undoubtedly have been many cases where there has been, through faith, an actual physical protection."[5]

---

1. Rooke, "Breeches of the Covenant: Gender, Garments and the Priesthood," 32.
2. *The Hebrew and Aramaic Lexicon of the Old Testament,* 1401. One may also review Welch and Foley, "Gammadia on Early Jewish and Christian Garments," 253–58, who present evidence regarding an L-shaped symbol that has been found on early Jewish and Christian garments and other textiles.
3. Asay, "The Temple Garment," 20; see also Marshall, "Garments," 2:534.
4. Ezra Taft Benson, Gordon B. Hinckley, Thomas S. Monson, First Presidency Letter, October 10, 1988, cited in Asay, "The Temple Garment," 22; emphasis in the original.
5. Kimball, *The Teachings of Spencer W. Kimball,* 539. Many other Church authorities have spoken regarding the protection of the temple garment. See for example, Hales, "Blessings of the Priesthood," 32.

An important discourse on the temple garment was written by Elder Carlos E. Asay (mentioned above). Among other teachings, he explained that "the piece of armor called the temple garment . . . strengthens the wearer to resist temptation, fend off evil influences, and stand firmly for the right. . . . And, to the degree it is honored, [it is] *a token of what Paul regarded as taking upon one the whole armor of God.*"[6]

GATE OF HEAVEN

Jacob's experience, as recorded in Genesis 28:10–22, was none other than a temple experience—"This is none other but the *house of God,* and this is the gate of heaven" (v. 17; emphasis added); Jacob "called the name of that place *Beth-el*" (Hebrew: "house of God") (v. 19; emphasis added), and "this stone, which I have set for a pillar, shall be *God's house*" (v. 22; emphasis added). Furthermore, this same text makes it clear that Jacob was in God's presence, because Jacob stated, "Surely the Lord is in this place" (v. 16; see also vv. 12–13). As Elder Marion G. Romney explained, "Temples are to us all what Bethel was to Jacob."[7]

"The gate of heaven" (v. 17; see also Hel. 3:28) means that the temple signifies an entryway into heaven. Every temple is, symbolically, a gate of heaven. Those who worthily enter the temple and receive the ordinances are enabled to enter into God's presence through the gate. "Temples really are the gateways to heaven,"[8] explains President Ezra Taft Benson.

---

6. Asay, "The Temple Garment," 20–21; emphasis in the original. See also Marshall, "Garments," 2:534.
7. Romney, "Temples—the Gates to Heaven," 16.
8. "Temple Memories," address given at Denver Colorado Temple dedication (October 25, 1986), cited in Monson, "Temple of the Lord," 5.

GATE, THE TABERNACLE

The gate of the tabernacle, located at the east end of the courtyard, was thirty feet wide and covered with a beautiful, colorful veil (or curtain). Its colors were blue, purple, and scarlet, and it was made of "fine twined linen, wrought with needlework" (Ex. 27:16) (see entry "Colors"). This gate reminds us of the Psalmist's words, the "gate of the Lord, into which the righteous shall enter" (Ps. 118:20).

Gatekeepers controlled access to this gate as well as other gates belonging to both ancient and modern temples (see, for example, 1 Chr. 9:22–27; 2 Chr. 8:14). The chief goals of these gatekeepers was to secure "the gates of the house of the Lord, that none which was unclean in any thing should enter in" (2 Chr. 23:19). See entry "Guards, Temple (Sentinels and Angels)."

The gate's colors, the gatekeepers, and the gate itself have symbolic significances. The gate calls to mind Jesus Christ. Not only is He "the door of the sheep" (John 10:7; see also v. 9), but He is the gate by which we must all enter in order to receive the blessings of the temple. Jesus Christ is also the chief gatekeeper, or the ultimate custodian of the way into the tabernacle (and also heaven). A Book of Mormon verse has application here: "The keeper of the gate is the Holy One of Israel . . . there is none other way save it be by the gate" (2 Ne. 9:41; see also Moses 7:53).

Beautiful and colorful gate to the model tabernacle courtyard.

The gate of the temple in heaven (celestial kingdom), too, is very beautiful. Joseph Smith records, "I saw the transcendent beauty of the gate through which the heirs of that kingdom will enter, which was like unto circling flames of fire" (D&C 137:2).

Mesa Arizona Temple panel, gathering of Israel.

GATHERING OF ISRAEL

The gathering of Israel is one of the most prominent topics both in the scriptures and among the living prophets. President Russell M. Nelson stated, "These surely *are* the latter days, and the Lord is hastening His work to gather Israel. That gathering is the most important thing taking place on earth today. Nothing else compares in magnitude, nothing else compares in importance, nothing else compares in majesty."[1]

And why the gathering? Its purpose, as the Prophet Joseph Smith taught, is to build temples so that God can reveal "the ordinances of his house and the glories of his kingdom, and teach the people the way of Salvation."[2] He also stated, "One of the most important points in the faith of the church of the Latter Day Saints, is . . . the gathering of Israel . . . The happy time when Jacob shall go up to the house of the Lord, to worship him in spirit and in truth, to live in holiness."[3]

---

1. Nelson, "Hope of Israel."
2. "History, 1838–1856, volume D-1 [1 August 1842–1 July 1843]," p. 1572, The Joseph Smith Papers, accessed March 27, 2019, https://www.josephsmithpapers.org/paper-summary/history-1838-1856-volume-d-1-1-august-1842-1-july-1843/217.
3. "History, 1838–1856, volume B-1 [1 September 1834–2 November 1838]," p. 680, The Joseph Smith Papers, accessed March 27, 2019, https://www.josephsmithpapers.org/paper-summary/history-1838-1856-volume-b-1-1-september-1834-2-november-1838/134.

Some temples set forth the gathering theme with architectural designs. For example, the Mesa Arizona Temple features eight panels on the temple's exterior that refer to Israel's gathering, as per Isaiah's words, "He shall set up an ensign for the nations, and shall assemble the outcasts of Israel, and gather together the dispersed of Judah from the four corners of the earth" (Isa. 11:12).

Various beautiful geometric designs, San Salvador Temple.

GEOMETRY, SACRED

Sacred geometry in the setting of temples pertains to the relative arrangement of lines and points that create a multitude of geometric symbols that belong to the exterior and interior parts of temples; these include circles, squares, rectangles, stars, concentric circles, squares within squares, circles within squares, and many more. Many (but certainly not all) of these geometric symbols are artistic expressions that provide symbolic understandings, conveying a variety of ideas, e.g., the concepts of earth, heaven, eternity, astronomical bodies, and others.

In association with sacred geometry, the scriptures portray God as the ultimate *Geometer*. When God created the earth, He utilized the following tools: the hollow of His hand, a span (the distance between the tips of the little finger and stretched out thumb), a measure, scales, and a balance: "Who hath measured the waters [of the sea] in the hollow of his hand (*sha'al*), and meted out heaven with the span (*zeret*), and comprehended the dust of the earth in a measure (*shalish*), and weighed the mountains in scales (*peles*), and the hills in a balance (*mozen*)?" (Isa. 40:12). God also used a geometer's tool called a compass (an instrument that creates circles and arcs): "When [God] established [*chaqaq*, 'marked out'] the heavens, I was there, when he inscribed a circle [*chug*, 'used a compass'] on the deep" (Prov. 8:27; translation by author; see also Job 26:10).

GESTURES OF APPROACH

"Gestures of approach" (or "threshold rituals") refer to sacred gestures, movements, or actions conducted by worshippers as they approach God in the temple. These gestures facilitate the transition from a profane setting to a sacred place and prepare the individual for entrance into holy, more holy, and most holy spheres; they also serve to spiritually elevate those who participate in the gestures. But note that it is only after participating in these gestures that the worshipper is permitted to approach God in His perfect state of holiness. There are many biblical texts that deal with sacred gestures.

The following is a brief list, representative and not comprehensive, of several gestures of approach in ancient Israelite temples. They are not necessarily listed in the order that they occurred by actual temple worshippers. Most of the gestures will be dealt with more fully below in subsequent sections.

The removal of profane items. For example, God commanded Moses to "put off thy shoes from off thy feet, for the place whereon thou standest is holy ground" (Ex. 3:5). Joshua also had a similar experience (see Josh. 5:15).

Ritual ablutions, or washing with water. This practice is referred to in a number of scriptural passages. For example, Exodus 29:4 states, "Aaron and his sons thou shalt bring unto the door of the tabernacle of the congregation, and shalt wash them with water" (see also Ex. 30:19–20; 40:12).

Anointing with olive oil (see Ex. 29:7; 40:13). This is a sacred rite that followed ritual ablutions but preceded the vesting rite.

Investiture of sacred vestments (see Ex. 28; 40:13). Rather than wear commonplace clothing, priests and high priests wore vestments that were holy (see Ex. 28:2–3), or set apart from the world.

Laying on of hand(s) on sacrificial animals. For example, "Aaron shall lay both his hands upon the head of the live goat, and confess over him all the iniquities of the children of Israel" (Lev. 16:21).

Offering of a variety of sacrifices for various occasions. The law of sacrifice is a very ancient institution. During the Mosaic period, these included burnt, grain, peace, sin, and trespass and guilt offerings.

Filling the priest's hand. For an explanation of filling the hand, see "Priests," Bible Dictionary.[1] This deals with Moses filling the hand of the priests.

Prayer with "uplifted hands." This is a well-attested biblical doctrine (see entry "Hands—Prayer with 'Uplifted Hands' [D&C 88:120; 109:17–19])."

Sprinkling with blood. The blood of sacrificial victims was sprinkled on the temple altar, on Aaron and his sons, on their garments, on the mercy seat, and on the cleansed leper.

Offering incense at the golden altar. Incense was burned on this altar twice daily, and once a year the high priest was commanded to "make an atonement upon the horns . . . with the blood of the sin offering" (Ex. 30:7–10).

Entering the veil. Leviticus 16 reveals instructions regarding entering the veil (see Lev. 16:2, 12, 15, 23).

---

1. Bible Dictionary, 708.

In our temples, both females and males participate equally in a series of gestures of approach.

Under the subheading of "Names, Signs, and Seals," Nibley explains how certain gestures were used in the ancient camp of Israel: "As one approaches the camp of Israel, carefully guarded in a dangerous environment, one first gives a sign to be seen from afar. Then, being recognized, one approaches and at closer range gives his name.

Cutaway of tabernacle illustrates locations of worshippers' gestures of approach and ceremonial movements as they approach God in the temple.

This establishes closer identity. *Nomen est omen:* every name is an epithet indicating exactly in the manner of a token above a distinguishing mark, indication, or characteristic trait, which distinguishes one from all other members of the society. . . . After the sign and the name comes the closest approach, an actual handclasp or embrace."[2]

So too, many of the world's great religions, including Buddhism, Christianity, Hinduism, Islam, Jainism, Judaism, Shintoism, Sikhism, and Taoism, utilize gestures of one sort or another during their religious services. For example, many adherents of the Catholic or the Orthodox (Eastern rite) Churches participate in religious services with one or more of the following gestures: bowing, standing, genuflection, sign of the cross, bowing the head, using holy water, striking the breast, and/or placing ashes on the forehead. Furthermore, the Trinitarian Blessing, the Christogram

---

2. Nibley, "On the Sacred and the Symbolic," 557–59.

(or IX XC Blessing, an abbreviation for the Greek words *Jesus Christ*), and the Benediction hand gestures are all conducted with the hand and fingers. Some of these gestures are entrance rituals, meaning they are gestured when one enters the church or cathedral. Some of the gestures belonging to the world's religions constitute altered remnants or echoes of the sacred gestures of ancient temples, as referred to in the Bible.

GETHSEMANE, TEMPLE SYMBOLISM IN

Because of the exceptional and significantly eternal events that took place in the Garden of Gethsemane, it was a hallowed place; in truth, the Garden of Gethsemane (similar to the Garden of Eden) contains several elements and symbols that make it a sacred space—a temple. The following consists of correspondences between the temple and Gethsemane:

(1) The temple is called a house of prayer; in Gethsemane, Jesus Christ prayed three times (see Matt. 26:36, 39, 42, 44).

(2) The temple is a place of sacrificial offerings; Jesus Christ offered Himself as the ultimate sacrificial offering, to the point that He bled from every pore: "Which suffering caused myself, even God, the greatest of all, to tremble because of pain, and to bleed at every pore, and to suffer both body and spirit" (D&C 19:18); in fact, "his sweat was as it were great drops of blood" (Luke 22:44). As it is well known, olive trees were present in Gethsemane, and while conducting a tour of the Rome Italy Temple, Elder David A. Bednar spoke of the olive tree in association with the Atonement: "One of the things I love most about this [Rome Italy Temple grand] staircase is the combining of the oval and the olive tree. . . . The olive tree recalls the garden of Gethsemane, that sacred site of the Savior's Atonement."[1]

---

1. David A. Bednar, "Two Apostles Lead a Virtual Tour of the Rome Italy Temple."

Olive tree in Gethsemane, Mount of Olives, Jerusalem.

(3) Some mountains serve as temples; Gethsemane was located on the western slope of the Mount of Olives, which exists east of Jerusalem.

(4) Priests and high priests wore sacred vestments; Christ's clothing was made sacred when it was touched by the blood of the infinite Atonement (see Luke 22:44).

(5) The temple consisted of a series of gradations of holiness, from less holy to most holy: the court, the holy place, and the Holy of Holies. Gethsemane was also divided into three gradations of holiness: "Then cometh Jesus with them unto a place called Gethsemane, and saith unto the disciples, Sit ye here [ZONE 1], while I go and pray yonder. And he took with him Peter and the two sons of Zebedee, and began to be sorrowful and very heavy. Then saith he unto them, My soul is exceeding sorrowful, even unto death: tarry ye here [ZONE 2], and watch with me. And he went a little further [ZONE 3], and fell on his face, and prayed,

saying, O my Father, if it be possible, let this cup pass from me: nevertheless not as I will, but as thou wilt" (Matt. 26:36–39). Jesus left eight of the Apostles in one area, three of His Apostles in a second area, and then He went by Himself to pray to the Father. Jesus's actions remind us of the high priest on the Day of Atonement, who went alone into the Holy of Holies to make an atonement.

(6) The temple housed the menorah, which provided light to the holy place; Jesus, Himself, is the light of the world (John 1:9; 8:12).

(7) The living waters are associated with the temple (Ezek. 47); Jesus is the waters of life, or "the fountain of living waters" (Jer. 2:13; 17:13).

(8) A laver of brass was set up in the tabernacle for ritual washings; specifically, the laver was for the priests (see Ex. 30:20–21). Where in the Garden of Gethsemane is the laver? Perhaps the laver symbolizes Jesus Christ, who washes us and cleanses us from sins.

(9) The temple is a place of revelation.

(10) The temple is a focal point of God's presence.

In sum, Elder Bruce R. McConkie instructed regarding Gethsemane, "This sacred spot . . . this holy ground is where the Sinless Son of the Everlasting Father took upon himself the sins of all men on condition of repentance.

"We do not know, we cannot tell, no mortal mind can conceive the full import of what Christ did in Gethsemane."[1]

GRADATIONS OF HOLINESS (LESS HOLY TO MOST HOLY)

The architectural plans and spatial layout of ancient Israelite temples demonstrate that each temple comprised graded divisions, including a holiest center (the Holy of Holies), a ceremonially unclean periphery (outside

---

1. McConkie, "The Purifying Power of Gethsemane," 9.

of the camp where lepers and ritually unclean souls dwelt), and gradations of holiness in between (e.g., the temple's court and holy place). The goal of graded space was to present a holiest zone for Deity, which was far away, in terms of both height and distance, from profane and corruptible space, persons, and objects. And as one moves from secular space to holy space, and then to an even holier space, he/she notices that there is an increase in light, splendor, and beauty, and a heightened awareness of spiritual feelings.

An ancient rabbinic record identifies the various gradations of holiness that existed in the temple of Herod:

> There are ten degrees of holiness:
> The land of Israel is holier than all the [other] lands. . . .
> The cities that are surrounded with walls are holier than it. . . .
> Within the wall of Jerusalem is holier than they [the foregoing]. . . .
> The Temple Mount is holier than it. . . .
> The Court of the Women is holier than it. . . .
> The Court of Israel is holier than it. . . .

Graded divisions of the tabernacle complex include the holiest center (the Holy of Holies), a ceremonially unclean periphery (outside of the camp where lepers and ritually unclean souls dwelt), and gradations of holiness in between (e.g., the temple's court and holy place).

> The Court of the Priests is holier than it. . . .
> [The space] between the porch and the altar is holier than it. . . .
> The sanctuary is holier than it. . . .
> The Holy of Holies is holier than them all. (m. Kelim 1:6–9)

In addition to divisions of sacred space in ancient Israelite temples, the chart designates that the holiness continuum also pertained to other aspects of the ancient temple, such as fabrics, priestly vestments, foods, persons, and rituals of approaching sacred space.

The entire idea of the continuum was to teach the Israelites that the innermost zone of the temple (where God's presence was found) was both superior and the most holy of spheres on the earth. This holiness was represented with the finest things—sacred vestments, fabric, sacrificial foods, and so forth. As priestly officiants or worshippers moved from a profane world outside of the holiness continuum toward the most holy zone, the visible things around them (fabric, vestments, temple furniture, vessels, foods, and so forth) were of better quality and more elaborate workmanship. All of these things served as teaching devices that pointed to the glories of heaven, where God Himself dwells in the temple of heaven.

Modern temples also display spatial layouts that demonstrate gradational divisions—from the profane world to the most holy. Richard Cowan, for example, points out that "the Logan, Manti, and Salt Lake Temples employed a series of rooms to present [the endowment]. Their walls were adorned with murals depicting distinctive stages in mankind's progress back into God's presence—the creation, the Garden of Eden, our present telestial world, the terrestrial state, and finally the celestial room, generally the most beautifully furnished space in the temple, representing the feelings of peace and joy in that glory. Typically one climbs a few stairs when going from one room to the next, representing progress forward and upward."[1]

---

1. Cowan, "Latter-day Saint Temples as Symbols," 5.

Gradations of Holiness—The Israelite Temple[2]

GRADATIONS OF HOLINESS

	Most Holy	Holy	Less Holy	Profane/Unclean
Space	Holy of Holies	Holy place	Court	Cemeteries, camp of lepers, etc.
Fabric	Very elaborate, superior work, with woven figures	Elaborate, multi-colored mixture of wool and linen, no figures	Less elaborate, no figures	
Persons	High priest	Priests	Levites, male and female Israelites	Persons w/ major or minor ritual impurities
Priestly Vestments	Very elaborate, superior work and fabric, gold and precious stones	Elaborate	Less elaborate	
Touching	Only the high priest is permitted to touch the ark	Only priests are permitted to touch furniture in the tabernacle; non-priests may not touch a priest when he is officiating or anointed with holy oil; outer veil may not be touched by non-priests	Only Levites may do the "work of the tent of meeting," transport the furniture, beams, etc., but only when the items are covered	
Sight	High priest, but the smoke of the incense tends to hide the ark in the Holy of Holies from the sight of the high priest	Non-priests may not view the furniture or items of the holy place; the priest covers them before they are transported.	Israelites only may see things in the court	

2. Information adapted from Haran, *Temples and Temple-Service in Ancient Israel,* 58–188.

GRADATIONS OF HOLINESS (continued)

	Most Holy	Holy	Less Holy	Profane/Unclean
Ore	Gold	Gold and silver	Copper (or bronze)	
Approach	Prophet and high priest	Priest	Non-Levites may not approach the furniture of the tabernacle or outer altar; laypersons (women and men) may be located in the "entrance to the tent of meeting" between the entrance and the altar	Non-Israelites are forbidden entry to temple
Furniture	Ark of the covenant	Lampstand, utensils, altar of incense, table of shewbread	Outer altar, laver, utensils	
Food	Sacrifices	Sacrifices, tithes	Pure food	Impure food (not permitted by law of Moses), carcasses

GUARDS, TEMPLE (SENTINELS AND ANGELS)

Temple guards or sentinels belong to four categories:

(1) *Gatekeepers of the ancient Israelite temple.* The Old Testament refers to gatekeepers of the Lord's house (King James Version reads "porters," but the Hebrew word *sho'er* refers to a gatekeeper). During the ministry of Samuel the seer, for example, there were 212 gatekeepers who "had the oversight of the gates of the house of the Lord, namely, the house of the tabernacle" (1 Chr. 9:23). These gatekeepers guarded the temple from all

cardinal directions: east, south, west, and north (see 1 Chr. 9:27; Num. 1:53; 2 Chr. 8:14; Jer. 35:4). The primary role of the gatekeepers was to secure "the gates of the house of the Lord, that none which was unclean in any thing should enter in" (2 Chr. 23:19).

(2) *Bishops and stake presidents as sentinels.* Lorenzo Snow taught, "Bishops and stake presidents are sentinels to guard the temples. . . . They should not allow any to pass by them into the temple that are unworthy. It is something like what we learn in the temple about a time that is coming when persons who go into the celestial kingdom will have to pass by the angels and gods."[1]

(3) *Angelic guards.* Multiple sacred accounts set forth that the Lord's angels protect the Saints who worship in His temple. Joseph Smith recorded, "Elder Roger Orton saw a mighty Angel riding upon a horse of fire with a flaming sword in his hand, followed by five others, encircle the house [Kirtland Temple], and protect the Saints, even the Lord's anointed from the power of satan and a host of evil Spirits, which were striving to disturb the Saints."[2]

Elder Vaughn J. Featherstone taught that in the temple, "unseen sentinels watch over us. . . . Surely angelic attendants guard the temples of the Most High God. It is my conviction that as it was in the days of Elisha, so it will be for us: 'Fear not: for they that be with us are more than they that be with them' (2 Kgs. 6:16.). . . . There are great unseen hosts in the temple. Joseph told the brethren, 'And I beheld the temple was filled with angels.' (History of the Church, 2:428.) I believe deceased prophets of all dispensations visit the temples. Those who attend the temple will feel their strength and companionship. We will not be alone in the house of the Lord."[3]

---

1. Snow, *The Teachings of Lorenzo Snow,* 99.
2. "History, 1838–1856, volume B-1 [1 September 1834–2 November 1838]," p. 699, The Joseph Smith Papers, accessed March 27, 2019, https://www.josephsmithpapers.org/paper-summary/history-1838-1856-volume-b-1-1-september-1834-2-november-1838/153.
3. Featherstone, *The Incomparable Christ,* 3–4.

Truman O. Angell wrote of seeing two angels who served as sentinels of the Kirtland Temple: "We walked out towards the [Kirtland] Temple. . . . We looked up and saw two Personages; one before each window, leaving and approaching each other like guards would do. . . . I have no doubt but the house was guarded."[1]

(4) *Angels as sentinels of the Temple in Heaven.* Some angels serve as sentinels who guard the way back to heaven, thus preventing unworthy or unauthorized persons from entering its sacred premises. Brigham Young taught that the endowment enables us to "[pass] the angels who stand as sentinels, being enabled to give them the key words, the signs and tokens, pertaining to the holy Priesthood, and gain your eternal exaltation in spite of earth and hell."[2] On another occasion, he spoke of the "laws and ordinances, by which we can be prepared to pass from one gate to another, and from one sentinel to another, until we go into the presence of our Father and God."[3]

John described the celestial city, which "had a wall great and high, and had twelve gates" (Rev. 21:12). John continues with his description in that verse and states that there are "at the gates twelve angels." The twelve angels are guardians or sentinels, assigned to prevent entrance into the city by "any thing that defileth" (v. 27).

HANDS AND COVENANTS

The *hand* or *hands* were regularly employed in ancient temple ritual—the laying on of hands of animals, filling the hands, cleansing the hands,

---

1. Angell, *Autobiography of Truman O. Angell,* 10–11.
2. Young, *Discourses of Brigham Young,* 416. Many Church authorities have cited President Young's statement. For example, see Kimball, "Things of Eternity—Stand We in Jeopardy?" 6; Haight, "Come to the House of the Lord," 15–16; Packer, "Come to the Temple," 20; and Nelson, "Prepare for Blessings of the Temple," 42.
3. *Teachings of Presidents of the Church: Brigham Young,* 15; less than a year later, Brigham spoke of these sentinels: see *Teachings of Presidents of the Church: Brigham Young,* 302.

the laying on of hands of persons, anointing with olive oil, clasping hands, sprinkling sacrificial blood, offering incense at the golden altar, the right hand, praying with uplifted hands, plus more. Additionally, the "wave offering" (Lev. 10:14–15; 23:17) and the heave offering (see Ex. 29:27–28, Lev. 7:13–14, 34) required the use of hands in ceremonial settings. In both ancient and modern temples, God instructs us perfectly through the utilization of hand rituals as we make covenants (consider, for example, the right arm to the square by the one conducting a baptism).

The Hebrew word *yad* denotes "hand" or "power."[4] When the laying on of hands is performed in various priesthood ordinations and rituals, the Lord's power is manifest through the hands of the mortal administering the ordination or ritual. The Lord revealed to Edward Partridge, "I will lay my hand upon you by the hand of my servant Sidney Rigdon" (D&C 36:2), meaning, the laying on of hands by Sidney Ridgon is as if the Lord had laid His hands on Edward Partridge. Similarly, Brigham Young explained, "When I lay hands on the sick, I expect the healing power and influence of God to pass through me to the patient. . . . When we are prepared, when we are holy vessels before the Lord, a stream of power from the Almighty can pass through the tabernacle of the administrator to the system of the patient, and the sick are made whole."[5] In sum, the *hand* is an agent of power that is utilized in both ancient and modern ordinances; the power comes from God, of course.

Sometimes God specifically commands His temple workers to use the right hand in sacred ceremonies and ordinances. For example, putting blood on the right ear, thumb, and foot (see Ex. 29:20; Lev. 8:24–25; 14:14); putting oil on the right ear, hand, and foot (see Lev. 14:17, 27–28); and sprinkling oil with the right finger (see Lev. 14:16, 26–27). It seems that the right hand is used more often in making covenants than is the left.

---

4. *A Hebrew and English Lexicon of the Old Testament,* 388–91; *The Hebrew and Aramaic Lexicon of the Old Testament,* 2:386–88.
5. *Teachings of Presidents of the Church: Brigham Young,* 252.

This reminds us of several scriptural passages that state that God's right hand (versus His left hand) is the prominent one: The right hand of God is associated with righteousness ("Thy right hand is full of righteousness," Ps. 48:10; see also Isa. 41:10) and power ("Thy right hand, O Lord, is become glorious in power," Ex. 15:6; see also v. 12; Ps. 89:13). With His right hand, the Lord executes justice (see 3 Ne. 29:4, 9), dispenses the law (see Deut. 33:2), and saves His people ("O thou that savest by thy right hand," Ps. 17:7; see also Ps. 20:6). With His right hand He created the heavens ("My right hand hath spanned the heavens," Isa. 48:13), makes oaths ("The Lord hath sworn by his right hand," Isa. 62:8), sustains (see Ps. 18:35), supports (see Isa. 41:10), and exalts (see D&C 109:71). In sum, "The right hand of the Lord is exalted: the right hand of the Lord doeth valiantly" (Ps. 118:16).

HAND, FILLING THE PRIEST'S

A number of passages in the King James Version of the Bible set forth the word *consecrate,* but the literal translation (from the Hebrew Bible) is "fill the hand." For example, KJV Exodus 28:41 reads: "Thou [Moses] shalt . . . consecrate [Aaron and his sons], and sanctify them." But a literal translation from the Hebrew reads: "Thou shalt . . . fill their hand, and sanctify them." The following passages signify literal translations from the Hebrew Bible: "Thou shalt fill the hand of Aaron and the hand of his sons" (Ex. 29:9); "to fill in them their hand" (Ex. 29:29); "seven days shalt thou fill their hand" (Ex. 29:35; see also Lev. 8:33); "he shall fill his hand to minister in the priest's office" (Lev. 16:32; see also Num. 3:3).

What is the meaning of "fill the hand"? It suggests that Moses placed something in the hand of Aaron and his sons. Whatever was placed in the hand remains unknown to us in the present day, although there are multiple possibilities:

(1) *Sacrificial offering* (e.g., fat, right shoulder or thigh, kidneys; see Bible Dictionary).[1]

(2) *Olive oil.* Compare Leviticus 14:15, where the priest pours oil into his own hand: "The priest shall take some of the log of oil, and pour it into the palm of his own left hand" (see also vv. 16–18).

(3) *Incense.* Several Old Testament verses read, "One golden spoon of ten shekels, full of incense" (Num. 7:26, 32, 38, etc.). The Hebrew word behind the KJV "spoon" is *kaf*, which literally reads "palm" or "hand." See also Rev. 8:4, where the "smoke of the incense . . . ascended up before God out of the angel's hand." Hugh Nibley explained that "incense was often burned in special holders made in the form of a cupped hand, the 'golden spoons' of Exodus 25:29. . . . The 'filled hand' (the Hebrew letter *kāp* means 'palm') is the widespread sign of offering sacrifice."[2]

HAND, RAISED IN OATH

The Old Testament exhibits instances of the raising of the hand—by God or by a mortal—when swearing an oath. David Seely wrote, "The image of the raised hand of God occurs seventeen times in the Hebrew Bible in the expression *ns' yd*. Fifteen of these occurrences are found in the context of God swearing an oath: ten times in the promise of the land (Exod 6:8; Num 14:30; Ezek 20:5 [bis], 6, 15, 28, 42; 47:14; Neh 9:15), and five times in oaths of judgment against Israel (Ezek 20:23; 44:12; Ps 106:26) and its enemies (Deut 32:40; Ezek 36:7). Translations often obscure the occurrence of this image of 'raised hand' in Hebrew by usually translating simply as 'swore.'"[3] A literal translation of Exodus 6:8 reads, "I [the Lord] will bring you in unto the land, which I lifted my hand to give

---

1. Bible Dictionary, 720–21.
2. Nibley, *Temple and Cosmos*, 106.
3. Seely, "The Raised Hand of God as an Oath Gesture," 411.

it to Abraham, to Isaac, and to Jacob" (translation by author). "I lifted my hand" is a sacred gesture, used by God when he swears an oath.

Isaiah stated, "The Lord hath sworn by his right hand, and by the arm of his strength" (Isa. 62:8). To swear by the right hand (the covenant hand) is to covenant unequivocally to fulfill one's promises. In the context of God swearing an oath, we recall also that Aaron's wife's name, *Elisheba*, literally means, "God is an oath."[1]

Seely gives an example of a mortal raising the hand when swearing an oath: "Genesis 14:22 has one occurrence of a human swearing an oath with the gesture of an upraised hand: Abram swears an oath, expressed with *hrym yad*."[2]

What is the symbolism behind the lifting of the hand in an oath gesture? The lifted hand points to heaven, the realm where God dwells; as Daniel 12:7 states, a heavenly messenger lifts his "right hand and his left hand unto heaven, and sware by him that liveth for ever," meaning his hands pointed *toward heaven*. Thus, in a religious or temple context, the lifted hand is directed to God Himself, with whom the oath is made.

HANDS, CLASPED

There are representations in stone of clasped hands on the exterior of the Salt Lake Temple,[3] located above the window on the west and east towers. These clasped hands are surrounded by rays of light (or an aureole). Elder Talmage explains, "The clasped hands [are] betokening the bond of brotherhood and the free offering of the right hand of fellowship."[4] This statement reminds us of a passage in Paul's epistle to the Galatians, where Paul states that Peter, James, and John "gave to me and Barnabas the right

---

1. *A Hebrew and English Lexicon of the Old Testament,* 45.
2. Seely, "The Raised Hand of God as an Oath Gesture," 411.
3. Oman, "Sculpting an LDS Tradition," 39.
4. Talmage, *The House of the Lord,* 150.

hands of fellowship" (Gal. 2:9). On January 16, 1836, a special meeting convened for the First Presidency and the Twelve. Toward the close of the meeting, they entered into a covenant, and "took each other by the hand in confirmation of our covenant and there was a perfect unison of feeling on this occasion."[5]

Handclasp, exterior of the Salt Lake Temple, west and east towers.

Several scriptural passages refer to the Lord taking the hand of mortals. In a passage about the temple, the Lord states, "In my house [temple] and within my walls I will give to them a hand and a name" (Isa. 56:5; translation by author). In some passages, the Hebrew verb *chzq* is employed, which a prominent Hebrew and English lexicon translates as "to grasp."[6] For example, "For I the Lord thy God will grasp your right hand, saying unto thee, Fear not; I will help thee" (Isa. 41:13); "I the Lord have called thee in righteousness, and will grasp your hand, and will keep you, and give you for a covenant of the people" (Isa. 42:6); and the Lord "has grasped me by my right hand" (Ps. 73:23).

David Seely asserts that in some Old Testament passages (e.g., Prov. 6:1; 11:15; 17:18; 22:25; Job 17:3), the Hebrew expression *tqʻ yd/kp* refers to a "handclasp."[7] That is to say, "striking the hands" refers to one taking another's hand when making "pledges, assurances, and oaths."[8]

---

5. "Minutes, 16 January 1836," p. 125, The Joseph Smith Papers, accessed March 27, 2019, https://www.josephsmithpapers.org/paper-summary/minutes-16-january-1836/7. Pratt, *Autobiography of Parley P. Pratt*, 97, 99, 105, wrote a handclasp is given in connection with an "oath and covenant."
6. When used in the *Hiphil*; see *A Hebrew and English Lexicon of the Old Testament*, 305.
7. Seely, "The Raised Hand of God as an Oath Gesture," 417.
8. Seely, "The Raised Hand of God as an Oath Gesture," 417. See also *A Hebrew and English Lexicon of the Old Testament*, 1075.

The uniting of the hands also reminds us of marriage, where a husband and wife join hands in marriage at the temple altar (see entry "Sacred Triangle").

Depictions of clasped hands are found in the ancient world, in art, on sarcophagi, in mosaics, on frescos, and elsewhere.[1] After researching the meaning of the handclasp in antiquity, Stephen Ricks summarized that "the clasping of the right hand was a solemn gesture of mutual fidelity and loyalty at the conclusion of an agreement or contract, the taking of an oath of allegiance, or reception in the mysteries, whose initiates were referred to as *syndexioi* ('joined by the right hand')."[2]

HANDS, LAYING ON OF

Laying on of hands (by a model on the head of a model) for the sacred work of the temple.

When the Levites were called to the service of the tabernacle, they were purified and then they offered a sacrifice of a young bullock. Afterward, "the whole assembly of the children of Israel" gathered together and laid "their hands upon the Levites" (Num. 8:9–10). The practice of laying on of hands in the setting of the temple could be interpreted to signify the transference of power from the mortal administering the ordination or ritual to the recipient of the blessing.

---

1. See the discussion and examples in Ricks, "*Dexiosis* and *Dextrarum Iunctio*," 431–36. See also Brown, "The Handclasp, the Temple, and the King," 5–9; Calabro, "The Divine Handclasp in the Hebrew Bible and in Near Eastern Iconography," 83–97; and Compton, "The Handclasp and Embrace as Tokens of Recognition," 1:611–42.
2. Ricks, "*Dexiosis* and *Dextrarum Iunctio*," 432.

HANDS, LAYING ON OF, ON SACRIFICIAL ANIMALS

The laying of hands on the head of certain sacrificial animals was a significant part of the ancient sacrificial system. "If any man of you bring an offering unto the Lord," then "he shall put his hand upon the head of the burnt offering; and it shall be accepted for him to make an atonement for him" (Lev. 1:2, 4; see also Lev. 3:2, 8, 13; 4:29); another example, "the Levites shall lay their hands upon the heads of the bullocks . . . to make an atonement for the Levites" (Num. 8:12; see also Lev. 4:24, 29; 16:21).

Laying on of hands and transference of sins onto bull's head.

The act of laying hands on sacrificial animals teaches the law of proxy, or the power for one to act as a substitute for another. Specifically, it symbolically transmits the sins of the human(s) onto the animal's head; the act of laying on of hands served as a conduit from the human to the animal. This symbolism is expressed in Leviticus 16:21–22, where the high priest transmitted Israel's sins and iniquities upon the goat's head: "Aaron shall lay both his hands upon the head of the live goat, and confess over him all the iniquities of the children of Israel, and all their transgressions in all their sins, putting them upon the head of the goat, and . . . the goat shall bear upon him all their iniquities."

This symbolic practice focused on Jesus Christ and His Atonement: "He shall put his hand upon the head of the burnt offering; and it shall be accepted for him to make atonement for him" (Lev. 1:4). That is to say, the practice of laying hands on the sacrificial animal points to Jesus Christ, who was the perfect divine sacrifice—He took upon Himself all of our sins and iniquities and He made Atonement for each of us. Each animal, then, symbolized Jesus Christ.

HANDS—PRAYER WITH "UPLIFTED HANDS"

The Prophet Joseph Smith's dedicatory prayer of the Kirtland Temple refers to hands "uplifted to the Most High" (D&C 109:19). The uplifted hands recall several biblical passages that refer to corresponding prayer positions in temple settings.[1] For example, when Solomon dedicated the temple that bore his name, he "stood before the altar of the Lord in the presence of all the congregation of Israel, and *spread forth his hands toward heaven:* And he said, Lord God of Israel" (1 Kgs. 8:22–23; emphasis added). The Psalmist commanded, "Lift up your hands in the sanctuary, and bless the Lord" (Ps. 134:2); also, "Hear the voice of my supplications, when I cry unto thee, when I lift up my hands toward thy holy oracle" (Ps. 28:2), with *oracle* meaning the temple's Holy of Holies. Also, using temple terminology, the Psalmist wrote, "Let my prayer be set forth before thee as incense; and the lifting up of my hands as the evening sacrifice" (Ps. 141:2).

In a temple context, Jesus Christ promised His disciples that they would "be endued with power from on high" and then "he *lifted up his hands,* and blessed them" (Luke 24:49–50; emphasis added). Consider also that the Apostle Paul instructed, concerning prayer, "I will therefore that men pray every where, *lifting up holy hands,* without wrath and doubting" (1 Tim. 2:8, emphasis added).

Several other scriptural passages refer to "uplifted hands":

---

1. In a BYU Religious Studies Center publication, David M. Calabro has written concerning prayer with uplifted hands; see Calabro, "Gestures of Praise: Lifting and Spreading the Hands in Biblical Prayer," 105–21.

- See Abraham, Facsimile No. 1, figure 2, where Abraham prays for deliverance.
- "Moses said . . . I will spread abroad my hands unto the Lord; and the thunder shall cease, neither shall there be any more hail; that thou mayest know how that the earth is the Lord's" (Ex. 9:29).
- "With his hands spread up to heaven" (1 Kgs. 8:54).
- "I will lift up my hands in thy name" (Ps. 63:4).
- "Let us lift up our heart with our hands unto God in the heavens" (Lam. 3:41).
- "When ye spread forth your hands" (Isa. 1:15).
- "When he held up his right hand and his left hand unto heaven, and sware by him that liveth for ever" (Dan. 12:7).
- "Stretch forth his hands towards heaven, and cry with a loud voice" (Alma 31:14).
- "With uplifted hands unto the Most High" (D&C 88:120; see also D&C 109:17–19).
- "Arise, cry out in the night . . . lift up thy hands toward him" (Lam. 2:19).
- "Stretch out thine hands toward him" (Job. 11:13).

HANNAH, ANNA, AND MARY

Hannah, Anna, and Mary, the mother of Jesus, are representative examples of the great importance of women in the temple setting during the period that the law of Moses ruled Israel (for more than a millennium). Unfortunately, we lack the historical records that recount the thousands and tens of thousands of faithful women who also served the Lord in the temple during this time period.

Hannah: 1 Samuel 1 is a Hannah-centric chapter. The setting for much of the chapter is the temple (tabernacle) at Shiloh. The following items demonstrate Hannah's important position in the temple, which would not only impact her own life, but that of the entire nation of Israel—Hannah's son Samuel was destined to become one of Israel's great prophets!

In the temple, Hannah prayed to the Lord (1:10–12); in her prayer, she vowed to give her son as a Nazarite (v. 11). It was Hannah's choice (not her husband's) to make Samuel a Nazarite. She informed her husband, "I will [dedicate] him as a Nazarite forever" (v. 22). The priest Eli witnessed her prayer and then conversed with her (see vv. 12–17). Afterward, the Septuagint (ancient Greek translation of the Bible) states that Hannah "entered her quarters," which was located near the temple (v. 18). Significantly, Hannah and others also "worshipped" in the temple (v. 19).

Hannah presents Samuel to Eli.

After Samuel's birth, Hannah journeyed back to the temple and presented him to Eli, thus fulfilling her vow (see 1 Sam 1:24–28); Hannah, and not her husband, is the catalyst who took Samuel to the temple—she "brought him [Samuel] unto the house of the Lord in Shiloh." On her journey to the temple, Hannah took a three-year-old bull (to be sacrificed), some flour, and wine (1:24). Then "they [Elkanah and Hannah?] slew a bullock, and brought the child to Eli" (1:25). Once again, Hannah worshipped at the temple (see v. 28). Hannah's impact on her family and the nation of Israel is immeasurable.

Anna: Luke describes this remarkably faithful woman: she was a prophetess, of "great age," widowed for decades, who belonged to the tribe of Asher (Luke 2:36). Anna was a quintessential temple worshipper—she "was a widow of about fourscore and four years, which departed not from the temple, but served God with fastings and prayers night and day" (v. 37). After the man named Simeon held the baby Jesus while in the temple and uttered prophecies (see vv. 25–35), Luke writes that Anna "coming in that instant gave thanks likewise unto the Lord, and spake of him to all that looked for redemption in Jerusalem" (v. 38). Evidently, Anna was blessed to see the baby Jesus in the temple at this time. In sum, Anna's life was temple-focused and full of service to God.

Anna, the prophetess of "great age."

Mary: Jesus Christ's mother (together with Joseph) fully complied with the law of Moses. Mary and Joseph "performed all things according to the law of the Lord" (Luke 2:39) while in Jerusalem, attending the temple; they also "went to Jerusalem every year at the feast of the passover" (2:41), which festival was celebrated, in part, in the temple.

After Jesus's birth, Mary was ceremonially unclean for forty days, meaning she could not touch sacred things or enter the temple for that period of time. Then, after the forty days (called "the days of her purifying," Lev. 12:4), Mary went to the temple "to offer a sacrifice according to that which is said in the law of the Lord, A pair of turtledoves, or two young pigeons" (Luke 2:24). According to the law, poor mothers presented two young pigeons or two doves, but those with economic means presented a lamb (see Lev. 12:6–8). Years later, when Jesus was twelve years old, Mary and Joseph "went up to Jerusalem after the custom of the feast [of the Passover]" (Luke 2:42). Surely Mary's careful and continual obedience to God's laws—including those that pertained to the temple—had a great impact on Jesus Christ, especially during His formative years. Her example, teachings, and temple-focused life no doubt prepared Him for His eternal and divine mission, that of being the Savior of the world.

HEIFER, RED

The sacrifice of the red heifer anticipated Jesus Christ's own sacrifice.

The sacrificial offering of the red heifer was different than others—the animal had to be a female, red in color, a heifer (one that has not given birth to a calf), with no spot or blemish, and which has never been attached to or pulled a yoke (see Num. 19:2–5, 17). Its purpose was to remove the defilement of death from people who have touched a dead body, bone, or grave (Num. 19:16). The sacrifice of the red heifer anticipated Jesus Christ's own sacrifice; He overcame death so that we could have immortality and eternal life (see entry "Animals, Female [Sacrificial Offerings]").

HIGH PRIEST, DEATH OF, AND THE CITIES OF REFUGE

One aspect of the law of Moses pertained to the cities of refuge (see Num. 35:9–34). The law stated that if someone accidentally killed another, he could flee for his life to one of the six cities of refuge, or alternatively, he could flee to the temple's altar of sacrifice and grasp one of its four horns (see 1 Kgs. 1:49–53; 2:28–34). Once the accidental slayer reached a city of refuge or grasped one of the horns, he obtained asylum from the "redeemer of blood" (KJV Numbers 35 reads "revenger of blood").

Three aspects of the laws of the cities of refuge have symbolisms that point to Jesus Christ and His Atonement.

(1) *The redeemer of blood* (mentioned six times in Numbers 35) may pursue and slay the person who accidentally killed his next of kin, therein cleansing the land of the blood that was shed (see vv. 33–34). The redeemer of blood foreshadowed Jesus Christ, who is the Great Redeemer. Both the redeemer of blood mentioned in Numbers 35 and the Great Redeemer administer justice; God administers perfect justice as the redeemer of blood when He cleanses the land of its pollutions and defilements.

(2) *Refuge.* The city of refuge could be interpreted to symbolize the Lord, who is our refuge from sin and from death. "O Lord: I said, Thou art my refuge" (Ps. 142:5; see also Deut. 33:27; Ps. 46:1); God is "my refuge, my saviour" (2 Sam. 22:3); "My refuge, is in God" (Ps. 62:7). Just as a person who accidentally killed another could flee for his life to one of the appointed cities of refuge ("that fleeing unto one of these cities he might live," Deut. 4:42), all of us may flee to the Lord Jesus from two of our greatest adversaries—sin and death. The Apostle Paul summed up, we "have fled for refuge to lay hold upon the hope set before us" (Heb. 6:18); that hope is Jesus Christ (see vv. 19–20). In other words, we have fled to Jesus, who is our refuge and laid hold upon the altar, that very sacred place of atonement in the temple.

(3) *The high priest.* In the law of Moses, the person who accidentally slew another would remain in a city of refuge until the death of the high priest who was anointed with holy oil (the anointed high priest who served in the temple). That high priest typified Jesus; just as the death of the ancient high priest freed the accidental killer from the confines of a city of refuge, allowing him to return to his homeland, so the death of Jesus Christ frees all humanity from the bondage of sin and death, allowing us to return to our heavenly homeland.

HOLINESS TO THE LORD

In the Old Testament, the high priest's crown had the significant inscription "Holiness to the Lord" written on it. This was placed prominently on the high priest's forehead, in view of women and men worshipping in the temple.

"Holiness to the Lord" is conspicuously placed on the exterior of our temples, usually written on a plaque, engraved on a wall or keystone, or established elsewhere, almost always on the temple's east side. President Russell M. Nelson states that the phrase "designates both the temple and its purposes as holy. Those who enter the temple are also to bear the attribute of holiness."[1]

Joseph Smith spoke of the blessed time of the Millennium that "even upon the bells of the horses shall be written *Holiness to the Lord*,"[2] meaning, even seemingly non-sacred things will be like unto the temple of the Lord during the Millennium.

HOLY OF HOLIES

In terms of sacred space, Israelite and modern temples were designed to exhibit graded divisions of holiness. Moving from the most holy to profane space, these divisions for Israelite temples included the Holy of Holies, the holy place, the courtyard, the Israelite camp, and then a ceremonially profane periphery, wherein were located cemeteries, lepers, and more. Out of all of the graded divisions of holiness, the Holy of Holies designated the holiest of all holinesses.

Why a Holy of Holies? This signified a most holy place for God to visit and to reveal His sacred word to His prophets (see Ex. 25:22; Lev. 16:2) or to the high priest (see Judg. 20:26–28) who served in the ancient

---

1. Nelson, "Personal Preparation for Temple Blessings," 32.
2. Smith, *HC* 2:358; citing Zechariah 14:20; emphasis in original.

(right) Doorknob of the Salt Lake Temple features "Holiness to the Lord" above symbol of a beehive.

temple. With regard to the Holy of Holies of the Salt Lake Temple, President Boyd K. Packer wrote, "Hidden away in the central part of the temple is the Holy of Holies, where the President of the Church may retire when burdened down with heavy decisions to seek an interview with Him whose Church it is. The prophet holds the keys, the spiritual keys and the very literal key to this one door in that sacred edifice."[1]

The Holy of Holies represents the highest degree of the celestial kingdom, the place where God dwells on His throne. It is only through the blood of Jesus that we can enter the Holy of Holies, or heaven itself: "Having therefore, brethren, boldness to enter into the holiest by the blood of Jesus" (Heb. 10:19).

Several temples, ancient and modern, feature a Holy of Holies, including the following:

(1) *Tabernacle*: The tabernacle's Holy of Holies was a perfect cube—its height, width, and length were each fifteen feet. A veil separated the holy place from the Holy of Holies. The high priest entered the Holy of Holies once a year, on the Day of Atonement, and therein conducted Atonement-focused rituals (see Lev. 15). The ark of the covenant resided in the Holy of Holies of the tabernacle and later Solomon's temple (see 1 Kgs. 8:1–8).

(2) *Solomon's Temple*: Two doors, made of olive wood, separated the holy place from the Holy

Model tabernacle Holy of Holies, viewing the ark and the veil from the inside.

---

1. Packer, *The Holy Temple*, 4.

of Holies, concealing this sacred space from unauthorized eyes. Carvings of cherubs, flowers, and palm trees decorated the doors—all of which were "overlaid . . . with gold" (1 Kgs. 6:31–32). Also, two very large cherubs made of olive wood, "each ten cubits high," resided in the Holy of Holies. These cherubs were also overlaid with gold (see vv. 23–28).

(3) *Kirtland Temple*: Joseph Smith's history refers to the Kirtland Temple's "most holy place,"[2] suggesting a space corresponding to the Holy of Holies.

(4) *Salt Lake Temple*: According to Elder Talmage, the Holy of Holies, located near the celestial room, is a room "of circular outline, 18 feet in diameter, with paneled walls, the panels separated by carved pillars supporting arches; it is decorated in blue and gold. . . . The ceiling is a dome in which are set circular and semicircular windows of jeweled glass."[3] Additionally, "On the south side of this room . . . is a window of colored glass depicting the appearance of the Eternal Father and his Son Jesus Christ to the boy Joseph Smith."[4] The Holy of Holies is "among the smaller rooms of the temple, by far the most beautiful."[5]

HORNS OF THE TWO ALTARS (SACRIFICE AND INCENSE)

The horns of the two altars, representative of power and strength (see 1 Sam. 2:10; Ps. 75:10; Jer. 48:25), typify God Himself: "The Lord is . . . the horn of my salvation" (2 Sam. 22:2–3; see also Ps. 18:2; Luke 1:69). Note also the following items concerning the two altars' horns.

The sacrificial altar had four horns, each having the same dimensions

---

2. "History, 1838–1856, volume B-1 [1 September 1834–2 November 1838]," p. 723, The Joseph Smith Papers, accessed March 27, 2019, https://www.josephsmithpapers.org/paper-summary/history-1838-1856-volume-b-1-1-september-1834-2-november-1838/177.
3. Talmage, *The House of the Lord,* 210.
4. Talmage, *The House of the Lord*, 210.
5. Talmage, *The House of the Lord*, 209.

Four horns of the altar of incense, in front of the tabernacle veil.

and appearance, with one horn located on each of the corners (see Ex. 27:1–2; 38:2). Each horn was overlaid with brass, giving it a striking, decorative, and shining appearance. The horns were fundamental to the atonement ceremony, for the priest took of the bullock's blood and placed it on the horns with his finger (see Ex. 29:12).

The incense altar (located in the holy place), also had four horns—one on each corner. Each horn was the same size and dimensions and each was overlaid with pure gold (see Ex. 30:1–3), providing the horns with a deep, yellow luster and splendid appearance. On the Day of Atonement, the high priest was required to "make an atonement upon the horns of it once in a year with the blood of the sin offering of atonements: once in the year shall he make atonement upon it throughout your generations: it is most holy unto the Lord" (Ex. 30:10).

HOSANNA SHOUT

The Hosanna Shout is a sacred ritual that belongs to temple dedications and other sacred assemblies. God revealed to Joseph Smith the order of the Hosanna Shout,[1] and it has been a sacred part of temple dedications in this dispensation beginning with the Kirtland Temple. According to President Gordon B. Hinckley, the Hosanna Shout constitutes "beautiful words of worship"[2] and a "sacred salute to the Father and the Son."[3]

Hosanna appears in the Old Testament, set in a temple context: "Save now [Hosanna]. . . . we have blessed you out of the house of the Lord" (Ps. 118:25–26). *Hosanna* is also manifest in the New Testament; when Jesus entered Jerusalem, several people "took branches of palm trees, and went forth to meet him, and cried, Hosanna: Blessed is the King of Israel that cometh in the name of the Lord" (John 12:12–13; see also Matt. 21:9, 15; Mark 11:9–10).

Joseph Smith concluded the dedicatory prayer of the Kirtland Temple with these words: "O hear, O hear, O hear us, O Lord! . . . that we may mingle our voices with those bright, shining seraphs around thy throne, with acclamations of praise, singing Hosanna to God and the Lamb!" (D&C 109:78–79). After the prayer, President Sidney Rigdon led the Saints in the Hosanna Shout; he "cried Hosannah, that all the congregation should join him, and shout hosanna to God and the Lamb, and glory to God in the highest."[4] Wilford Woodruff revealed that "angels on high" joined with mortals in the Hosanna Shout on this occasion.[5]

On April 6, 1892, Lorenzo Snow, President of the Quorum of the

---

1. "History, 1838–1856, volume B-1 [1 September 1834–2 November 1838]," p. 702, The Joseph Smith Papers, accessed March 27, 2019, https://www.josephsmithpapers.org/paper-summary/history-1838-1856-volume-b-1-1-september-1834-2-november-1838/156.
2. Hinckley, "'An Humble and a Contrite Heart,'" 89.
3. Hinckley, "This Great Millennial Year," 69.
4. "History, 1838–1856, volume B-1 [1 September 1834–2 November 1838]," p. 699, The Joseph Smith Papers, accessed March 27, 2019, https://www.josephsmithpapers.org/paper-summary/history-1838-1856-volume-b-1-1-september-1834-2-november-1838/153.
5. Wilford Woodruff, Wilford Woodruff's Journal, 1:132–33.

Twelve Apostles, was assigned to lead more than forty thousand Saints in expressing the Hosanna Shout at the laying of the capstone of the Salt Lake Temple. To prepare the Saints for the shout, President Snow explained, "This is no ordinary order, but is—and we wish it to be distinctly understood—a sacred shout, and employed only on extraordinary occasions like the one now before us. We wish it also to be distinctly understood that we want the brethren and sisters not only to express the words, but that their hearts shall be full of thanksgiving to the God of heaven." After demonstrating the order of the Hosanna Shout, President Snow then directed the Saints, "Now when we go before the Temple, and this shout goes forth, we want every man and every woman to shout these words to the very extent of their voices, so that every house in this city may tremble, the people in every portion of this city hear it, and it may reach to the eternal worlds."[1]

HOUSE OF LIFE, THE TEMPLE IS A

The temple is the *House of Life*![2] This is evident from several teachings connected with both ancient and modern temples that deal with the doctrines of rebirth, resurrection, immortality, and eternal life. Correspondingly, the three garden temples—Eden, Gethsemane, and the Tomb—are associated with various themes connected with life; the focal point of each garden temple is Jesus Christ, who is the *Life*.

HOUSE OF PRAYER

Twice the Lord through Isaiah called the temple a "house of prayer": I will "make them joyful in my *house of prayer* . . . for mine house shall

---

1. *Teachings of Presidents of the Church: Lorenzo Snow*, 138, citing *Millennial Star*, July 4, 1892, 418.
2. Lundquist, *The Temple: Meeting Place of Heaven and Earth*, 24–26, writes regarding Ancient Near East temples and the "house of life."

be called an *house of prayer* for all people" (Isa. 56:7, emphasis added); so, too, the mortal Jesus Christ said, "It is written, My house shall be called the house of prayer" (Matt. 21:13). Why is the temple called a house of prayer, when prayer can be uttered anywhere and at any time? Because the temple is the ultimate, sacred, set-apart space where the Lord's Atonement is manifest, conspicuous, and fully evident. Another reason the temple is the house of prayer is that after the worshipper appropriately and worshipfully offers the gestures of approach, then she/he is spiritually prepared to pray. In short, the temple is a quintessential place of prayer.

The Psalmist captured the significance of the temple as a place of prayer: "One thing have I desired of the Lord . . . that I may dwell in the house of the Lord all the days of my life, to behold the beauty of the Lord, and to enquire in his temple" (Ps. 27:4). On one occasion David prayed for deliverance from his enemies and then stated that the Lord heard David's prayers from His temple: "In my distress I called upon the Lord, and cried to my God: and he did hear my voice out of his temple, and my cry did enter into his ears" (2 Sam. 22:7).

Joseph Smith's dedicatory prayer of the Kirtland Temple presented the concept that the temple is a crucial place to pray: "Establish a house, even a house of prayer . . . That your incomings may be in the name of the Lord, that your outgoings may be in the name of the Lord, that all your salutations may be in the name of the Lord, with uplifted hands unto the Most High" (D&C 109:8–9). In the same dedicatory prayer, the Prophet expressed these powerful words about prayer in the temple setting: "O Lord God Almighty, hear us in these our petitions, and answer us from heaven. . . . O hear, O hear, O hear us, O Lord! And answer these petitions" (D&C 109:77–78).

Many of the Lord's ancient people, when they were not able to pray within the temple, would pray toward the temple (see "Prayer, Directional [Praying toward the Temple]").

HOUSE OF THE LORD

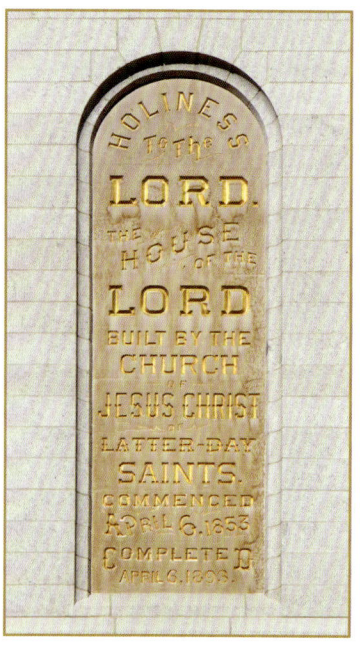

"The House of the Lord," Salt Lake Temple.

The expression "House of the Lord," found more than two hundred times in the Old Testament, refers to God's temple. *House of the Lord* is also found prominently on the exterior of our modern temples; President Russell M. Nelson wrote, "A temple is literally the house of the Lord."[1] Just as a *house* is a structure designed for human habitation, even so the house of the Lord is a building that is dedicated to the Lord. John A. Widtsoe taught, "*The temple is a house or home of the Lord. Should the Lord visit the earth, he would come to his temple.*"[2]

HYSSOP

The hyssop plant was used anciently in various sacred ceremonies, including rituals associated with the temple. For example, hyssop was utilized in the red heifer sacrifice, specifically, to cleanse someone who'd had contact with a dead body or a grave (see Num. 19:6, 18); Moses used hyssop and other items in a covenantal scene (see Heb. 9:19; Ex. 24:6–8), and hyssop was an important component in the ritual of cleansing the leper and the leper's house (see Lev. 14:4–6; 14:49–52). Additionally, at Passover, Israelite faithful dipped a clump of hyssop in the lamb's blood and struck their door's two side posts and lintel to prevent the destroyer from smiting them (see Ex. 12:23).

---

1. Nelson, "Prepare for Blessings of the Temple," 41.
2. Widtsoe, "Looking toward the Temple," 708; emphasis in original.

The Psalmist provided the symbolic significance of hyssop: "Wash me thoroughly from mine iniquity, and cleanse me from my sin. . . . Purge me with hyssop, and I shall be clean: wash me, and I shall be whiter than snow" (Ps. 51:2, 7; see also Ps. 26:6).

Using hyssop to place lamb's blood on door posts (modeled here) kept the destroyer away.

INCENSE AT THE GOLDEN ALTAR

The high priest burned incense on the golden altar twice daily (see Ex. 30:7–9), and once a year he was commanded to "make an atonement upon the horns . . . with the blood of the sin offering" (v. 10). Located directly in front of the temple's veil, the altar of incense was the quintessential place of prayer (represented by incense): "Let my prayer be set forth before thee as incense; and the lifting up of my hands as the evening sacrifice" (Ps. 141:2); also, "the smoke of the incense, which came with the prayers of the saints, ascended up before God" (Rev. 8:4). Zacharias, the father of John the Baptist, was burning incense in the temple when the angel Gabriel appeared to him; Gabriel stood at the right side of the altar of incense (see Luke 1:7–19). According to verse 10, "the whole multitude of the people [those worshipping in the temple] were praying without at the time of incense."

Anciently, offering incense (and prayer) was an essential course of action before the high priest could approach God through the veil and enter into the Holy of Holies (see Ex. 30:1–10; Lev. 16:12–13).

High priest (model) offers incense at the altar of incense.

JACOB'S LADDER ("FLIGHT OF STEPS")

Jacob's dream of the "ladder" (also translated as "flight of steps"[1]) is set in the context of a temple (see Gen. 28:12–19). Jacob stated "this is none other but the house of God, and this is the gate of heaven"; Jacob also called the place *Bethel* (Hebrew: "house of God"), and he testified, "Surely the Lord is in this place" (Gen. 28:16–17). Furthermore, in the dream, God made covenants with Jacob that pertain to the Abrahamic covenant. Note also Joseph Smith's correlation of the "three principal rounds of Jacob's Ladder" with "the Telestial, the Terrestrial, and the Celestial glories or Kingdoms."[2] As we keep our temple covenants, we move from the earth (telestial) upward to heaven (celestial).

JESUS CHRIST-FOCUSED, TEMPLE IS

President Russell M. Nelson expressed succinctly, "The temple teaches of Christ."[3] And Elder David A. Bednar adds these words, "The temple is the house of the Lord. Everything in the temple points us to our Savior, Jesus Christ."[4] This volume sets forth scores of symbols that pertain directly to Jesus Christ. Many of the symbols belong to ancient Israelite temples, and others are associated with modern temples.

JESUS CHRIST, SYMBOLS OF, IN THE TABERNACLE OF MOSES

Various components of the tabernacle foreshadow aspects of Jesus Christ's divine ministry and atoning sacrifice. These components include the tabernacle furniture (laver of brass, altars, lampstand, ark of the

---

1. Koehler and Baumgartner, *The Hebrew and Aramaic Lexicon of the Old Testament*, 758.
2. "History, 1838–1856, volume D-1 [1 August 1842–1 July 1843]," p. 1556, The Joseph Smith Papers, accessed March 25, 2019, https://www.josephsmithpapers.org/paper-summary/history-1838-1856-volume-d-1-1-august-1842-1-july-1843/199.
3. Nelson, *Teachings of Russell M. Nelson*, 367.
4. Bednar, "Prepared to Obtain Every Needful Thing," 103.

covenant), sacrifices (burnt, peace, sin, trespass offerings), foods (portions of sacrificial offerings, shewbread), sacred objects (jar of manna, tablets of the law, rod of Aaron), and diverse parts of the tabernacle (veil, horns of the altar). The rituals and performances (i.e., anointings, washings, sprinkling of blood, laying on of hands), too, typified Jesus Christ and His mission. The tabernacle building itself, and later the temple of Jerusalem, also served as types of Jesus Christ. For a discussion of most of these components, see the individual entries.

JOSEPH SMITH: RESTORER OF THE ANCIENT TEMPLE

As part of the "whole and complete and perfect union, and welding together of dispensations" (D&C 128:18), the Prophet Joseph Smith restored ancient truths, doctrines, and ordinances regarding God's ancient temples.[5] These truths are manifest in numerous ways in our modern temples. For example, the Prophet restored the concept of gradational sacred space, moral qualities for temple entrance, the temple as a Jesus Christ–focused institution, a large receptacle of water situated on the backs of twelve oxen, the temple as the Lord's "house," and the significance of sacred space. Altogether, the abundance of restored truths forms a remarkable attestation of the seership of the Prophet. In fact, Elder Widtsoe once wrote, "It may

A portrait of Joseph Smith Jr., from 1830 to 1844; painted by Danquart Anthon Weggeland.

---

5. For a review of the restoration of the temple in this dispensation, see Cowan, "Joseph Smith and the Restoration of Temple Service," 109–22.

be that the temple endowment and the other temple ordinances form the strongest available evidence of the divine inspiration of the Prophet Joseph Smith."[1]

We note, however, that there also exist notable differences between ancient and modern temples. For example, work for the dead did not exist in the ancient temples before Jesus Christ's death and Resurrection.

How did Joseph Smith know to restore these ancient truths, doctrines, and ordinances? It was not from academic learning in a school or university, or from scrutinizing books or weighty tomes. Hugh Nibley asks, "Did the Prophet Joseph Smith reinvent all this by reassembling the fragments—Jewish, Orthodox, Masonic, Gnostic, Hindu, Egyptian, and so forth? In fact, few of the fragments were available in his day, and those poor fragments do not come together of themselves to make a whole. Latter-day Saints see in the completeness and perfection of Joseph Smith's teachings regarding the temple a sure indication of divine revelation."[2]

No, Joseph Smith did not learn about the temple through formal educational training. Rather, God, angels, and spirits revealed the doctrines of the temple to Joseph over a period of time; "Who instructed [Joseph Smith] in . . . baptisms for the dead. . . ? Angels and spirits from the eternal worlds."[3] Furthermore, Joseph Smith acknowledges God's hand in all great things, "If there was anything great or good in the World it came from God. The construction of the first vessel was given to Noah, by revelation. . . . The architectural designs of the temple at Jerusalem, together with its ornament and beauty, were given of God."[4]

---

1. Widtsoe, "Temple Worship," 59.
2. Nibley, "Meanings and Functions of Temples," 4:1462.
3. Pratt, "Spiritual Communication," *JD* 2:44.
4. "History, 1838–1856, volume C-1 Addenda," p. 34, The Joseph Smith Papers, accessed March 25, 2019, https://www.josephsmithpapers.org/paper-summary/history-1838-1856-volume-c-1-addenda/34

Tabernacle of Moses/Temple of Solomon— Correspondences with Our Temples (Representative Examples)

Theme/Concept	Tabernacle of Moses/Temple of Solomon and Our Temples
Moral Qualities for Temple Entrance	Psalms 15 and 24 set forth the moral qualities of those who wish to enter the temple. We must have a temple recommend to enter our temples.
Dedicatory Prayer	For Solomon's temple (1 Kgs. 8); for Kirtland Temple (D&C 109).
Sacred Ceremonies and Ordinances	These include washings, anointings, various rituals, and consecration of priesthood members (Ex. 29), and others (D&C 124:37, 39).
Built after a Divine Pattern	The Lord revealed the pattern of the tabernacle to His prophet, Moses (Ex. 25:8–9), the pattern of Solomon's temple to King David (1 Chr. 28:11–13, 19), and the pattern of the Kirtland and Nauvoo Temples to Joseph Smith (D&C 95:14–15; HC 6:197).
Jesus Christ	The temple is a Jesus Christ–focused institution.
Large Receptacle of Water (KJV, "molten sea"), Set on the Backs of Twelve Oxen	Anciently, a large receptacle of water rested on the backs of twelve oxen in Solomon's temple (1 Kgs. 7:23; 2 Chr. 4:2, 6); this receptacle, together with the twelve oxen, resembles the baptismal fonts that exist in our temples.
"Holiness to the Lord"	These words existed on the high priest's crown (written in Hebrew) (Ex. 39:30). "Holiness to the Lord" is placed prominently on the exterior of our temples, almost always on the temple's east side.
Gradations of Holiness (Less Holy to Most Holy)	The goal of graded space is to present a holiest zone for God, which was far away, in terms of both height and distance, from profane and corruptible space, persons, and objects. Our temples also demonstrate gradations of holiness.
Priesthood	Priesthood ministered in ancient and modern temples and managed the affairs therein: "I will show unto my servant Joseph [Smith] all things pertaining to this house, and the priesthood" (D&C 124:42).
Temple and Zion	In the scriptures, the concepts of temple and Zion are collocated (Ps. 20:2; 48; 76; 84; Isa. 2:3; D&C 4:32; 119:2; 124:36, 39; 133:12–13).
Atonement	See various entries in this volume.

Theme/Concept	Tabernacle of Moses/Temple of Solomon and Our Temples
The Temple as "House" (i.e., House of the Lord)	Ancient temples were denominated "the house of the Lord." So, too, modern temples are named the Lord's house.
The Temple as a Place to Worship God	Both ancient (Ps. 99:1–9; 116:17–19; 132:1–18) and modern temples (D&C 109:14, 24; 115:8) are quintessential places for humankind to worship God.
Gatekeepers	For more information, see entry "Guards, Temple (Sentinels and Angels)."
Eastward Orientation	Both ancient and modern temples emphasize the cardinal direction east.
Temple as a Place of Prayer	Twice Isaiah called the temple a "house of prayer" (Isa. 56:7; see also Ps. 27:4). Each of our temples is also "a house of prayer" (D&C 109:8–9, 16–19).
Holy of Holies	The Mosaic tabernacle, temple of Solomon (1 Kgs. 6:23–32), and Salt Lake Temple have a Holy of Holies.
Temple Is Called Holy	Both the tabernacle and Solomon's temple were called "holy" (Lev. 16:33; Ps. 5:7; 65:4), as are our temples (D&C 109:12–13).
Sacred Vestments	Ancient temple workers wore sacred vestments (Exodus 28, 39) as they do in our temples (see churchofjesuschrist.org).
Temple Is a Place of Divine Revelation	This includes the tabernacle (Lev. 1:1; Ex. 25:21–22; 29:42–43; 30:6, 36; Num. 17:4), Solomon's temple (Ps. 27:4), Herod's temple (Acts 22:17), and our temples (D&C 97:15–16; 110:7–8; 124:39).
Altar	Both ancient and modern temples feature a holy altar.
Temple Is Associated with Power	*Power* is collocated with *temple* in several scriptural passages (Ps. 63:2; 150:1; Rev. 15:8; D&C 84:20–21; 109:13, 22, 35; 132:7).

KEYS

Keys pertain to two aspects of temples and temple service:

(1) *Keys of the kingdom*: Ancient prophets restored these keys to Joseph Smith and Oliver Cowdery in the Kirtland Temple (see D&C 110). Church presidents in our dispensation "have received and exercised

the priesthood keys of the kingdom, including the keys which authorized them to perform in the holy temples of God the ordinances essential for the salvation of both the living and the dead. Those ordinances, which center on our Savior Jesus Christ and his divine mission, can be had in no other place."[1]

(2) *Certain signs*: On May 1, 1842, Joseph Smith taught: "I preached in the grove on the keys of the Kingdom, Charity, &c The keys are certain signs and words by which false spirits and personages may be detected from true, which cannot be revealed to the Elders till the Temple is completed. The rich can only get them in the Temple—the Poor may get them on the Mountain top as did Moses."[2]

KINGS, QUEENS, CORONATION, AND ENTHRONEMENT

In a masterful way, John the Revelator linked the concepts of (temple) *washing* and *kingship*: "Jesus Christ . . . washed us from our sins in his own blood, And hath made us kings and priests unto God and his Father" (Rev. 1:5–6; see also Rev. 5:10). The feminine counterpart of the words "kings and priests"—queens and priestesses—applies equally to females. Careful searches of several scriptural passages reveal that temples are closely associated with the concept of kings and queens. Key words to look for include *king, queen, throne, sceptre, crown, kingdom, dominion, power, royal, robe,* etc. Of course, not all of these key words reveal sacred temple concepts.

In our day, Church authorities have connected the temple with the concept of kings and kingship. Joseph Smith taught, "Those holding the fulness of the Melchizedec priesthood are kings and Priests to the most

---

1. Haight, "Symbol of Sacrifice, Monument to Life," 11; see also Packer, "Come to the Temple," 21.
2. "History, 1838–1856, volume C-1 [2 November 1838–31 July 1842]," p. 1326, The Joseph Smith Papers, accessed March 27, 2019, https://www.josephsmithpapers.org/paper-summary/history-1838-1856-volume-c-1-2-november-1838-31-july-1842/500

high God, holding the keys of power and blessings."[1] Furthermore, he explained, "as soon as the Temple and baptismal font are prepared, we calculate to give the Elders of Israel their washings and anointings, and attend to those last and more impressive ordinances . . . men may receive their endowments, and be made kings and Priests unto the most High God, having nothing to do with temporal things."[2]

In their article "King, Coronation, and Temple: Enthronement Ceremonies in History," Latter-day Saint scholars Ricks and Sroka demonstrate that coronation and enthronement ceremonies of both religious and secular societies (both ancient and medieval) echo things belonging to God's ancient temples. Ricks and Sroka dealt with such topics as anointing, sacrifice, new name, rebirth, royal vestments, crown, regalia, throne, feasts, dominion, and promises.[3]

The coronation ceremony of Emperor Nicholas II and Empress Alexandra Fedorovna (the Czar and Czarina), which took place on May 26, 1896, in the Church of the Annunciation in Moscow, echoes many sacred biblical rituals and temple practices: the metropolitan (a supreme ecclesiastical leader of the Russian Orthodox Church) anointed the czar "with the sacred unguent on the forehead, the eyelids, the nostrils, the lips, the ears, the breast, and the arms, with the words, 'The seal of the gift of the Holy Ghost.'" Other ecclesiastical leaders gave the czar a "mantle of imperial purple," which could be interpreted to signify both royalty and protection; the metropolitan instructed the czar, "Cover and protect the people as this robe covers and protects thee." The metropolitan took the crown and put it on the head of the czar; as an archbishop gave the sceptre

---

1. "History, 1838–1856, volume E-1 [1 July 1843–30 April 1844]," p. 1708, The Joseph Smith Papers, accessed March 27, 2019, https://www.josephsmithpapers.org/paper-summary/history-1838-1856-volume-e-1-1-july-1843-30-april-1844/80
2. "History, 1838–1856, volume E-1 [1 July 1843–30 April 1844]," p. 1982, The Joseph Smith Papers, accessed March 25, 2019, https://www.josephsmithpapers.org/paper-summary/history-1838-1856-volume-e-1-1-july-1843-30-april-1844/354
3. Ricks and Sroka, "King, Coronation, and Temple," 259. See also the extensive bibliography, 264–71.

and orb to the czar (the sceptre in the right hand and the orb in the left), he pronounced the words, "in the name of the Father, the Son, and the Holy Ghost." An archdeacon pronounced upon the czar his new name-titles: *Mighty Sovereign, Exalted Autocrat, Czar, Lord, Prince, Grand Prince,* and *Ruler.*

At one point in the ceremony, the archbishop led "the Czar by the hand into the Holy of Holies, where the Czar receive[d] the sacrament after the manner of the clergy, not of secular communicants" (the czar now has both kingly and priestly authority and privileges). Then an Archbishop attended "to the ablution [washing] of his Majesty." The czarina participated in many of these events, but not all. After all of these things, the czar and czarina joined a procession to remember their dead and showed "reverence at the tombs of the Russian sovereigns."[4]

LAMPSTAND, GOLDEN (MENORAH OR CANDLESTICK)

The seven-branched lampstand (in the King James Version called "candlestick"), because of its remarkable qualities, was a magnificent, elegant, and inspiring wonderment. Why so magnificent? Because God Himself revealed its pattern to Moses (see Num. 8:4). The scriptures set forth its construction (see Ex. 25:31–40; 37:17–24), consecration (see Ex. 30:27; 40:9), placement in the tabernacle (see Ex. 25:37; Num. 8:2–3), and the manner of transporting it (see Num. 3:31; 4:9). It was made of pure gold (see Ex. 25:31) and it weighed a talent! The lampstand's fuel was pure olive oil that was beaten, not ground in a mill (see Ex. 27:20). Exodus 25:31–40 describes the menorah as an almond tree; it had the appearance of an almond tree, with its trunk-like base, seven branches, and blossoms or flowers. The lampstand was placed in the tabernacle's holy place, situated on

---

4. "Coronation of the Czar," *New York Times* (April 5, 1896).

High priest (model) in sacred vestments pours olive oil into lampstand (in the holy place).

the south side (see Ex. 40:24). The light produced by the lampstand was the only source of light in the tabernacle's holy place.

Various parts of the lamp bring Jesus Christ to mind—olive oil points to Christ, who is the Anointed One, or, the one anointed with olive oil; light points to Jesus, who is "the light of the world" (John 8:12; see also 1:9); the seven branches form a tree, conveying the idea of Jesus as the tree of life, and the number of branches—seven—could be interpreted to signify perfection, pointing to Jesus's perfection. With regard to the almond (Hebrew: *sha-ked,* "to arise early") and almond tree possibly representing Jesus, see entry "Rod of Aaron."

LAVER OF BRASS

Ablution, or ritual washing (see Heb. 9:10), marks the cleansing of the soul from sin; it was one method the Lord employed to express washing away the filth of His people (see Isa. 4:4). Such washings were conducted in the laver (or basin) of brass. *Laver* is from the same root as *lavatory*

(Latin: *lavatorium*, "place for washing"), a compartment or room where there is a sink or washbasin.

The laver and its stand were made of brass (see Ex. 30:18). Moses anointed the laver with anointing oil to sanctify it (see Lev. 8:10–11). It was located between the tabernacle and the sacrificial altar (see Ex. 30:18). The purpose of the laver was for washings with water (see Ex. 40:30); specifically, Aaron and his sons (the high priest and the priests) were commanded to wash their hands and feet at the laver (see Ex. 30:19). If they failed to wash at the laver, they were subject to death ("that they die not" is twice mentioned; Ex. 30:20–21).

High priest (model) washes at the laver, located in front of the tabernacle of Moses.

Anciently the priests washed in water, but the water symbolized Jesus's blood. As John wrote, Jesus Christ has "washed us from our sins in his own blood" (Rev. 1:5; see also entry "Washing with Water").

LAW OF MOSES

Scores of the regulations and ordinances of the law of Moses pertained to the tabernacle, as is shown in various entries in this book. According to several Book of Mormon passages (Jacob 4:5; Jarom 1:11; Mosiah 3:15; 16:14–15; Alma 25:15; 34:14; 3 Ne. 9:17), the chief objective of the law was to focus the Israelites' attention on Jesus Christ and His Atonement.

Speaking of the law of Moses, Elder Jeffrey R. Holland wrote, "This historic covenant, given by the hand of God himself and second only to the fulness of the gospel as an avenue to righteousness, should be seen rather as the unparalleled collection of types, shadows, symbols, and prefigurations of Christ that it is. For that reason it was once (and still is, in its essence and purity) a guide to spirituality, a gateway to Christ."[1]

LEPER

Leprosy was "the disease [that] was regarded as a living death."[2] This can be seen from Aaron's description of his sister Miriam when she became leprous: "Let her not be as one dead, of whom the flesh is half consumed when he cometh out of his mother's womb" (Num. 12:12). In Leviticus, the leper's awful state is described: "He is a leprous man, he is [ceremonially] unclean: the priest shall pronounce him utterly unclean" (Lev. 13:44).

Leviticus 13–14 deals with multiple laws regarding lepers and leprosy; specific terms in these chapters pertain directly to the temple, including *priest(s)* (93 times), *atonement* (7 times), *tabernacle* (twice), sacrificial *blood* (7 times), and sacrificial *offerings* (25 times). Furthermore, *clean, unclean,* and *cleanse* (these three words are used a total of 74 times in these chapters) are technical terms that pertain to ceremonial purity or impurity, rather than the temporal concepts of one being soiled, unhygienic, or smudged with dirt or grime.

Many of the symbols in Leviticus 13–14 are evident: the priest making atonement for the cleansed leper expresses Jesus making atonement for each of us; the sacrificial animal and its blood points to Jesus's infinite sacrifice and His blood; the ceremonially unclean leper points to a spiritually unclean person; and the death-like symptoms of the leper suggest a spiritually dead person.

---

1. Holland, *Christ and the New Covenant,* 137 (see also 135–57).
2. Bible Dictionary, 680.

LEVITES

The Levites (descendants of Levi, the third son of Jacob and Leah) had special assignments in the tabernacle and temple during the period that the law of Moses was in force. They served as substitutes for Israelite first-born sons (see Num. 3:11–13; 8:16–18) and were consecrated by means of a series of sacred rituals (see Num. 8:5–13). Their cleansing and consecration consisted of the following: one with authority would "sprinkle water of purifying upon them"; they had to shave "all their flesh"; they were required to "wash their clothes"; Israelites "put their hands upon the Levites" (laying on of hands); and the Levites offered a sacrifice to the Lord (see Num. 8:5–15).

The Levites' service began at the age of twenty-five and continued until the age of fifty (see Num. 8:24–26). They were assigned to serve in weekly courses, and then they returned home for the remainder of the year and maintained regular occupations. Part of the time, the Levites were supported by the tithes of the Israelites (see Num. 18:21, 24). The Levites served as porters (see 1 Chr. 23:2–4), gatekeepers (see 1 Chr. 26:1–19), treasurers (see 1 Chr. 9:26), musicians and members of the choir (see Num. 3:6–9; 1 Chr. 23:5), and assistants to the priests (see 1 Chr. 23:28). They also dismantled, transported, and set up the tabernacle and its furnishings and vessels (see Num. 1:48–54; 4:3–15). Most importantly, the Levites were required "to do the service of the children of Israel in the tabernacle of the congregation, and to make an atonement for the children of Israel: that there be no plague among the children of Israel, when the children of Israel come nigh unto the sanctuary" (Num. 8:19).

Under the Mosaic order, the ancient Levites correspond to deacons and teachers of our day, and the ancient priests correspond to priests of our day: "From the departure of Moses to the coming of Christ, the organized theocracy of Israel was that of the Lesser or Aaronic Priesthood, comprising the office of priest, which was confined to the lineage of Aaron,

and the lesser offices of teacher and deacon, which were combined in the Levitical order."[1]

LIGHT, QUINTESSENTIAL PLACE OF

The Lord's temples are quintessential places of light. President Packer shared this important insight: "The house of the Lord, bathed in light, standing out in the darkness, becomes symbolic of the power and the inspiration of the gospel of Jesus Christ standing as a beacon in a world that sinks ever further into spiritual darkness."[2] In point of fact, the Psalmist prayed that God's light and truth would bring him to the temple: "Send out thy light and thy truth: let them lead me; let them bring me unto thy holy mountain, and to thy tabernacles" (Ps. 43:3, translation by author). In multiple ways the temples are places of light:

(1) *The light of God's presence*: The light that emanates from God's presence, when He visits His holy temples, marks the most significant of all illuminations that are associated with temples—ancient and modern. When the Lord visited Joseph Smith and Oliver Cowdery in the Kirtland Temple, "his countenance shone above the brightness of the sun" (D&C 110:3).

(2) *The endowment itself is a source of light*: Mercy R. Thompson, from Nauvoo, explained, "I received my endowments by the direction of the Prophet Joseph, his wife Emma officiating in my case. In his instructions to me at that time, he said, 'This will bring you out of darkness into marvelous light.'"[3] Millions of worshippers who enter the temple receive light, glory, and intelligence when they receive the endowment.

(3) *Supernatural light*: Anciently God sent a "pillar of fire" to

---

1. Talmage, *Jesus the Christ*, 598.
2. Packer, *The Holy Temple*, 43.
3. *Encyclopedia of Joseph Smith's Teachings*, 217. See also *Teachings of Presidents of the Church: Joseph Smith*, 414.

(left) Rome Italy temple at sunset.

accompany ancient Israel and the tabernacle, which gave ancient Israel direction "to go by . . . night" (Ex. 13:21). During our dispensation, some individuals witnessed "a bright light like a piller of Fire resting upon the [Kirtland] Temple."[1] Eliza R. Snow provided this description: "A sense of divine presence was realized by all," and "on subsequent occasions" there was "a pillar of light . . . several times seen resting down upon the roof."[2]

(4) *Architectural symbols depict light*: A number of our temples feature images (made of stone or stained-glass windows) of the sun, moon, and stars. The images are variegated; for example, some star images portray five-, six-, eight-, ten-, or even thirty-two-pointed stars.

(5) *Formal ceremonies manifest light*: Two examples are the laying of the southeast cornerstone, which designates the corner where "there is the most light,"[3] and the dramatization of the Creation narrative, which emphasizes light: "God said, Let there be light: and there was light. . . . God said, Let there be lights in the firmament of the heaven. . . . God made two great lights" (Gen. 1:3, 14–16).

(6) *Natural light*: Inspired temple architects utilize natural light (via stained, etched, and art glass) to illuminate various areas of the temple's exterior and interior, to the end that light flows upon worshippers.

(7) *Artificial light*: Temple architects also utilize artificial lights to illumine sacred spaces for the benefit of men and women worshipping therein. Anciently, the tabernacle menorah's seven branches of light illuminated the holy place; in modern days, decorative lamps and magnificent chandeliers serve temple attendees.

---

1. "History, 1838–1856, volume B-1 [1 September 1834–2 November 1838] [addenda]," p. 4 [addenda], The Joseph Smith Papers, accessed March 26, 2019, https://www.josephsmith papers.org/paper-summary/history-1838-1856-volume-b-1-1-september-1834-2-november -1838/307.
2. Jenson, *Historical Record* 5 (June 1886), 79.
3. Young, "The Temple Cornerstones—The Apostles," *JD* 1:133.

LINEN

Linen clothing, which is associated with ancient temples and temple worship, could be interpreted as the righteousness of women and men: "For the fine linen is the righteousness of saints" (Rev. 19:8).

Once a year, on the Day of Atonement, the high priest wore linen garments, consisting of a tunic, undergarments, sash, and headpiece. Wearing linen clothing was an essential part of the work of the atonement: the high priest "shall make the atonement, and shall put on the linen clothes, even the holy garments" (Lev. 16:32; see also v. 23). Note, too, that priests wore linen garments (see Lev. 6:10; 16:4).

Levitical musicians wore white linen in the temple when they sang and played their musical instruments, comprised of cymbals, harps, and lyres (see 2 Chr. 5:12).

The seven angels in the temple in heaven were "clothed in pure and white linen, and having their breasts girded with golden girdles" (Rev. 15:6). The high rank of the angels is deduced from the golden girdles (or sashes) they wear, which are like that worn by Christ Himself (see Rev. 1:13). In addition, Daniel saw a heavenly "man clothed in linen, whose loins *were* girded with fine gold of Uphaz" (Dan. 10:5).

In the great scene that is revealed in Revelation 19, two different entities are clothed in "fine linen." The Lamb's bride (which is the Church) is "arrayed in fine linen, clean and white" (Rev. 19:8), and the armies in heaven that follow Jesus Christ while riding on white horses are "clothed in fine linen, white and clean" (Rev. 19:14).

MERCY SEAT (THRONE OF ATONEMENT)

The mercy seat (see Ex. 25:17–22; 30:6; Lev. 16:2), situated on the ark of the covenant, was a magnificent appointment and its appearance was glorious to behold—it was made of pure gold and measured two and a half cubits long by a cubit and a half wide (about 54 inches by 27 inches). Two elaborate cherubim, also made of gold, were situated at either end of the mercy seat, their wings stretched forth and their faces looking at each other (see Ex. 25:17–20).

The mercy seat was a focal point of atonement, grace, and revelation. On the Day of Atonement, the high priest took blood from the sacrificed bull and goat, entered through the veil into the Holy of Holies, and sprinkled the blood on the mercy seat (see Lev. 16:14–15). The Hebrew underlying the English "mercy seat" is *kapporet*, which is derived from the Hebrew root *kpr* ("to atone"). *Kapporet* has the sense of "[throne of] atonement" or "instrument of atonement."[1] Regardless of the lid's name, it is clear that it served as God's throne: "He sits between the cherubs" (2 Sam. 6:2; Isa. 37:16).

The ark was the quintessential place of grace; Paul wrote, "Let us therefore come boldly unto the *throne of grace,* that we may obtain mercy, and find grace to help in time of need" (Heb. 4:16; emphasis added). The mercy seat was also a supreme place of revelation, where God communicated with His prophet. God said, "There I will meet with thee, and I will commune with thee from above the mercy seat, from between the two cherubims which are upon the ark of the testimony, of all things which I will give thee in commandment unto the children of Israel" (Ex. 25:22; see also 30:6; Lev. 16:2; Num. 7:89).

MIRRORS

Many of our temple sealing rooms have mirrors on opposite sides of the room, which enable newly married couples to view multiple images of themselves, as if they are glimpsing into eternity. Elder Gerrit W. Gong calls these "temple mirrors of eternity."[2] In 2016, Elder Quentin L. Cook

---

1. *A Hebrew and English Lexicon of the Old Testament*, 498.
2. Gong, "Temple Mirrors of Eternity: A Testimony of Family," 37–38.

spoke of temple marriages and mirrors, stating that after a husband and wife "enter into [temple] covenants, they can 'see themselves in the temple' mirrors that face each other. . . . These reflected images help us contemplate parents, grandparents, and all previous generations. They help us recognize the sacred covenants that connect us to all generations that follow. This is incredibly significant, and it starts when you see yourself in the temple."[3] The mirrors, of course, are not part of the actual ordinance or covenant of marriage.

MOONSTONES

Fifty moonstones encircle the Salt Lake Temple, enhancing and beautifying it. They represent the lunar month cycle—new moon, first-quarter moon, full moon, and last-quarter moon—for the year 1878. More than coincidentally, this new moon cycle places the month of April at the east side of the temple, perhaps making a correspondence between Jesus's April birth[4] and eastward direction, or the direction of the sunrise (see the following diagram).

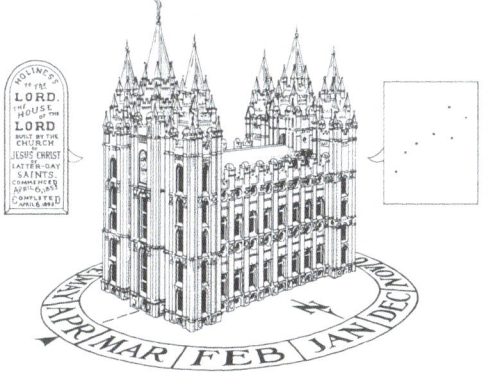

Phases of the moon (moonstones) focus on the month of April, Salt Lake Temple.

Not only are moonstones part of the architectural structure of the Salt Lake Temple, but they belong to the original Nauvoo Temple, the newly built Nauvoo Illinois Temple, the St. Louis Missouri Temple, and other temples.

The moonstones of the Salt Lake Temple, together with sunstones and

---

3. Cook, "See Yourself in the Temple," 99.
4. Lee, "Strengthen the Stakes of Zion," 2; see also Kimball, "Remarks and Dedication of the Fayette, New York, Buildings," 54.

Two of several moonstones, Salt Lake Temple.

starstones, could be interpreted to signify the three degrees of glory (see 1 Cor. 15:40–42; D&C 76).[1] Additionally, the moon representations of our modern temples may recall the new moon observances associated with ancient Israel and their temple (2 Chr. 2:4; see also 1 Chr. 23:31; 2 Chr. 8:13; Ezra 3:5).

MORONI, ANGEL

The statue of the angel Moroni, which is situated on the top of scores of temples, stands large and visible to millions who view the temples throughout the world. Moroni conveys the idea of a herald to the world that the gospel has been restored to the earth. President Gordon B. Hinckley wrote, "John the Revelator 'saw another angel fly in the midst of heaven, having the everlasting gospel to preach unto them that dwell on the earth. . . .' That angel has come. His name is Moroni. His is a voice

---

1. Cowan, "Latter-day Saint Temples as Symbols," 7.

speaking from the dust, bringing another witness of the living reality of the Lord Jesus Christ."²

Furthermore, Moroni's trump, which blows loudly and clearly, calls each of us to attend the temple. Sister Elaine S. Dalton edified us with these words: "From my window in the Young Women office, I have a spectacular view of the Salt Lake Temple. Every day I see the angel Moroni standing atop the temple as a shining symbol of not only his faith but ours. . . . I feel somehow he stands atop the temple today, beckoning us to have courage, to remember who we are, and to be worthy to enter the holy temple—to 'arise and shine forth,' to stand above the worldly clamor, and to, as Isaiah prophesied, 'Come . . . to the mountain of the Lord'—the holy temple."³

Here are several details about the angel Moroni statues:

The first temple to feature an angel Moroni statue was the Salt Lake Temple.

Most of the Moroni statues are oriented eastward, looking toward the rising sun and also looking forward to the Second Coming; exceptions include the Manila Philippines, Nauvoo Illinois, Seattle Washington, Spokane Washington, and Taipei Taiwan Temples.

Several of the temples feature Moroni holding gold plates, including Jordan River Utah, Los Angeles California, Mexico City Mexico, Seattle Washington, and Washington D.C.

Moroni with trumpet, Salt Lake Temple.

---

2. Hinckley, "Stay the Course—Keep the Faith," 70.
3. Dalton, "Now Is the Time to Arise and Shine!" 123.

Some of the temples feature Moroni holding a scroll, including Anchorage Alaska, Bismarck North Dakota, Caracas Venezuela, Columbus Ohio, and Kona Hawaii.

Most Moroni statues depict Moroni wearing a robe (Joseph Smith described Moroni's robe in JS–H 1:31), which is belted at the waist. The Los Angeles California Temple is an exception; it features Moroni depicted in a Mayan robe and having facial features of a Native American.

The Moroni statues of the Salt Lake and Nauvoo Temples face each other in a symbolic manner. President Hinckley explains, "Today, facing west, on the high bluff overlooking the city of Nauvoo, thence across the Mississippi, and over the plains of Iowa, there stands Joseph's temple, a magnificent house of God. Here in the Salt Lake Valley, facing east to that beautiful temple in Nauvoo, stands Brigham's temple, the Salt Lake Temple. They look toward one another as bookends between which there are volumes that speak of the suffering, the sorrow, the sacrifice, even the deaths of thousands who made the long journey from the Mississippi River to the valley of the Great Salt Lake."[1]

MOUNTAIN AS "TEMPLE" AND TEMPLE AS "MOUNTAIN"

Symbolically, all temples of the Lord are mountains—they are made of mountain materials (granite, marble, etc.), they reach to the sky, they appear to be "mountain-like," and those who worship in them ascend, step by step, from profane to sacred space, as if they are climbing a mountain. Correspondingly, some actual mountains have served as temples; these include Mount Simeon, Mount Shelem, Mount Sinai, the Mount of Transfiguration, and others.

On occasion, prophets and others have conducted temple rituals on

---

[1]. Hinckley, "'O That I Were an Angel, and Could Have the Wish of Mine Heart,'" 6.

mountains. Some biblical passages refer to the temple as a mountain: Isaiah refers to "the house of the God of Jacob" as "the mountain of the Lord" (Isa. 2:3; see also Ezek. 20:40), and Psalm 68:16 mentions "the mountain which God desireth to dwell in; yea, the Lord will dwell in it forever" (translation by author). Similarly, the Psalmist says: "Exalt the Lord our God, and worship at his holy mountain; for the Lord our God is holy" (Ps. 99:9; translation by author).

Hills leading up to the Arequipa Peru Temple.

Several prophets and others had temple experiences on mountains, including the following:

- "I [Nephi] was caught away in the Spirit of the Lord, yea, into an exceedingly high mountain" (1 Ne. 11:1).
- "The brother of Jared . . . went forth unto the mount, which they called the mount Shelem, because of its exceeding height" (Ether 3:1).
- "Moses went up into the mount of God" (Ex. 24:13; see also Moses 1:42).
- "The Lord made the top of the Mount Simeon a sanctuary and there appeared to Enoch who saw Him face to face"[2] (see Moses 7:2–3).
- "Thou [Lord] will bring them [thy people] and plant them on the mountain that is thine own, in the place, O Lord, which thou hast made for thee to dwell in, in the Sanctuary [*miqdas*], O Lord, which thy hands have established" (Ex. 15:17; translation by author).

---

2. Smith, "The Mission of the Kirtland Temple," 204.

- "Then Solomon began to build the house of the Lord at Jerusalem in mount Moriah" (2 Chr. 3:1).
- "He carried me [John] away in the spirit to a great and high mountain" (Rev. 21:10).
- "The spirit lifted me [Ezekiel] up between the earth and the heaven, and brought me in the visions of God to Jerusalem" (Ezek. 8:3).
- "Then the eleven disciples went away into Galilee, into a mountain where Jesus had appointed them. And when they saw him, they worshipped him" (Matt. 28:16–17).
- On July 21, 1849, President Brigham Young permitted Addison Pratt to receive his endowments on Ensign Peak, which is located just north of Salt Lake City.[1]

MOUNT OF TRANSFIGURATION

Many great and sacred things happened on the "high mountain apart," which is known as the "Mount of Transfiguration" (see Matt. 17:1–3, 5). Peter called this mountain "the holy mount" (2 Pet. 1:18). One event of particular eminence is that Peter, James, and John received their endowments on this mount. President Joseph Fielding Smith stated that Jesus Christ "took the three disciples up on the mount, which is spoken of as the 'Mount of Transfiguration,' he there gave unto them the ordinances that pertain to the house of the Lord and that they were endowed. That was the only place they could go. That place became holy and sacred for the rites of salvation which were performed on that occasion."[2] Decades before this teaching, President Heber C. Kimball affirmed, "Jesus took Peter, James and John into a high mountain, and there gave them their endowment....

---

1. See Roberts, *A Comprehensive History of The Church of Jesus Christ of Latter-day Saints*, 3:386.
2. Smith, *Doctrines of Salvation*, 2:170; see also 2:165, 223; see also McConkie, *Doctrinal New Testament Commentary*, 1:400.

For the same purpose has the Lord called us up into these high mountains, that we may become endowed with power from on high."[3]

A second event of eminence that took place on this same mount was that "the Savior, Moses, and, Elias, gave the keys to Peter, James and John on the Mount, when they were transfigured before him."[4] These keys included the authority to conduct temple work. Almost two thousand years later, Moses, Elijah, and others appeared to Joseph Smith and Oliver Cowdery in the Kirtland Temple and gave them the "same keys."[5]

MOUNT SINAI—TEMPLE SYMBOLISM

The Sinai texts, set forth in Exodus 19–20, 24, 34, reveal that Mount Sinai was a natural temple. Elder Marion G. Romney taught that "Sinai became a temporary sanctuary from which he taught Moses."[6] And President Joseph Fielding Smith explained, "The Lord made of Sinai a temple and there gave to Moses the Gospel and the Law."[7] Temple elements at Sinai included the mountain itself, sacrificial offerings, religious laws, the waters of life, divine revelation, a sacred meal, gradations of holiness, God's law, plus more.[8]

Additionally, Mount Sinai was divided into three zones of holiness, which prefigured the gradations of holiness that were attached to the tabernacle and Solomon's temple. Biblical scholar Jacob Milgrom explains,

> Mount Sinai is the archetype of the Tabernacle, and is similarly divided into three gradations of holiness. Its

---

3. Heber C. Kimball, "Proclamation of the Gospel to the Dead," *JD* 9:327.
4. "History, 1838–1856, volume C-1 [2 November 1838–31 July 1842] [addenda]," p. 11 [addenda], The Joseph Smith Papers, accessed March 25, 2019, https://www.josephsmithpapers.org/paper-summary/history-1838-1856-volume-c-1-2-november-1838-31-july-1842/546.
5. Bednar, "The Hearts of the Children Shall Turn," 24. See also Haight, "Keys of the Kingdom," 73–75.
6. Romney, "The House of the Lord," 119.
7. Smith, "The Mission of the Kirtland Temple," 204.
8. Parry, "Sinai as Sanctuary and Mountain of God," 1:482–500.

Mount Sinai at sunrise.

summit is the Holy of Holies; God's voice issues forth from there (Exodus 19:20) as from the inner shrine (Exodus 25:22; Numbers 7:89); the mountaintop is off limits to priest and layman alike (Exodus 19:24) and its very sight is punishable by death (Exodus 19:21), and so with its Tabernacle counterpart (cf. Leviticus 16:2 and Numbers 4:20); finally, Moses alone is privileged to ascend to the top (Exodus 19:20; see 34:2) just as later, the high priest is permitted to enter the inner shrine under special safeguards (Leviticus 16:2–4). The second division of Sinai is the equivalent of the outer shrine, marked off from the rest of the mountain by being enveloped in a cloud (Exodus 20:21; 24:15–18) just as the cloud overspreads the entirety of the Tabernacle (Numbers 9:15–22).... Below the cloud is the third division.... Here is where the altar and stelae are erected (Exodus 24:4). It is equivalent to the courtyard, the sacred enclosure of the Tabernacle.[1]

---

1. Milgrom, *Studies in Levitical Terminology*, 44–45.

MUSIC—PRAISING THE LORD IN HIS TEMPLE

Music and praising the Lord belong to ancient and modern temples. "Praise God in his sanctuary," wrote the Psalmist. "Praise him with the trumpet, harp, and cymbals" (Ps. 150:1–6). The scriptures refer to a choir singing in the tabernacle (see 1 Chr. 6:31–32) and the Jerusalem temple (see 2 Chr. 5:12–14; 29:25–30), song and music on the occasion of the laying of the temple's foundation (see Ezra 3:10–12), and a song of thanksgiving and praise that is sung at the Jerusalem temple dedication (see 2 Chr. 5:12–14; 1 Chr. 13, 15, 16). In our day, the Saints praise God through music during cornerstone and temple dedications and on other sacred occasions.

NAMES

In the context of ancient and modern temples, names have a vital role—for both women and men.[2] The most eminent name associated with temples, of course, is that of the Lord, but our own names are also exceptionally significant and powerful in the temple setting.

The Lord's name: All temples are "built unto [his] name" (D&C 105:33); in fact, the Lord commands us to build temples to His name (see D&C 124:39). Joseph Smith's Kirtland Temple dedicatory prayer refers to the Lord's name multiple times (see D&C 109:2–3, 9, 22). After the temple dedication, the Lord declared, "For behold, I have accepted this house, and my name shall be here" (D&C 110:7).

Regarding the Lord's name and the holy temples, President Dallin H. Oaks explained, "The Old Testament contains scores of references to the name of the Lord in a context where it clearly means the authority of the Lord. Most of these references have to do with the temple. . . . The

---

2. For names in the temple setting, see Porter and Ricks, "Names in Antiquity: Old, New, and Hidden," 501–22.

scriptures speak of the Lord's putting his name in a temple because he gives authority for his name to be used in the sacred ordinances of that house."[1] Elder David A. Bednar spoke of temple ordinances and Jesus's name: "Thus, in the ordinances of the holy temple we more completely and fully take upon us the name of Jesus Christ."[2]

Jesus Christ's new name: Jesus Christ, at His Second Coming, will have "a name written, that no man knew, but he himself" (Rev. 19:12).

The "new name": Several scriptural passages refer to the significance of our names in the setting of the temple—this pertains equally to women and men. In a passage that has multiple temple themes, Revelation 2–3 twice uses the term "new name": "To him that overcometh will I give to eat of the hidden manna, and will give him a white stone, and in the stone a new name written, which no man knoweth saving he that receiveth it" (Rev. 2:17); "Him that overcometh will I make a pillar in the temple of my God, and he shall go no more out: and I will write upon him the name of my God . . . and I will write upon him my new name" (Rev. 3:12). These passages in Revelation may be associated with another passage, in which the Lord revealed, "A white stone is given to each of those who come into the celestial kingdom, whereon is a new name written, which no man knoweth save he that receiveth it. The new name is the key word" (D&C 130:11).

In Isaiah 56, the Lord refers to His temple via a variety of expressions (see vv. 1–7), then in verse 5 the Lord states that He will give temple worshippers a hand and a name: "I will give to them in my house [e.g., the temple] and within my walls a hand and a name" (translation by author).

Just as a change of vestments—from secular street clothes to sacred vestments—indicates a favorable change of status, a new name also denotes an elevation of stature for all participants in the temple ordinances—females and males.

---

1. Oaks, "Taking upon Us the Name of Jesus Christ," 81.
2. Bednar, "Honorably Hold a Name and Standing," 98.

OLIVE OIL

Anciently, priests and high priests who served in the tabernacle and temple were anointed with olive oil, as were various items that belonged to the tabernacle (see "Anointing [with Olive Oil]"). In our day, as President Boyd K. Packer has explained, both "washings and anointings" are "associated with the endowment."[3] What symbolic quality is associated with olive oil?

A number of scriptures associate olive oil with the Holy Ghost.[4] Luke, for example, wrote that "God anointed Jesus of Nazareth with the Holy Ghost and with power" (Acts 10:38; see also D&C 45:56–57; Matt. 25:1–14). John associated the anointing of oil with the Holy Ghost or with receiving divine truth and being taught from on high (see JST, 1 John 2:20–27). Paul also made a direct connection between the anointing and the Holy Ghost when he wrote that he who "hath anointed us,

Horn serving as the receptacle for the sacred anointing oil.

is God; Who hath also sealed us, and given the earnest of the Spirit in our hearts" (2 Cor. 1:21–22). Similarly, Old Testament passages connect the Holy Ghost with olive oil and the anointing (see 1 Sam. 16:13; 18:12; Isa. 61:1; Luke 4:18, 21).

In the Old Testament, a horn served as the receptacle for the sacred anointing oil. Zadok the priest utilized a horn of oil from the tabernacle when he anointed King Solomon (see 1 Kgs. 1:39), and Samuel the

---

3. Packer, *The Holy Temple*, 154.
4. See Tvedtnes, "Olive Oil: Symbol of the Holy Ghost," 427–59.

prophet used a horn of oil when anointing King David (see 1 Sam. 16:13). The horn of oil was of such significance that the Psalmist wrote, "But my horn shalt thou exalt like the horn of an [wild ox]: I shall be anointed with fresh oil" (Ps. 92:10).

ORDINANCES, UNDERSTANDING

An ordinance is a "prescribed religious rite" (from the Latin *ordinare*, "put in order"). Gospel ordinances include baptism, the sacrament, temple ordinances, and others. President Boyd K. Packer informs us that "the ordinances we perform in the temples include washings, anointings, the endowment, and the sealing ordinance—both the sealing of children to parents, and the sealing of couples, spoken of generally as temple marriage."[1] These ordinances, writes President Gordon B. Hinckley, "represent the ultimate in our worship" and "become the most profound expressions of our theology."[2]

From whence came the temple ordinances? Doctrine and Covenants 124 makes it clear and unambiguous that the Lord revealed the temple ordinances to the Prophet Joseph Smith: "Verily I say unto you, let this house [Nauvoo Temple] be built unto my name, that *I may reveal mine ordinances* therein unto my people. . . . *I will show unto my servant Joseph all things pertaining to this house*" (vv. 40–42; emphasis added).

The following important truths help us to better understand ordinances:

(1) Ordinances are centered on Jesus Christ and His Atonement. Compare also Mosiah 13:30–33; Alma 13:16.

(2) Officiants who conduct ordinances use the name of Jesus Christ. As examples, consider the multiple divine names in the sacrament and baptism prayers.

---

1. Packer, "Come to the Temple," 20.
2. Hinckley, "Of Missions, Temples, and Stewardship," 53.

(3) Ordinances are performed with the proper authority. Individuals conducting ordinances "must be [1] called of God, [2] by prophecy, and [3] by the laying on of hands by those who are in authority, to preach the Gospel and administer in the ordinances thereof" (Articles of Faith 1:5). God's prophet, the Church president, authorizes and delegates the authority: "The Presiding High Priest over the High Priesthood of the Church. From the same comes the administering of ordinances and blessings upon the church, by the laying on of the hands" (D&C 107:66–67).

(4) Temple ordinances are concerned with the celestial kingdom. Joseph Fielding Smith instructed that "all of the ordinances of the gospel pertain to the celestial kingdom, and what the Lord will require by way of ordinances, if any, in the other kingdoms he has not revealed."[3]

(5) Ordinances require the faith of those who participate. John A. Widtsoe explained this important doctrine: "In the end all ordinances are derivatives of faith."[4]

(6) Ordinances generally entail a sacred gesture with the hand(s) or arm(s). Many examples exist in the Old and New Testaments, including partaking of the sacrament, baptism, and administering to the sick (see entry "Hands and Covenants").

(7) Ordinances are built around symbolism. Most ordinances are attached to one or more symbols. Obvious examples include the ordinances of baptism and the sacrament.

(8) Objects or materials are often required in the performances of ordinances. For instance, the sacrament requires bread and water, baptism requires water, administering to the sick requires olive oil, and animal sacrifices pertain to blood, which was utilized in different ways by ancient priests in the setting of the tabernacle.

(9) Many of the ordinances are eternal. Joseph Smith taught that God

---

3. Smith, *Doctrines of Salvation*, 2:329. "No man will receive of the celestial glory except it be through the ordinances of the House of God," Wilford Woodruff, "Faith," *JD* 19:361.
4. Widtsoe, "What Is the Need of Ordinances?" 97.

"set the ordinances to be the same for ever and ever, and set Adam to watch over them, to reveal them from heaven to man or to send angels to reveal them."[1] And again, "Ordinances instituted in the heavens before the foundation of the World in the Priesthood for the Salvation of men, are not to be altered or changed, all must be saved on the same principles."[2]

(10) In the ordinances, "the power of godliness is manifest" (D&C 84:20).

(11) The ordinances enable us to know God. Based on Doctrine and Covenants 84:19–21, which deals with the ordinances and "the key of the knowledge of God," Elder Dennis Neuenschwander explained that "through personal participation in sacred gospel ordinances we come to know God."[3]

(12) Ordinances are closely connected with covenants. President Russell M. Nelson taught, "With each ordinance is a covenant—a promise. . . . Covenants do not hold us down; they elevate us beyond the limits of our own power and perspective."[4]

(13) All ordinances are essential. Brigham Young instructed that "there is no ordinance that God has delivered by his own voice, through his Son Jesus Christ, or by the mouths of any of his Prophets, Apostles or Evangelists, that is useless. Every ordinance, every commandment and requirement is necessary for the salvation of the human family."[5]

(14) Most ordinances are for both the living and the dead. For this reason, we have work for the dead. As Joseph Fielding Smith explained,

---

1. "History, 1838–1856, volume C-1 [2 November 1838–31 July 1842] [addenda]," p. 16 [addenda], The Joseph Smith Papers, accessed March 25, 2019, https://www.josephsmith papers.org/paper-summary/history-1838-1856-volume-c-1-2-november-1838-31-july -1842/551.
2. "History, 1838–1856, volume D-1 [1 August 1842–1 July 1843]," p. 1572, The Joseph Smith Papers, accessed March 25, 2019, https://www.josephsmithpapers.org/paper-summary /history-1838-1856-volume-d-1-1-august-1842-1-july-1843/217.
3. Neuenschwander, "Ordinances and Covenants," 23.
4. Nelson, "Personal Preparation for Temple Blessings," 34.
5. Young, *Discourses of Brigham Young*, 152.

"These sacred ordinances are administered for the living and on a proxy basis for the dead also."[6]

(15) Ordinances serve to reveal our true relationship with God. Joseph Smith explained this profound truth: "Could we read and comprehend all that has been written from the days of Adam on the relation of man to God and Angels in a future state, we should know very little about it. Reading the experience of others, or the revelation given to *them,* can never give *us* a comprehensive view of our condition and true relation to God. Knowledge of these things can only be obtained by experience through the ordinances of God set forth for that purpose."[7]

(16) The ordinances pertain to "the signs of things in the heavens." As Heber C. Kimball informed us, "All the ordinances are signs of things in the heavens. Everything we see here is typical of what will be hereafter."[8]

OVAL

Several temples feature ovals, architecturally, both on interior and exterior designs. For example, various artistic and architectural patterns of the Rome Italy Temple reflect ancient Roman building styles and designs as well as Italian Renaissance culture and art; one prominent symbol—manifested in the temple's magnificent domes, stained-glass windows, Perlato Svevo stone floors, ceilings, and the grand staircase—is the oval. The oval is reminiscent of Italy's Piazza del Campidoglio (located near Rome's Capitoline Hill), designed by the acclaimed Michelangelo (1475–1564). The oval represents eternity. As Elder David A. Bednar explained,

---

6. *Doctrines of Salvation,* 2:252–57.
7. "History, 1838–1856, volume E-1 [1 July 1843–30 April 1844]," p. 1750, The Joseph Smith Papers, accessed March 27, 2019, https://www.josephsmithpapers.org/paper-summary/history-1838-1856-volume-e-1-1-july-1843-30-april-1844/122 (emphasis in original).
8. Heber C. Kimball, "Address to My Children," cited in *Enc. of Mormonism* 4:1444.

"The oval reminds us that the Lord's course is one eternal round, that His ways are endless."[1]

Molten sea on twelve oxen, Solomon's temple.

OXEN, TWELVE

Both the ancient "molten sea" of Solomon's temple (1 Kgs. 7:23, 25) and the baptismal fonts of our modern temples feature twelve oxen, which face outward to the four cardinal directions—east, south, west, and north. Important symbols are attached to these fixtures:

Oxen: Elder David A. Bednar explained, the "oxen represent the twelve tribes of Israel, and they also represent the strength and the power of the gospel of Jesus Christ."[2] Why oxen instead of other animals? Because oxen are beasts of burden that possess great power—so great, in fact, that Numbers 23:22 compares God's very strength to that of a wild ox: "God . . . hath as it were the strength of [a wild ox]"[3] (see also Num. 24:8). The house of Israel, like twelve mighty oxen, have the privilege and

---

1. Bednar, "Two Apostles Lead a Virtual Tour of the Rome Italy Temple."
2. Bednar, "Two Apostles Lead a Virtual Tour of the Rome Italy Temple"; see also https://www.lds.org/church/temples/why-we-build-temples/inside-the-temple?lang=eng.
3. The King James Version incorrectly reads "unicorn" in this passage.

burden of taking the gospel and its ordinances (including baptism) to the families and nations of the earth.[4]

Twelve: Featuring twelve oxen points to the tribes of Israel. The high priest's breastplate's twelve stones and Elijah's rebuilt altar with "twelve stones" also point to the twelve tribes (Ex. 39:8–14; 1 Kgs. 18:30–31).

Cardinal directions: The four cardinal directions represent the totality of the earth and her inhabitants. The ordinance of baptism is designed for all inhabitants who accept the gospel and who repent. The Lord's missionaries go forward in all directions to preach the gospel (see also entry "Sea, Molten [Bronze]").

PATHWAY OF PROGRESSION

Both ancient and modern temples have a literal pathway, or a course of direction that leads worshippers from profane to sacred space. For the tabernacle and Israelite temples (Solomon's, Ezekiel's, Herod's), the path began outside the courtyard's walls and continued to the Holy of Holies. The path traversed through three chief horizontal zones—the courtyard(s), the holy place, and the Holy of Holies. The pathway features architectural safeguards, gradations of holiness, and various rites (gestures of approach). The path represents the way to approach the temple's most sacred center—the Holy of Holies. Biblical scholar J. G. Davies, who has researched the topic of the pathway in sacred monumental architecture, calls this pathway "the path that signals a direction."[5] Latter-day Saint temples, too, feature a literal pathway, which begins at the temple's exterior door and continues to the celestial room.

Beyond the literal pathway, both ancient and modern temples also feature a symbolic pathway. At the St. Louis Missouri Temple dedication, President Russell M. Nelson spoke of "a symbolic pathway of progression"

---

4. See Brandt, "Why are oxen used in the design of our temples' baptismal fonts?" 55; see also Fetzer, "Could you tell me a little about the history of our temple baptismal fonts?" 26–28.
5. Davies, "Architecture," 4:387.

(but his words apply to all Latter-day Saint temples). "In this temple there is a symbolic pathway of progression. The baptismal font is located in the lowest part of the temple, symbolizing the fact that Jesus was baptized in the lowest body of fresh water on planet earth. There He descended below all things to rise above all things. In Solomon's temple, the baptismal font was supported by twelve oxen that symbolized the twelve tribes of Israel. . . . From the baptismal font of the temple, we progress upward through the telestial and terrestrial realms to the room that represents the celestial home of God."[1]

PASSOVER

Passover was one of the three ancient pilgrimage festivals, wherein ancient Israelites would journey to the temple of Jerusalem, according to the command of the Lord (see Ex. 23:14–17). The Passover festival, as set forth in Exodus 12, reveals Jesus Christ's atoning sacrifice. This festival encompasses rituals and commandments that anticipate Jesus's death—His blood would spill on the cross, His legs would not be broken, He would be killed after noon, and a large assembly would kill Him. In fact, the correspondences between the Passover and Jesus Christ's death are so notable that Paul named Jesus "Our Passover" (1 Cor. 5:7) and John called Jesus "the Lamb of God" (John 1:29).

The Passover lamb had to be without physical blemishes.

---

1. Nelson, *Teachings of Russell M. Nelson*, 371–72.

Correspondences between the Passover and Jesus

Passover	Jesus Christ
The Passover offering was a lamb (Ex. 12:3)	Jesus is "the Lamb of God" (John 1:29)
The lamb was called "the Lord's Passover" (Ex. 12:11)	Jesus was called "Passover" (1 Cor. 5:7)
The Passover lamb was a male (Ex. 12:5)	Jesus is a male
The Passover lamb was without blemish (Ex. 12:5)	Christ was "without blemish and without spot" (1 Pet. 1:18–19)
The lamb was sacrificed at Passover (Ex. 12:6)	Jesus was sacrificed at Passover (John 19:14)
The Passover lamb was killed after noon (Ex. 12:6)	Jesus was killed after noon (Matt. 27:46)
Israel ate bitter herbs (Ex. 12:8)	Jesus drank from the bitter cup (D&C 19:18)
The token of the lamb's blood saved ancient Israel from death (Ex. 12:13)	Christ's atoning blood saves souls from the grave and from spiritual death (Hel. 5:9)
Lamb's blood was struck on the door's vertical posts and horizontal beam (Ex. 12:7)	Christ's blood fell on the cross's vertical post and horizontal beam
Israel ate the "flesh" of the lamb (Ex. 12:8)	Sacramental bread, which is eaten, represents Christ's body (Matt. 26:26)
The whole assembly killed the Passover lamb (Ex. 12:6)	The entire nation slew Jesus (Matt. 27:20–23; Luke 23:1, 10, 13, 23, 35)
No bones of the sacrificial lamb were broken (Ex. 12:46)	Christ's bones were not broken on the cross (John 19:33)
The Passover released Israel from bondage (Ex. 12:31)	The Atonement releases mortals from the bondage of sin and death (D&C 84:49–53; 2 Ne. 9:12)
The Passover provided temporal deliverance to those who smeared the lamb's blood on their door posts (Ex. 12:7)	Jesus provides spiritual deliverance to those who accept His blood (Matt. 1:21; Luke 4:18)

PILLARS OF TEMPLES

All nine of the tabernacle's pillars were overlaid with gold; five of the nine stood at the tabernacle entrance to the holy place and the other four separated the holy place from the Holy of Holies (see Ex. 26:32, 37; 36:36, 38). Solomon's temple featured two massive, elaborate, brass pillars that were erected on either side of the porch; each pillar was eighteen cubits high, each had a large capital built on top, and each capital was decorated with lily-work and images of pomegranates. The two pillars were named—the pillar located on the right was named *Jachin* ("may he establish") and the left pillar was called *Boaz* ("in strength" or "in him is strength") (1 Kgs. 7:15–22).

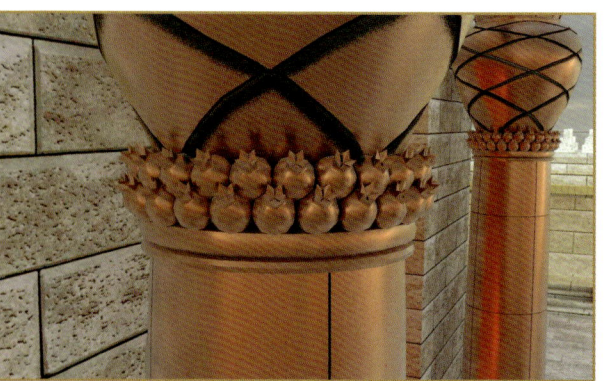
Solomon's temple featured two massive, brass pillars (named Jachin and Boaz); each capital was decorated with pomegranates.

These massive temple pillars may serve as symbols of faithful souls who abide in the Lord's house. Thus the Lord revealed to John, "Him that overcometh will I make a pillar in the temple of my God, and he shall go no more out" (Rev. 3:12). Paul also wrote, "James, Cephas, and John, . . . seemed to be pillars." (Gal. 2:9).

PLAGUES, AND THE ATONEMENT

The Atonement, in association with the temple, had the power to protect the Israelites from plagues. The Lord gave "the Levites as a gift . . . to make an atonement for the children of Israel: that there be no plague among the children of Israel, when the children of Israel come nigh unto the sanctuary" (Num. 8:19). An example of how the Atonement stopped a plague is recorded in Numbers 16. As a consequence of the Israelites committing great sins against the Lord, He smote them with a plague, wherein fourteen thousand, seven hundred people died. To halt the plague, Aaron offered up incense, then he "made an atonement for the people. And he stood between the dead and the living; and the plague was stayed" (Num. 16:46–48).

The Lord sometimes allowed plagues to serve as punishments for immorality and sin during Old Testament times. For example, an Israelite male brazenly brought a Midianite woman into the Israelite camp for immoral purposes. His and others' sexual sins and idolatrous practices resulted in a plague that killed twenty-four thousand Israelites (see Num. 25:1–14). To halt the plague and the resulting deaths, the priest Phinehas, Aaron's grandson, "made an atonement for the children of Israel" (Num. 25:13), and because Phinehas did this, the Lord blessed him and his posterity.

As another example, King David asked Ornan to allow him to build an altar on Ornan's threshingfloor in order to stop a plague. "Then David said to Ornan, Grant me the place of this threshingfloor, that I may build an altar therein unto the Lord: thou shalt grant it me for the full price: that the plague may be stayed from the people" (1 Chr. 21:22). The altar, of course, is a place of sacrifice and atonement. And a significant fact—this place of the threshingfloor later became the site of the temple of Solomon.

POMEGRANATE

Skillful workers embroidered representations of pomegranates into the hem of the high priest's robe; the pomegranates were alternated with bells of gold (see Ex. 28:33–34). Additionally, hundreds of images of pomegranates existed on the columns

Pomegranates of blue, purple, and scarlet on the high priest's robe.

of Solomon's temple (see 1 Kgs. 7:20; see also 7:18, 42; 2 Chr. 3:16; Jer. 52:22–23).

The pomegranate may have three symbolic values: (1) The pomegranate's calyx (sepals) has the appearance of a crown, which is suggestive of kings, queens, and royalty (queenship/kingship is also associated with the temple). (2) During the spring season, the pomegranate tree is covered with lovely scarlet flowers; scarlet serves as a reminder of the blood of Christ. Similarly, the pomegranate juice is blood red, also an image of Jesus's blood. (3) The pomegranate's numerous seeds suggest fertility and eternal increase (*granate* [from pome*granate*] originates from Latin, meaning "having many seeds").

Pomegranate and seeds; calyx has the appearance of a crown.

PRAYER CIRCLE (ANCIENT AND MODERN)

In May 1977, President Spencer W. Kimball spoke to a general conference audience and referred to "a solemn prayer circle."[1] Almost a decade later, Jeffrey R. Holland wrote of "the prayer circle of the First Presidency and Council of the Twelve."[2] That the prayer circle is conducted in the temple was made clear by President N. Eldon Tanner: "As the First Presidency enters this room at ten o'clock on Thursday mornings, we shake hands with all members of the Twelve, then change to our temple robes. We sing, kneel in prayer, and then join in a prayer circle at the altar."[3]

Hugh Nibley has provided evidence for the existence of a prayer circle

---

1. Kimball, "The Lord Expects His Saints to Follow the Commandments," 4.
2. Holland, "President Thomas S. Monson," 16.
3. Tanner, "The Administration of the Church," 43, 47–48.

in ancient times, especially among early Christians.[4] The exact nature of a prayer circle, of course, is too sacred to discuss outside of the temple. For the symbolism of the circle, see entry "Circle."

PRAYER, DIRECTIONAL (PRAYING TOWARD THE TEMPLE)

Directional prayer, or prayer directed toward the temple, serves to make the temple prominent in the minds of those who are worshipping through prayer. A number of times during his temple dedicatory prayer (at least seven!), Solomon directed worshippers to pray *toward* the temple:

> That thou mayest hearken unto the prayer which thy servant shall make toward this place.... when they shall pray toward this place.... if they pray toward this place.... What prayer and supplication soever be made by any man, or by all thy people Israel ... and spread forth his hands toward this house.... when he shall come and pray toward this house.... and shall pray unto the Lord toward the city which thou hast chosen, and toward the house that I have built for thy name.... pray unto thee toward their land, which thou gavest unto their fathers, the city which thou hast chosen, and the house which I have built for thy name (1 Kgs. 8:29–30, 35, 38, 42, 44, 48; emphasis added).

Other biblical texts also refer to worshipping toward the Lord's house. David wrote in a psalm, "I will ... worship toward thy holy temple" (Ps. 5:7); and again, "I will worship toward thy holy temple" (Ps. 138:2). Jonah, in his extreme condition of tribulation, prophesied, "I will look again toward thy holy temple" (Jonah 2:4).

---

4. Nibley, "Early Christian Prayer Circle," 45–99; see also Tate, "Prayer Circle," 1120–21.

Other writers have also instructed worshippers regarding directional prayer. The Prophet Joseph Smith referred to Daniel's custom of prayer (see Dan. 6:10) and taught: "You must make yourselves acquainted with those men who like Daniel pray three times a day to the House of the Lord Look to the Presidency and receive instruction."[1] From the dedicatory prayer of the Salt Lake Temple: "Heavenly Father, when Thy people shall not have the opportunity of entering this holy house to offer their supplications unto Thee, and they are oppressed and in trouble, surrounded by difficulties or assailed by temptation and shall *turn their faces towards this Thy holy house* and ask Thee for deliverance, for help, for Thy power to be extended in their behalf."[2] Jewish texts also refer to directional prayer, or praying in the direction of the temple (see B. T. Berakoth 30a; M. Berakoth 4:5–6).

The idea of directional prayer underscores the significance of the temple, because even when female and male worshippers were situated outside of the temple, they could have the temple uppermost in their minds and in their hearts, meaning, they would direct their sympathy, emotions, love, innermost feelings, etc., to the temple.

PRAYER ROLL

Religious Jews from around the world travel to Jerusalem, write prayers on small pieces of paper, and then place them in the cracks of the huge Herodian stones of the famous Western Wall. This wall is a very sacred site to Judaism because it is a remnant of the ancient Temple Mount (not the temple itself), and, furthermore, some Jews hold that the Divine Presence resides at the wall. In some ways, these prayer notes remind us of

---

1. "History, 1838–1856, volume C-1 [2 November 1838–31 July 1842] [addenda]," p. 13 [addenda], The Joseph Smith Papers, accessed March 27, 2019, https://www.josephsmith papers.org/paper-summary/history-1838-1856-volume-c-1-2-november-1838-31-july -1842/548.
2. April 6–24, 1893, Wilford Woodruff.

A woman places a prayer note in a crack of the Western Wall, Jerusalem, while other women pray.

the "prayer roll" of our temples, spoken of by President Dallin H. Oaks[3] and others. Jews also pray at the wall and worship with deep emotion and spiritual passion.

PRIESTESSES

Eliza R. Snow, denominated "poetess-presidentess-priestess-prophetess"[4] by a historian, served as the second General President of the Relief Society (1866–87). On a certain occasion she addressed the sisters: "Inasmuch as we continue faithful, we shall be those that will be crowned in the presence of God and the lamb. You, my sisters, if you are faithful, will become Queens of Queens, and Priestesses unto the Most High God."[5] Years later, Bathsheba W. Smith, the fourth General President of the Relief Society (1901–10), provided these words: "When I had my

---

3. See Oaks, "Healing the Sick," 50.
4. Mulvay, "Eliza R. Snow and The Woman Question," 252.
5. Mulvay, "Eliza R. Snow and The Woman Question, 264.

Eliza R. Snow, the second General President of the Relief Society (1866–87).

endowments Brother Joseph [Smith] was there. . . . I have always been pleased that I had my endowments when the Prophet lived. He taught us the true order of prayer. . . . He wanted to make us, as the women were in Paul's day, 'A kingdom of priestesses.'"[1] In point of fact, on March 31, 1842, Joseph Smith spoke to the Relief Society and told them that "he was going to make of this Society a kingdom of priests an [as] in Enoch's day—as in Pauls day."[2]

John the Revelator wrote that Jesus Christ "hath made us kings and priests unto God and his Father; to him be glory and dominion for ever and ever" (Rev. 1:6). John's words—*kings* and *priests*—refer to both males and females. The expression "hast made us unto our God kings and priests" is so significant that it will become part of a "new song" that will be sung in heaven: "And they sung a new song, saying, Thou [Jesus Christ] art worthy to take the book, and to open the seals thereof: for thou wast slain, and hast redeemed us to God by thy blood out of every kindred, and tongue, and people, and nation; And hast made us unto our God kings and priests" (Rev. 5:9–10). According to this passage, persons from "every kindred, and tongue, and people, and nation" are made kings and priests (and *priests*, here, refers to the "order of Melchizedek" and not that of Aaron [Ps. 110:4; see also Heb. 5:10; 7:11, 21]). This glorious and eternal

---

1. Clawson, "Pioneer Stake," 14.
2. "Nauvoo Relief Society Minute Book," p. 22, The Joseph Smith Papers, accessed December 14, 2019, https://www.josephsmithpapers.org/paper-summary/nauvoo-relief-society-minute-book/19.

blessing is for all worthy women and men, not a single family or tribe, as it was during periods of the Old Testament.

President John Taylor sets forth the distinction between a king and a priest: "Kings and Priests—Priests to administer in the holy ordinances pertaining to the endowments and exaltation; and Kings, under Christ, who is King of Kings and Lord of Lords, to rule and govern, according to the eternal laws of justice and equity, those who are thus redeemed and exalted."[3]

A number of our prophets have taught regarding the significance of kings and priests and queens and priestesses. In 1966, President Spencer W. Kimball spoke on "Kings and Priests" at a Brigham Young University devotional. He said, "Now, you 10,000 priests and priestesses, where do you stand? You are heirs to great fortunes, for eternal life is the greatest gift. What will you do with it? You are entitled to a kingdom or a queendom. You are princesses and princes. . . . Claim your throne, hold tightly to the scepter, keep your inheritance inviolate. You will be priests and priestesses, kings and queens, throughout all eternity, may you precious young people never abdicate."[4] And President Joseph Fielding Smith wrote of faithful men and women, "They have been promised that they shall become sons and daughters of God, joint heirs with Jesus Christ, and if they have been true to the commandments and covenants the Lord has given us, to be kings and priests and queens and priestesses, possessing the fulness of the blessings of the celestial kingdom."[5]

---

3. Taylor, *Mediation and Atonement*, 158–59.
4. Kimball, "Kings and Priests," BYU devotional, Feb. 15, 1966, https://speeches.byu.edu/talks/spencer-w-kimball_kings-priests/. See also President Kimball's teachings in *The Teachings of Spencer W. Kimball*, 331.
5. Smith, *Answers to Gospel Questions,* 4:61. See also Joseph Fielding Smith's teachings in "Relief Society—An Aid to the Priesthood," 5–6.

PRIESTS AND HIGH PRIESTS

During the period of the law of Moses, the high priest was the ranking temple official. He, together with the priests, held the Aaronic Priesthood (but God's prophets held the Melchizedek Priesthood). Every worthy priest and high priest during ancient times served as figures or symbols of Jesus Christ, who is "a high priest . . . a minister of the sanctuary, and of the true tabernacle" (Heb. 8:1–2; see also 2:17; 3:1; 4:14; 9:11), and "an high priest after the order of Melchisedec" (Heb. 5:10) (meaning, Jesus was a high priest of the Melchizedek Priesthood).

Priest (model) dressed in sacred vestments stands beside the altar of incense (veil in background).

The high priests of the Mosaic order were required to be holy and undefiled and to maintain personal and ritual purity (see Lev. 21; Num. 16:5); Christ was a "high priest . . . who is holy, harmless, undefiled, separate from sinners" (Heb. 7:26). The high priest entered into the Holy of Holies as part of his duties on the Day of Atonement (see Lev. 16), but "Christ is not entered into the holy places made with hands, which are the figures of the true; but into heaven itself, now to appear in the presence of God for us" (Heb. 9:24). Priests and high priests were workers of the Atonement for Israel and for their sins: "The priest shall make an atonement for them, and it shall be forgiven them" (Lev. 4:20), as Christ would perfectly work out the Atonement.

Elder Jeffrey R. Holland affirms: "God has ordained priests 'after the order of his Son.' . . . They have been ordained in a way that serves as a type and shadow of Christ, letting the people know in what manner they may look forward to the Son of God for redemption."[1]

PRISON-TEMPLE

During the winter of 1838–39, Joseph Smith and others were imprisoned in Missouri's Liberty Jail. Some Church authorities have referred to this prison as a "prison-temple."[2] So how was it a "prison-temple"? Elder Holland summarizes, "You can have sacred, revelatory, profoundly instructive experience with the Lord *in the most miserable experiences of your life*—in the worst settings, while en-

Liberty Jail, 1888.

during the most painful injustices, when facing the most insurmountable odds and opposition you have ever faced."[3]

PULPITS

The Kirtland Temple features a large assembly hall with a series of pulpits situated on the east (designed for the Aaronic Priesthood) and additional pulpits located on the west (for the Melchizedek Priesthood). The

---

1. Holland, *Christ and the New Covenant*, 116.
2. Holland, "Lessons from Liberty Jail," 3.
3. Holland, "Lessons from Liberty Jail," 3–4, italics in original.

Kirtland Temple pulpits.

pulpits express hierarchical relationships and demonstrate the importance of the Aaronic and Melchizedek Priesthoods in the temple complex. The St. George, Logan, Manti, Los Angeles, and Washington D.C. temples also feature pulpits that set forth hierarchical meanings.

RECOMMEND, TEMPLE

Temple recommends serve to keep unclean persons who would pollute the temple from entrance (see D&C 109:20; compare D&C 97:15–16). President Russell M. Nelson taught, "Our Redeemer requires that His temples be protected from desecration. No unclean thing may enter His hallowed house.... Because the temple is the house of the Lord, standards for admission are set by Him. One enters as His guest. To hold a temple recommend is a priceless privilege and a tangible sign of obedience to God and His prophets."[1]

Although the Old Testament lacks specific mention of a temple recommend, there existed strict requirements regarding who could enter the Lord's house. For example, Ezekiel 44:9 states, "Thus saith the Lord God; No stranger, uncircumcised in heart, nor uncircumcised in flesh, shall enter into my sanctuary." The strict requirements are reflected in three biblical scriptural passages—Psalm 15, Psalm 24, and Isaiah 33:14–17—all of which are written in poetic form.[2] These passages share the same goal: that of inviting women and men worshipping in the temple to be morally and ethically worthy to enter the temple. These three hymns share the same structure addressed to temple visitors—(1) two rhetorical questions, (2) a rhetorical response to the two questions, and (3) a promise of a blessing to the faithful.

In addition, the authors of all three texts utilize multiple symbols. For example, Psalm 15:1 calls the temple a *holy hill* (Hebrew: "holy mountain") and in Psalm 24:3 refers to it as the *hill of the Lord* (Hebrew: "mountain of the Lord"). Isaiah uses the terms *devouring fire* and *everlasting burnings* to express the great glory that exists in the heavenly temple, or celestial kingdom. This is consistent with teachings of Joseph Smith, who taught, "God dwells in everlasting burnings"[3] and "flesh and blood cannot go there <for> all corruption is devoured by the fire."[4]

Psalms 15 and 24 are addressed to those who wish to enter the earthly temple; Isaiah 33:14–17 is addressed to those who wish to enter the

---

1. Nelson, "Personal Preparation for Temple Blessings," 33.
2. For a discussion of the three hymns, see Parry, "'Who Shall Ascend into the Mountain of the Lord?': Three Biblical Temple Entrance Hymns," 729–42.
3. *Teachings of Presidents of the Church: Joseph Smith*, 224.
4. "Discourse, 12 May 1844, as Reported by Thomas Bullock," p. [2], The Joseph Smith Papers, accessed March 25, 2019, https://www.josephsmithpapers.org/paper-summary/discourse-12-may-1844-as-reported-by-thomas-bullock/2.

heavenly temple, or the celestial kingdom. Portions of the three temple entrance hymns are as follows:

	Psalm 15:1–5	Psalm 24:3–5	Isaiah 33:14–17
Two Questions	Lord, who shall abide in thy tabernacle? Who shall dwell in thy holy hill?	Who shall ascend into the hill of the Lord? . . . Who shall stand in his holy place?	Who among us shall dwell with the devouring fire? Who among us shall dwell with everlasting burnings?
Response	He that walketh uprightly, and worketh righteousness . . .	He that hath clean hands, and a pure heart . . .	He that walketh righteously, and speaketh uprightly . . .
Blessing	He that doeth these *things* shall never be moved	He shall receive the blessing from the Lord, and righteousness from the God of his salvation	He shall dwell on high . . .

REFUGE, TEMPLE IS A PLACE OF

Throughout the centuries, many religious institutions—churches, synagogues, and sanctuaries—have served as places of refuge. Individuals and groups have fled to these sacred places during times of war and natural disaster, to seek political asylum, or to avoid arrest from officers of the law. Conceivably, these places of refuge emerged based on the concept of ancient, biblical cities of refuge (see Num. 35), where certain individuals could find refuge (see entry "High Priest, Death of, and the Cities of Refuge").

In ways similar to ancient and medieval places of refuge, our modern temples function as a refuge to faithful Saints who seek the peace, calm, and tranquility that can only be found in the Lord's house. For them, the temple is the ultimate safe haven from the confusion, chaos, and evil of the world.

A number of Church authorities have identified our temples as places of refuge. Elder Quentin L. Cook testified, "The temple is . . . a place of refuge. . . . Throughout my life it has been a place of tranquility and peace in a world that is literally in commotion. It is wonderful to leave the cares of the world behind in that sacred setting."[1] And President Gordon B. Hinckley's words at the Portland Oregon Temple dedication (19 August 1989) have application to all of the Lord's temples: "It is a place of peace and holiness, a refuge from the storms of life, a sanctuary in which to worship thee 'in spirit and in truth.'"[2]

As an important sidenote, the Laie Hawaii Temple has been called a "temple of refuge" because "in ancient times, the area had served as a city of refuge for Hawaiians seeking protection from the tyrannical rulers of the kingdom."[3]

Although temples serve as places of refuge, the Lord, of course, is our ultimate place of safety—He is "my refuge, my saviour" (2 Sam. 22:3); also, O Lord, "thou hast been a strength to the poor, a strength to the needy in his distress, a refuge from the storm" (Isa. 25:4).

REVELATION IN THE TEMPLE

Jean B. Bingham testified, "Like a massive telescope focused on stars beyond our immediate sight, the temple opens our minds to a higher and broader vision."[4] Indeed, sacred spaces, which include mountaintops and temples, are quintessential places for mortals to receive divine revelation. Nephi (see 1 Ne. 11:1), the brother of Jared (see Ether 3:10), Moses (see

---

1. Cook, "See Yourself in the Temple," 99.
2. Hinckley, Dedicatory Prayer, https://www.churchofjesuschrist.org/temples/details/portland-oregon-temple/prayer/1989-08-19?.
3. Pratte, "Temple of Refuge in the Pacific," 26.
4. Bingham, "The Temple Gives Us Higher Vision," 38.

Moses 1:42), Enoch (see Moses 7:2–3), and others received mighty revelations on mountains. Sacred revelatory experiences are also common occurrences in temples, both ancient and modern. On multiple occasions, Moses received the word of the Lord in the tabernacle (see, for example, Lev. 1:1; Ex. 25:21–22; 29:42–43; 30:6, 36; Num. 17:4). Phinehas, Aaron's grandson, asked the Lord while in the temple's Holy of Holies whether or not Israel should war against the Benjaminites (see Judg. 20:26–28). The Psalmist visited the Lord's house "to inquire in his temple" (Ps. 27:4). Also, Paul the Apostle prayed in the temple and had a vision: "While I prayed in the temple, I was in a trance" (Acts 22:17).

Several texts establish that the temple is the quintessential place to receive the highest form of communication from God to mortals. The Lord spoke concerning the Kirtland Temple: "I will manifest myself to my people in mercy in this house. *Yea, I will appear unto my servants, and speak unto them with mine own voice,* if my people will keep my commandments, and do not pollute this holy house" (D&C 110:7–8; emphasis added). Also, "If the Lord has occasion to visit any particular part of his kingdom, the place where he will come will be the sanctuary that is appointed, the house that has been dedicated to him, the house that is his.... All who are entitled to see the face of the Lord will receive that blessing in the House of the Lord."[1]

In addition to divine communications with God Himself, the temple is the place where "the living might hear from the dead." Elder Parley P. Pratt wrote, "Ye are assembled here today, and have laid these Corner Stones [of the Salt Lake Temple], for the express purpose that the living might hear from the dead; and that we may prepare a holy sanctuary, where 'the people may seek unto their God; for the living to hear from the dead,' and that heaven, and earth, and the world of spirits, may commune

---
1. McConkie, "The Promises Made to the Fathers," 48.

together."[2] Eliza R. Snow, too, explained, the temple is "a portal for angels, a threshold for God."[3]

President Gordon B. Hinckley related how the temple is "a place of revelation" for both Church leaders and lay members: "The temple is also a place of personal inspiration and revelation. Legion are those who in times of stress, when difficult decisions must be made and perplexing problems must be handled, have come to the temple in a spirit of fasting and prayer to seek divine direction. Many have testified that while voices of revelation were not heard, impressions concerning a course to follow were experienced at that time or later which became answers to their prayers."[4]

"I believe that the busy person on the farm, in the shop, in the office, or in the household, who has his worries and troubles, can solve his problems better and more quickly in the house of the Lord than anywhere else. . . . That is the gift that comes to those who enter the temple properly, because it is a place where revelations may be expected."[5]

RITUAL (SACRED CEREMONY)

In both the Old and New Testaments, God teaches us through ritual, or sacred ceremony (which also includes the sacred ordinances of our day). In fact, the revelations make it clear that God does not simply suggest, but He *commands* His covenant people to participate in ritual. During the period of the Mosaic law, for example, these sacred rituals included the laying on of hands; the act of anointing oil on individuals and things; washing with water; smearing sacrificial blood on the body parts of the priests; offering incense; sprinkling sacrificial blood on things; and sacrificing certain animals to make atonement for the people. New Testament rituals

---

2. Pratt, "Oration," 3.
3. Snow, "The Temple," 254.
4. Hinckley, "The Salt Lake Temple" 6.
5. Widtsoe, "Temple Worship," 63–64.

include baptism; the laying on of hands; breaking, blessing, and partaking of sacramental bread; anointing the sick with oil followed by the laying on of hands; and many other rituals.

Drawing upon the understanding of ritual in both ancient and modern temples from various religious faiths of the world, biblical scholar John Lundquist summarizes the meaning of ritual: "Ordinary mortals, indeed priests too, approach the temple through ancient, carefully prescribed ritual preparations, including purification, special clothing, certain ritual movements and gestures . . . ritual speech . . . visual symbols . . . and group interaction. These rituals are not something recently thought up or devised in popular religious or artistic movements (although traditional forms of ritual may well appear in these media). They bear the stamp of tradition, are often passed on by elderly members of a society, are usually considered to be secret, and are purposefully kept from the knowledge of outsiders, or those who have not been initiated."[1]

Ritual symbols, including those attached to clothing, gestures, speech, and movements, create a sacred environment wherein participants transcend profane time and space and enter into the realms of the sacred, where God and angels reside. Ritual also removes individuals from a worldly environment and allows them to enter into God's presence, where eternal light and manifold glories exist.

SACRED TRIANGLE

In the October conference of 1952, Elder Matthew Cowley spoke of the sacred triangle, which consists of God and a wife and husband. This sacred triangle is fully established in a covenantal setting when the wife and husband hold hands at the temple's altar. Elder Cowley said, "We . . . who have knelt at the sacred altar and on that altar clasped the hand of a

---

1. Lundquist, *The Temple: Meeting Place of Heaven and Earth*, 19.

sainted companion and have entered an eternal triangle, not a companionship of two, but of three—the husband, the wife, and God—the most sacred triangle man and woman can become a part of. . . . I thank God for the symbol of the handclasp, with all of its eternal significance. God grant that I may always have the strength to clasp the hand of my companion wife and that she will always have the strength to hold my hand as if it were in a vise."[2]

SACRIFICES—SYMBOLS OF JESUS'S ATONING SACRIFICE

The Atonement of Jesus Christ was typified by sacrifice from the very beginning. Adam and Eve were commanded to "offer the firstlings of their flocks, for an offering unto the Lord" (Moses 5:5). Later an angel appeared to Adam and explained: "This thing is a similitude of the sacrifice of the Only Begotten of the Father, which is full of grace and truth" (v. 7). Joseph Smith explained, "Whenever the Lord revealed himself to men in ancient days, and commanded them to offer sacrifice to him . . . it was done that they might look forward in faith to the time of his coming, and rely upon the power of that atonement for a remission of their sins."[3]

The sacrifices under the law of Moses—burnt, grain, peace, sin, and trespass offerings—were ordered as symbols of Jesus Christ's atoning sacrifice (see Moses 5:4–8, 2 Ne. 11:4). The sacrifices focused on animals—sheep, goats, birds, bulls—and the shedding of their blood. Or, if the offerer's economic status did not permit the sacrifice of an animal, then flour or grain served as acceptable substitutes. Some offerings were voluntary and others were mandatory; some dealt with the unintentional transgressions

---

2. Cowley, "The Sacred Triangle," 916–17.
3. "Letter to the Church, circa March 1834," p. 143, The Joseph Smith Papers, accessed March 25, 2019, https://www.josephsmithpapers.org/paper-summary/letter-to-the-church-circa-march-1834/2.

of the children of Israel and others atoned for their willful or deliberate sins.

SACRIFICES UNDER THE LAW OF MOSES—SIX ACTS

Animal sacrifices under the law of Moses consisted of a six-part process,[1] which focused on Jesus Christ and His Atonement. The accompanying chart lists these six acts, together with a brief explanation for each one.

Action #	Action	Three Acts Conducted by the Worshipper
1	Presentation of the Sacrifice	The worshipper presented the sacrifice at the door of temple or on the north side of the altar (Lev. 1:3; 3:2)
2	Laying on of Hands	The worshipper laid his hands on the sacrifice to consecrate the offering to God and to make the sacrifice the offerer's substitute (Lev. 1:4; 16:21; Num. 8:10; 27:18, 20)
3	Slaughter of the Animal	The worshipper or priest slaughtered the animal
		Three Acts Conducted by the Priests
4	Sprinkling or Pouring of the Blood	For most animal sacrifices, the priest collected the animal's blood and sprinkled a portion of it on the sides of the altar and poured the remainder at the altar's base (Ex. 29:12; Lev. 1:5; 3:2; 4:7; 8:15; Num. 18:17; cf. Lev. 17:11)
5	Burning of the Sacrifice	Depending on the sacrifice, the priest burned all or part of the animal on the altar
6	Partaking of the Sacrificial Meal	Participants of the sacrificial meal included, depending on the sacrifices, (a) Worshippers and priests, in the case of the peace offerings (Lev. 7:11–36); (b) Only the priests and their wives and children (Lev. 10:14; 22:10–12; Num. 18:11–13); (c) Only the priests (Lev. 6:16, 26; 7:6; 24:9)

1. See Bible Dictionary, 720.

Note that worshippers conducted acts one through three, and acts four and five pertained to the priests. Act six, partaking of the sacrificial meal, pertained to priests and worshippers.

SACRIFICIAL MEALS, PARTAKING OF

Sacrificial sheep (representative) beside the altar of sacrifice.

Priests and Israelite worshippers had the privilege of partaking of a portion of the sacrificial offerings of the temple. This was not simply a way to enjoy a meal or to eat to satiate; this was part of an extraordinarily sacred ceremony. The Mosaic code set forth a number of regulations regarding partaking of the sacrificial meat or animal's flesh (see, for example, Ex. 12:4, 11, 46–48; Lev. 6:16, 18, 23–30; 7:11–36; 10:11–15). The Lord revealed who, where, what, and when they were to partake of the sacrifices. The Lord also instructed that individuals could not partake if they had uncleannesses, otherwise they would "be cut off" (Lev. 7:20).

In multiple ways, the ancient sacrificial meal was similar to our sacrament: (1) Both ancient and modern Saints partook/partake in holy places (anciently, the temple precinct; in modern days, the chapel); (2) Both ancient and modern Saints must be clean or worthy to partake; (3) Both the terms *sacrifice* and *sacrament* originate from the Latin *sacer*, meaning "sacred"; (4) Most importantly, both the sacrificial meat and the sacrament bread symbolize Jesus Christ's flesh. President Boyd K. Packer explained, "Both sacrifice before, and the sacrament afterward, are centered in Christ, the shedding of His blood, and the atonement He made for our sins."[2]

---

2. Packer, "The Aaronic Priesthood," 31.

A priest (model) takes the scapegoat into the wilderness (see Lev. 16:10).

SCAPEGOAT

The term *scapegoat*, used in modern times to blame someone for others' mistakes or wrongdoings, originates in the Old Testament. Anciently, the scapegoat, which prefigured Jesus Christ's atoning sacrifice, had an important role in the Day of Atonement procedures. The scapegoat was presented in the temple "alive"; it served "to make an atonement" for the people. The high priest laid his hands upon the scapegoat's head and then he confessed over the scapegoat "all the iniquities of the children of Israel, and all their transgressions in all their sins" (Lev. 16:21); in this manner, the high priest transferred their sins "upon the head of the goat" (Lev. 16:21; see also 16:8, 10, 21–22, 26).

SEA, MOLTEN (BRONZE)

A large receptacle or basin of water ("molten sea"), set upon the backs of twelve oxen, existed in Solomon's temple courtyard. The basin was so large that the Hebrew scriptures called it a "sea" (Hebrew: *yam*). The basin was fifteen feet in diameter, a height of seven and one-half feet, and the circumference was forty-five feet (see 2 Chr. 4:2). The basin "stood upon twelve oxen, three looking toward the north, and three looking toward the west, and three looking toward the south, and three looking toward the east" (2 Chr. 4:4; 1 Kgs. 7:23, 25). The heads of the oxen faced outward.

This large basin was used for ritual washings: "The sea was for the priests to wash in" (2 Chr. 4:6). Joseph Fielding Smith stated that the basin was used for ceremonial purposes, perhaps for washings or baptisms for the living.[1] This receptacle, together with the twelve oxen, resembled the baptismal fonts that exist in our temples, which fonts are used for baptisms for the dead (see "Baptismal Font").

Molten sea on twelve oxen, Solomon's temple, by Melantrich.

SEALING ORDINANCE

The sealing ordinance in our temples pertains to the eternal uniting of a husband and wife and of children to their parents. This sealing is possible because of Jesus Christ's Atonement and the restoration of priesthood keys. On 3 April 1836, Elijah appeared to Joseph Smith and Oliver Cowdery and "bestowed upon them the sealing power, the power to use

---

1. Smith, *Doctrines of Salvation* 2:323; McConkie, *Mormon Doctrine*, 69–70. See also Fetzer, "Could you tell me a little about the history of our temple baptismal fonts?" 26–28.

the priesthood to bind on earth and seal in heaven."[1] This sealing power, states Joseph F. Smith, is "an everlasting, unbreakable covenant," which "can never be broken by death, by time, or distance, because God has confirmed it, it is sealed by His power for time and for all eternity."[2] Of the various gospel ordinances, "blessing, baptism, confirmation, ordination, and endowment," expressed President Russell M. Nelson, "the sealing ordinances are supreme. . . . The ordinance of sealing is an absolute."[3]

In the Old Testament, prophets, kings, or others with authority sometimes used seals or signet rings to seal and to give authentication to official documents.[4] Once the document was sealed, "the purpose [of the seal] might not be changed" (Dan. 6:17) and "no man [may] reverse" (Esther 8:8) its purpose. In the gospel, when ordinances are sealed by the Holy Spirit of Promise (see Eph. 1:13), then the purpose of the ordinance cannot be changed. No spirit or mortal, including the power of evil, has the authority or the power to change it. Such is the case for all temple ordinances that are sealed by the Holy Spirit of Promise.

The Lord's words are clear in this matter; He revealed through Joseph Smith that if a husband and wife marry "by my word, which is my law, and by the new and everlasting covenant, and it is sealed unto them by the Holy Spirit of promise . . . [it] shall be of full force when they are out of the world" (D&C 132:19). These words impact every single bride and groom who come to the Lord's house to receive this covenant.

SEEING THE LORD IN THE TEMPLE

There are many examples of theophany (or appearances of God) in the Old Testament;[5] and the place where God generally visits His people is in

---

1. Smith, "Magnifying Our Callings in the Priesthood," 65.
2. Smith, in Conference Report, Oct. 1913, 9.
3. Nelson, *Teachings of Russell M. Nelson*, 366–67.
4. *A Hebrew and English Lexicon of the Old Testament*, 368.
5. Skinner, "Seeing God in His Temple," 270–90.

a temple setting (e.g., on a mountaintop), or in the temple itself (see Ex. 24:9–1; 29:42–46; Ps. 17:15; 42:2; 63:2; 84:7; Amos 9:1). For example, Isaiah testified, "I saw also the Lord sitting upon a throne, high and lifted up, and his train filled the temple" (Isa. 6:1).

Modern temples are also sacred spaces for theophanies. Joseph Smith's dedicatory prayer of the Kirtland Temple states that the Saints had built the temple so "that the Son of Man might have a place to manifest himself to his people" (D&C 109:5). We recall that Joseph Smith and Oliver Cowdery saw the Lord in the Kirtland Temple (D&C 110:1–4). Also, Lorenzo Snow reported to Allie Young Pond, his granddaughter, that he saw the resurrected Lord in the Salt Lake Temple standing "about three feet above the floor" and remarked that "it looked as though he stood on a plate of solid gold."[6] Doctrine and Covenants 97:15–16 promises, "Inasmuch as my people build a house unto me in the name of the Lord, and do not suffer any unclean thing to come into it, that it be not defiled, my glory shall rest upon it; Yea, and my presence shall be there, for I will come into it, and all the pure in heart that shall come into it shall see God."

SEVEN PROMISES "TO HIM THAT OVERCOMETH"

Revelation 2–3 submits the seven-fold phrase "to him that overcometh," which is directed to individuals—females and males—who overcome the world and its wickedness. Each phrase, found in the letters to the seven churches (see Rev. 2:11, 17, 29; 3:6, 13, 22; 13:9), is followed by one or more promises (shown in italics), which pertain directly to the temple.[7] For example:

"*Eat of the tree of life*" (Rev. 2:7). Through the Atonement of Jesus

---

6. Lorenzo Snow, *Deseret News*, April 2, 1938.
7. For a discussion of the seven promises, see Draper and Parry, "Seven Promises to Those Who Overcome: Aspects of Genesis 2–3 in the Seven Letters," 121–42.

Christ, all who overcome death receive the promise and blessing to "eat of the tree of life."

"Will I give to eat of the hidden manna" (Rev. 2:17). The hidden manna refers to Jesus (see John 6:48–51).

"Give him a white stone" (Rev. 2:17). Written upon this white stone will be a new name, which is "the key word" (D&C 130:10–11).

"New name" (Rev. 2:17; see also D&C 130:10–11). The new name, similar to the white robe (see Rev. 3:5, 6:11, and 7:9), conveys the idea of a new existence, or a new life.

"Will I give power over [many kingdoms]" (Rev. 2:26). "Many kingdoms" refers to eternal, not temporal kingdoms. The Saints are invited to "come up unto the crown prepared for you, and be made rulers over many kingdoms" (D&C 78:15).

"The same shall be clothed in white raiment" (Rev. 3:5). These are they who are transformed into new persons by Jesus's atoning sacrifice; they "have washed their robes, and made them white in the blood of the Lamb" (Rev. 7:14). The white clothing, with the new name, signifies a new state of existence.

"Will I make a pillar in the temple of my God" (Rev. 3:12). Exalted men and women are compared to the pillars of a temple, which are stable, strong, and permanent fixtures of the temple precinct. These Saints will stand forever in the heavenly temple, never to be removed by evil forces.

"I will write upon him the name of my God" (Rev. 3:12; see also Rev. 14:1; D&C 132:20; 133:18). The righteous will take the name of the Lord.

"I will write upon him my new name" (Rev. 3:12). Christ will give the righteous His own new name.

SHEWBREAD (BREAD OF GOD'S PRESENCE)

The table of shewbread, situated in the tabernacle's holy place, was called the "pure table" (Lev. 24:6; 2 Chr. 13:11). The table was somewhat small, measuring three feet by one and a half feet, with a height of about two feet. The table was constructed with acacia wood and then overlaid with pure gold. The priests covered the table with a blue cloth and then placed various dishes, utensils, and the shewbread on the cloth (Num. 4:7).

Shewbread, an archaic word, literally means "bread of the face" (from Hebrew), probably meaning "bread of the face of God." The bread was made of fine flour; every Sabbath, the priests placed twelve loaves on the table, arranged in two rows, with six loaves per row. Pure frankincense was placed on each row "that it may be on the bread for a memorial, even an offering made by fire unto the Lord" (Lev. 24:7). High priests and priests ate the bread while in the holy place. The bread was considered "most holy" and "a perpetual statute" (Lev. 24:9).

Although the bread was not the sacrament, it did look forward to the Lord's eternal sacrifice. In fact, Jesus would later teach, "I am the bread of life" (John 6:35). "Bread of the face [of God]" suggests that the priests were eating the bread in God's presence. The number twelve signifies the twelve tribes of Israel.

Shewbread and incense on the table of shewbread, tabernacle of Moses.

SHOES, REMOVING

In the narrative of the burning bush, the Lord commanded Moses to "put off thy shoes from off thy feet, for the place whereon thou standest is holy ground" (Ex. 3:5). Joshua was similarly commanded (see Josh. 5:15). Shoe removal was an important gesture that could be interpreted to signify a transition from a worldly to a spiritual and sacred setting. Shoe removal correlates with the priests changing from their nonreligious clothing into sacred vestments.

President Gordon B. Hinckley cited Exodus 3:5 and then referred to our temples: "We do not ask our people to remove their shoes when they come into the chapel. But all who come into the Lord's house should have a feeling that they are walking and standing on holy ground and that it becomes them to deport themselves accordingly."[1]

SINS, INTENTIONAL AND UNINTENTIONAL, AND THE ATONEMENT

Two categories of sins are dealt with in the law of Moses: (1) willful sins, or those of an intentional, premeditated, or rebellious nature; and (2) inadvertent or unintentional sins, or those that are committed through ignorance or thoughtlessness. For example, if a man borrowed a tool from his neighbor and forgot to return it, that man has committed an unintentional sin. Or, if a person failed to properly enclose his ox and it gored a neighbor, then the ox's owner has sinned through carelessness. The Lord's laws regarding unintentional sins pertained to priests, the entire congregation of Israel, rulers, and individuals (see Lev. 4:1–35; 5:14–19; Num. 15:22–29). In these cases, atonement had to be made to maintain order in the community.

All sins—minor or major, willful or unintentional—separate sinners

---

1. Hinckley, "Reverence and Morality," 45–46.

from God and His glory and excellence because all sins, even those that some individuals may deem inconsequential, represent an infraction of one of God's laws. Therefore, an atonement must be made for both willful and unintentional sins. Temple sacrifices expressed means and ways of atoning for both types of sins.

We can look at these atonement sacrifices as a means of understanding Christ's great and last sacrifice for our sins, recognizing that His Atonement paid the price for both our intentional sins and our unintentional sins.

SOLEMN ASSEMBLY

The solemn assembly has its roots in the Old Testament, when faithful Israelite males and females met together in association with the Feasts of Passover and Tabernacles (see Lev. 23:33–36; Deut. 16:8, 16; Neh. 8:18). On certain occasions, both anciently and in modern times, the Lord commands His people to convene a solemn assembly in the temple. For example, Joel 1:14 states: "Sanctify ye a fast, call a solemn assembly, gather the elders and all the inhabitants of the land into the house of the Lord your God." And in our day, "Call your solemn assembly, as I have commanded you" (D&C 109:6; see also 95:7). On March 27, 1836, the Saints met together in the Kirtland Temple for a solemn assembly; at that time the Saints sustained the Church leaders, and Joseph Smith dedicated the temple.[2]

Our Church presidents have convened solemn assemblies at various times, including at the dedication or rededication of temples, or when General Authorities meet in the temple with local leaders. A solemn assembly also refers to general conference sessions where a new President of the Church is sustained.

---

2. Smith, *HC* 2:410–28.

The Salt Lake Temple pinnacles are symbolic of Church leaders.

SPIRES AND STEEPLES

The most symbolic aspect of spires and steeples pertains to the way that they reach heavenward; as worshippers approach the temple, these great structures compel us to look upward, toward heaven and toward God who dwells there. Several temples feature these spires or steeples, which are significant architectural monuments.

In addition to temple spires and steeples, the Salt Lake Temple features several pinnacles, of which Church architect Truman O. Angell wrote, "Each tower has a spire and twelve pinnacles (emblematical of the First Presidency, Twelve Apostles, High Council, Bishops and their Counselors)."[1]

Johannesburg South Africa Temple spires.

---

1. Angell, "The Salt Lake City Temple," 274.

SQUARES AND THE SQUARED CIRCLE

With four right angles and four equal sides, a square[2] is an important geometrical shape attached to various symbolisms. Perhaps for this reason, both ancient and modern temples feature squares; some are practical in design and others are purely ornamental. A multitude of our temples feature square designs, patterns, and figures on either exterior architectural components or interior spaces. The Mosaic tabernacle and Solomon's temple featured many squares—the altars (sacrificial and incense) were built in the form of a perfect square (referring to the width and length); the Holy of Holies of both the Mosaic tabernacle and Solomon's temple formed a perfect cube, with a three-dimensional, symmetrical shape—six equal squares.

Squared circle—the circular font rests on the backs of the twelve oxen, which face the four cardinal directions (thus forming a square).

Also, a square communicates the idea of the earth, with its four corners. "Four corners" of the earth is a scriptural term (Isa. 11:12; Acts 10:11; Rev. 7:1; D&C 124:3), which pertains to all individuals who live on the earth; thus Isaiah wrote, "He shall set up an ensign for the nations, and shall assemble the outcasts of Israel, and gather together the dispersed of Judah from the four corners of the earth" (Isa. 11:12; see also D&C 124:3).

Squared circles, or circles located within a square, are architectural symbols that belong to many temples. Inasmuch as a circle expresses the idea of eternity (or heaven) and a square may be interpreted to signify the earth (and its inhabitants),[3] then a squared circle seems to point the

---

2. Nibley, *Temple and Cosmos*, 139–73.
3. For a study of circles and squares in the context of the temple, see Nibley, "The Circle and the Square," in *Temple and Cosmos*, 139–73; and Brown and Smith, *Symbols in Stone*, 153–54.

Squared Circle, Las Vegas Temple.

meeting of heaven and earth. A significant example of a squared circle is the molten sea of Solomon's temple and also the baptismal font of our temples. The twelve oxen form a square, and the font that rests on their backs generally form a circle: The twelve oxen face outward to the four cardinal directions—east, south, west, and north—or to the four corners of the earth (hence, forming a square).

STAIRS/STAIRCASES

While most stairs in temples have a utilitarian function, some have a symbolic value, serving as a method to ascend from one sacred space to the next, or from one ordinance room to another. Ascension is a vital aspect of sacred space (see entry "Ascension"). The Salt Lake Temple has a series of stairs that lead from one level to the next; these include the grand staircase, four corner-tower spiral staircases, and other steps and staircases. Monumental stairs and staircases are also part of the Manti Utah, Mesa Arizona, Payson Utah, and several other temples. In Manti, two renowned spiral staircases wind up five stories in the octagonal towers on the temple's west side. Considered to be pioneer engineering marvels, they are open-centered and self-supporting.

STARS/STARSTONES

Many of our temples feature decorative starstones or star images on the exterior of the buildings; the stars are variegated, portraying five-, six-, eight-, ten-, or even thirty-two-pointed stars. The stars may be located in the temple's cornerstone, walkway, wrought-iron fences, entrance doors, entryway, exterior temple walls, stained-glass windows, steeple glass, or glass doors.

The stars depicted on temples may possibly represent a few things: (1) Stars may symbolize people. "The morning stars" of Job were eminent persons (Job 38:7; see also 1 Ne. 1:9–10; D&C 128:23), with morning stars denoting spheres whose light continues for a period lengthier than the remaining stars of heaven. (2) Of all the stars, Jesus Christ is the preeminent and the greatest, "the bright and morning star" (Rev. 22:16). He is also the "Star out of Jacob" (Num. 24:17). (3) Beyond the symbolism of people, the brightness of the light of the stars has been compared to the glory that will exist in the telestial kingdom (see 1 Cor. 15:40–41; D&C 76:98). By way of contrast, the light of the sun is comparable to the glory of the celestial kingdom.

Just as the North Star has helped travelers for millennia to orient themselves during their journeys, temples assist us as we journey through mortality and back to Heavenly Father's presence. And the North Star symbol reminds us of that journey.

President Gordon B. Hinckley likened the North Star to Jesus Christ: "Like the polar star in the heavens, regardless of what the future holds, there stands the Redeemer of the world, the Son of God, certain and

Glass-etched series of eight-pointed stars, San Diego Temple.

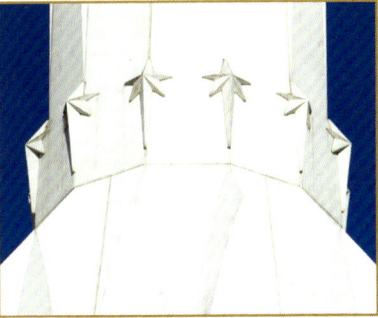
Star images on steeple, Portland Temple.

Glass-window star image facing starstone (upper), Nauvoo Illinois Temple.

sure as the anchor of our immortal lives. He is the rock of our salvation, our strength, our comfort, the very focus of our faith."[1]

SUNSTONES/SUN IMAGES

Sunstones and sun images are prominently and beautifully featured on several temples, including Albuquerque New Mexico, Las Vegas Nevada, Nauvoo Illinois, Omaha Nebraska, Salt Lake, St. Louis Missouri, Washington D.C., and Winter Quarters Nebraska. Inspired artisans creatively present diverse and unique sunstones and images; for example, each of the Salt Lake Temple sunstones features forty rays; the Nauvoo Illinois Temple sunstones give prominence to a face, rays, and two trumpets each held by a hand; and the Las Vegas Temple sunstone is an artistic circle, with fifty-two rays.

Regarding the Nauvoo Temple moonstones, starstones, and sunstones, Richard Cowan explained, "They undoubtedly reminded Latter-day Saints of the three degrees of glory spoken of by Paul and elaborated in latter-day revelation."[2]

Sunstones also remind us of Jesus Christ, who is "the light of the world" (Alma 38:9; see also John 12:46); also, "This is the light of Christ. As also he is in the sun, and the light of the sun, and the power thereof by which it was made" (D&C 88:7; see also vv. 8–13). In powerful ways,

---

1. Hinckley, "We Look to Christ," 90.
2. Cowan, "Latter-day Saint Temples as Symbols," 7. So, too, Nibley wrote, "The series of stars, moon, and sunstones on the buttresses indicate the levels of . . . glory," Nibley, *Temple and Cosmos*, 367.

(left) Sun image, Washington D.C. Temple. (middle) Sunstone, Nauvoo Illinois Temple. (right) Sun image, Preston England Temple.

divine light draws us to the Lord's house. As the Psalmist reminds us, "O send out thy light and thy truth: let them lead me; let them bring me unto thy holy hill [Hebrew: "mountain"], and to thy tabernacles" (Ps. 43:3).

SYMBOLS, DIVERSE

In the dedication of the St. Louis Missouri Temple, President Russell M. Nelson set forth a number of diverse symbols that pertain to a chandelier, altar, sculptured carpets, white clothing, and "similarity of our dress": "In the temples symbols are utilized to teach us spiritual things. For example, we admire that beautiful chandelier in the celestial room. . . . Look at the many innumerable pieces in that chandelier, each one made beautiful as it reflects the light behind it. Can you see that each piece in that chandelier could represent some of the lineage of Abraham, Isaac, and Jacob illuminated by the light of the Lord?

Chandeliers in temples can represent the light of the Lord.

"Elsewhere in the temple we admire the altars. They become more important to us when they symbolize the importance of prayer. The sculptured carpets on the floor signify the sure foundation of truth, below which we do not descend, as devoted Latter-day Saints. . . .

"The whiteness of temple clothing suggests purity, and the similarity of our dress symbolizes the fact that we are all sons and daughters of God. In the temple there is no segregation according to position held, color, wealth, or the lack of it."[3]

---

3. Russell, *Teachings of Russell M. Nelson*, 371.

TABERNACLE (PORTABLE TEMPLE), SYMBOLISM OF

God commanded the children of Israel to build the tabernacle so that He "may dwell among them" (Ex. 25:8).[1] He revealed to Moses the tabernacle's pattern together with its instruments, furniture, and sacred vestments. The tabernacle served ancient Israel for some 400 to 500 years and was erected in the wilderness, Gilgal, Shiloh, Nob, Gibeon, and Jerusalem.

Image of tabernacle structure and altar of sacrifice in the courtyard.

After Solomon's temple was built, the tabernacle no longer served Israel.

The chief builders of the tabernacle were genuine artisans, Bezalel, of the tribe of Judah and Oholiab, from the tribe of Dan (see Ex. 31:1–11). The tabernacle complex consisted of a courtyard (measuring 75 feet by 150 feet) that was surrounded by a fence (height 7.5 feet) made of linen hangings. The tabernacle building (45 feet long by 15 feet wide) itself existed within the courtyard; it was a bipartite structure consisting of the holy place (30 feet long by 15 feet wide) and the Holy of Holies (a perfect cube, 15 feet on all sides). A veil separated the holy place from the Holy of Holies.

The tabernacle and all of its appurtenances signified a place of atonement par excellence. It was a Jesus Christ–focused space where sinful men and women could approach God with sacrifices and worship, and therein find peace and grace.

---

1. This tabernacle was a portable temple, and not to be confused with certain regional buildings called "tabernacles," which the pioneers built in various places.

The tabernacle building itself brings to mind Christ's body, the perfect tabernacle or temple (see Heb. 8:2). In his epistle to the Hebrews, Paul called Jesus "a greater and more perfect tabernacle, not made with hands" (Heb. 9:11), versus the actual tabernacle that the Israelites built. The very best temple builders created Jesus, the "perfect tabernacle"—Mary and God!

TEMPLE, DESIGN OF, REVEALED BY GOD

According to a number of scriptural and historical records, God has revealed to His prophets the plan or design of many of His temples. Here are several examples:

Mosaic Tabernacle. The tabernacle's precise architectural dimensions and plans were so essential to the Israelite community that God revealed its pattern or technical plan to Moses: "Let them make me a sanctuary. . . . according to all that I shew thee, after the pattern of the tabernacle" (Ex. 25:8–9; see also Heb. 8:5). The Lord also revealed "the pattern of all the instruments thereof" (Ex. 25:8–9, 40; Num. 8:4) and the details and description of the priestly vestments (see Ex. 28 and 39).

Temple of Solomon. God delivered to King David "by the Spirit" instructions concerning the details and measurements of the temple; David then conveyed the pattern to his son Solomon. "All this, said David, the Lord made me understand in writing by his hand upon me, even all the works of this pattern" (1 Chr. 28:11–13, 19).

Temple of Ezekiel. An angel revealed to Ezekiel the design of Jerusalem's future temple (see Ezek. 40–46).

Kirtland Temple. The Lord revealed the pattern to Joseph Smith and others: "Let the house be built . . . after the manner which I shall show unto three of you" (D&C 95:13–14). Elder Orson Pratt explained that Joseph Smith received divine knowledge regarding "the order of the pulpits, and in fact everything pertaining to it was clearly pointed out by

234 | TEMPLE, DESIGN OF, REVEALED BY GOD

Nauvoo Temple drawing.

revelation. God gave a vision of these things, not only to Joseph, but to several others, and they were strictly commanded to build according to the pattern revealed from the heavens."[1]

Nauvoo Temple. God revealed the plan to Joseph Smith: "I have seen in vision the splendid appearance of that building illuminated and will have it built according to the pattern shewn me."[2] Once William Weeks (temple architect) considered semicircular windows to be appropriate, but Joseph Smith maintained that round ones would be used because of the vision that he had received.[3]

Far West Temple. Doctrine and Covenants 115:14–15 states concerning this temple, "Let a house be built unto my name according to the

---

1. Pratt "The Latter-Day Work," *JD* 13:357; see also "Order," 14:273.
2. "History, 1838–1856, volume E-1 [1 July 1843–30 April 1844]," p. 1876, The Joseph Smith Papers, accessed March 27, 2019, https://www.josephsmithpapers.org/paper-summary/history-1838-1856-volume-e-1-1-july-1843-30-april-1844/248.
3. "History, 1838–1856, volume E-1 [1 July 1843–30 April 1844]," p. 1876, The Joseph Smith Papers, accessed March 27, 2019, https://www.josephsmithpapers.org/paper-summary/history-1838-1856-volume-e-1-1-july-1843-30-april-1844/248.

pattern which I will show unto them. And if my people build it not according to the pattern which I shall show unto their presidency, I will not accept it at their hands."

Salt Lake Temple. Brigham Young saw the Salt Lake Temple in vision: "I . . . saw in the Spirit the Temple not ten feet from where we have laid the Chief Corner Stone. I have not inquired what kind of a Temple we should build. Why? Because it was represented before me. I have never looked upon that ground, but the vision of it was there. I see it as plainly as if it was in reality before me."[4]

TEMPLE IN HEAVEN

The concept of the temple in heaven is taught in several Old Testament passages (see, for example, Ps. 11:1–7; 102:19; 150:1; Isa. 6:1–8; 1 Kgs. 22:19; Ezek. 1, 10)[5] as well as throughout the book of Revelation.[6] In fact, John the Revelator explicitly refers to the heavenly temple with such expressions as, "Another angel came out of the temple which is in heaven" (Rev. 14:17), and, "There came a great voice out of the temple of heaven" (Rev. 16:17; see also 7:15; 14:15; 15:5–8). And in our own dispensation, President Wilford Woodruff once saw and spoke with Joseph Smith and other deceased individuals "at the door of the temple in heaven."[7]

Ancient Israelite temples have a particular relationship with the temple in heaven; for example, (1) Jesus Christ and His Atonement are the focus of both ancient temples and the temple in heaven; (2) various aspects of ancient Israelite temples are symbolic representations of things in the

---

4. Young, "The Temple Corner Stones—The Apostleship, &c." *JD* 1:133.
5. Biblical scholar Brazil de Souza, *Toward a Theology of the Heavenly Sanctuary*, examines more than two dozen Old Testament passages that deal with the temple in heaven. See also his extensive bibliography.
6. See, for example, Parry and Parry, "The Temple in Heaven: Its Description and Significance," 515–32.
7. Woodruff, *Deseret Weekly* 53 (November 7, 1896), 642–43; also in Stuy, *Collected Discourses* 5:238.

heavenly temple; and (3) John touched on several ancient temple rituals as he wrote regarding the temple of heaven (see the following chart). The chart sets forth relationships, similarities, and differences between ancient temples and the temple in heaven.

Temple on Earth		Temple in Heaven	
Description	References	Description	References
Called "worldly sanctuary"	Heb. 9:1–2	Called "true tabernacle" or "temple in heaven"	Heb. 8:2; Rev. 7:15; 14:17; 15:5; 16:17
Seven-branched lamp stand	Ex. 26:35	Seven-branched lamp stand	Rev. 1:12
Altar of sacrifice	Ex. 27:1–2; 39:39	Altar of sacrifice	Rev. 6:9
Sacred vestments	Ex. 29; 39	Sacred vestments	Rev. 4:4; 6:11; 15:6
Altar of incense	Ex. 30:1–6; 39:38	Altar of incense	Rev. 8:3, 5
Four horns of the altar	Ex. 30:10	Four horns of the altar	Rev. 9:13
Ark of the covenant	Ex. 25	Ark of the covenant	Rev. 11:19
Golden censer	1 Kgs. 7:50	Golden censer	Rev. 8:3–5
Incense	Ex. 30:34–36	Incense	Rev. 5:8; 8:4
Throne (mercy seat)	Ex. 25:22; Lev. 16:2	Throne	Ps. 11:4; Rev. 7:9; 16:17
Holy place	1 Kgs. 7:50	Holy place	Heb. 9:11–12, 24
Holy of Holies	Ex. 26:25–33	Holy of Holies	Rev. 4:1–10
Priestly officiants	Ps. 110:4; Heb. 7:17	Priestly officiants	Rev. 8:2–5
Rituals	Throughout	Rituals	Rev. 4:8–11; 8:2–5; 15:1–8
24 priestly courses	1 Chr. 23:3–6	24 elders	Rev. 4:4, 10
Cherubim	Ex. 25:18, 22; 1 Kgs. 6:23–28	Four living creatures	Rev. 4:6–8 (cf. Ezek. 1, 10)
Worshippers	Throughout	Worshippers	Rev. 5:11; 7:9; 19:6
Sacrifice of lambs	Ex. 29:39	Lamb of God	Rev. 5:6

TEMPLES, CATEGORIES OF

The scriptures identify several categories of temples, which may be divided into three groups:

Group 1: Temples Built by God

Temple Category	Representative Examples
Gardens	Garden of Eden, Garden of Gethsemane, and Garden Tomb
Mountains	Sinai, Transfiguration, Simeon, and Shelem
Temple in Heaven	As described by John and others

Group 2: Temples Built by Women

Temple Category	Representative Examples
God as Temple	Jesus Christ is a holy temple; Mary was His mother
Man/Woman as Temple	Men and women are holy temples of God, grown and birthed by women
Jesus, Saints, Apostles, and Prophets	As described by Paul in Ephesians 2:19–22

Group 3: Temples Built by Mortal Builders

Temple Category	Representative Examples
Structures built by mortal builders	Tabernacle of Moses, Solomon's temple, Ezekiel's temple, modern-day temples

All categories of temples are designed to serve God's divine purposes and exist for the salvation of the human family. There is a formal connection among all temple types—God (Himself a holy temple) reveals sacred laws and rituals to His children (who are holy temples) within holy temple buildings or within natural temples. That is to say, temple buildings and natural temples accommodate God and His children in spaces that are holy, or separate, set apart from the world.

"TEMPLES EVERYWHERE"

God's ancient temples have had such an extraordinary and exceptional impact on the world and its religions that remnants of the temple can be found "everywhere"[1] in today's civilization. Stated differently, significant components from ancient temples have diffused throughout the ancient, medieval, and modern world so that now virtually each of the world's major religions, to a lesser or greater extent, have incorporated such components into its own religious system. As Nibley explained, "One can easily detect familiar echoes of the endowment in religious institutions and practices throughout the world.... Students of comparative religion have now come around to the same conclusion, namely, that the real endowment has been on earth from time to time and has also been spread abroad in corrupted forms so that fragments from all parts of the world can be traced back to common beginnings."[2]

Elder John A. Widtsoe explained the matter this way: "Let me suggest that the reason why temple building and temple worship have been found in every age, on every hand, and among every people, is because the gospel in its fullness was revealed to Adam, and that all religions and religious practices are therefore derived from the remnants of the truth given to Adam and transmitted by him to the patriarchs. The ordinances of the temple in so far as then necessary, were given, no doubt, in those early days, and, very naturally, corruptions of them have been handed down the ages. Those who understand the eternal nature of the gospel—planned before

---

1. "Temples Everywhere" is the title of Hugh Nibley's presentation given at the "Temples through the Ages" conference held at BYU, Dec. 4, 1999. For examples of temples "everywhere," see Lyon, *Understanding Temple Symbols Through Scripture, History, and Art*; Gaskill, *Sacred Symbols: Finding Meaning in Rites, Rituals, and Ordinances*; Lundquist, *The Temple: Meeting Place of Heaven and Earth*; and several of Nibley's writings, including "Looking Backward."
2. Nibley, "On the Sacred and the Symbolic," 575–76.

the foundations of the earth—understand clearly why all history seems to revolve about the building and use of temples."[3]

What remnants or categories of components did various religious groups appropriate from God's ancient temples? Architecture (various synagogues, churches, cathedrals, and shrines have components that recall ancient temples), furniture (including such items as altars and ritual ablution basins or fonts), rituals, gradations of holiness, sacred gestures in the liturgy, ceremonial terminology and expressions, and much more. These items deserve serious study. For example, dozens of religious faiths—ancient, medieval, and modern—utilize sacred vestments; many of these faiths have created sacred vestments based (often loosely) on biblical passages, such as Exodus 28 and 39.

In sum, the Lord's temples have impacted postbiblical religious institutions in numerous ways, and the diffusion of aspects of the temple is evident in many faiths and religions throughout the world.

TEMPLES, FUTURE

Both modern and ancient prophets have prophesied that there will be temples in the last days and even beyond, as the following statements demonstrate:

Brigham Young: "To accomplish this work there will have to be not only one temple but thousands of them, and thousands and tens of thousands of men and women will go into those temples and officiate for people who have lived as far back as the Lord shall reveal."[4]

Wilford Woodruff: "When the Savior comes, a thousand years will be devoted to this work of redemption; and Temples will appear all over this

---

3. Widtsoe, "Symbolism in the Temples," 163.
4. Young, "The Gifts of Prophecy and Tongues," *JD* 3:372. See also Cowan's discussion of temple work that will occur during the Millennium, in *Temples to Dot the Earth*, 277–80.

land of Joseph—North and South America—and also in Europe and elsewhere."[1]

Isaiah: "It shall come to pass in the *last days,* that the mountain of *the Lord's house shall be established* in the top of the mountains" (Isaiah 2:2; emphasis added).

Ezekiel: The Lord states, "I will make . . . an everlasting covenant with them . . . and *will set my sanctuary in the midst of them for evermore*" (Ezek. 37:26–27; emphasis added). Ezekiel chapters 40 through 46 describe a future temple.

Zechariah: "The man whose name is The Branch . . . *shall build the temple of the Lord;* and he shall bear the glory, and shall sit and rule upon his throne" (Zech. 6:12–13; emphasis added; see also vv. 14–15; 1:16–17).

TEMPLES, GOD'S PEOPLE ALWAYS COMMANDED TO BUILD

The great importance of temples is supported by the fact that the Lord has "always commanded" His covenant people to build them (D&C 124:39). Joseph Smith taught: "The object of gathering the Jews together or the people of God in any age of the world . . . was to build unto the Lord an house whereby he could reveal unto his people the ordinances of his house and glories of his kingdom & teach the people the ways of salvation."[2]

The most famous Israelite temples of the Old World are the tabernacle of Moses, Solomon's temple, and Herod's temple. However, Biblical scholar Menahem Haran has produced evidence that temples also existed in Shiloh, Dan, Bethel, Gilgal, Mizpah, Hebron, Bethlehem, Nob, hill-country of Ephraim, Ophrah, Gibeah, Arad, and Jerusalem.[3]

---

1. Wilford Woodruff, "Not Ashamed of the Gospel," *JD* 19:230.
2. "Discourse, 11 June 1843–A, as Reported by Wilford Woodruff," p. [42–43], The Joseph Smith Papers, accessed March 27, 2019, https://www.josephsmithpapers.org/paper-summary/discourse-11-june-1843-a-as-reported-by-wilford-woodruff/1.
3. Haran, *Temples and Temple-Service in Ancient Israel,* 26–42.

Calgary Canada Temple.

Additionally, two Jewish temples existed in Egypt: the Temple of Onias at Leontopolis (about 200 BC) and the temple of Elephantine (about 500 BC). It is unknown which temples identified by Haran and the two in Egypt were authorized by and accepted by the Lord.

The Nephites built temples in the New World,[1] and the first generation of Latter-day Saints in the last days built temples in Kirtland, Nauvoo, Manti, Logan, St. George, and Salt Lake City. Later generations of Saints have built scores of temples in multiple lands and countries on the face of the earth.

Elder Widtsoe summarizes, "All people of all ages have had temples in one form or another. . . . There are evidences that even in patriarchal days, in the days of Adam, there was the equivalent of temples, for the priesthood was held in its fulness, as far as the people needed it; and there is every reason to believe that from Adam to Noah, temple worship was in operation. After the flood the Holy Priesthood was continued; and we have reason to believe, in sacred places, the ordinances of the temple were given to those entitled to receive them."[2]

TEMPLE TEXTS—REPRESENTATIVE EXAMPLES

There are literally hundreds of scriptural texts that pertain to the temple, to a greater or lesser degree; this is owing to the fact that the temple is such a significant religious institution and eternally consequential to God and His covenant people. The following are representative examples of scriptural references of temple texts, followed by a brief description of their contents. The list is not comprehensive, nor does the list set forth various words or passages that call to mind the temple, including various nuances or words that pertain to the temple. For example, the double

---

1. Welch, "The Temple in the Book of Mormon," 297–387.
2. Widtsoe, "Temple Worship," 52–53.

attestation of "hands"[3] in KJV Isaiah 1:15 recalls two different aspects of the temple. A cursory reading will miss the temple-context of this passage.

- Genesis 1–2:4; Moses 2:1–3:25; Abraham 4:1–5:25, Creation accounts
- Genesis 2:4–3:24, Garden of Eden narrative
- Genesis 15:7–18, Abraham sacrifices animals and has a sacred experience
- Genesis 22:1–8, Abraham offers Isaac on Mount Moriah
- Genesis 32:24–32, Jacob "wrestling" with the angel
- Genesis 35:1–15, Jacob at Bethel
- Exodus 12:2–20, Passover
- Exodus 19–20, 24, 34, Sinai texts (see "Mount Sinai—Temple Symbolism")
- Exodus 26–27, 30–31, 33, 36–38, 40, Tabernacle texts
- Exodus 29, Washing, anointing, and consecration of priesthood members
- Exodus 28, 39, Sacred vestments (description and rites)
- Leviticus 16, 23:33–43, Day of Atonement
- Leviticus 1:1–7:38, The law of sacrifice
- Leviticus 8:1–10:20, The need for priestly mediators
- Leviticus 11:1–15:33, Separating the clean from the unclean
- Leviticus 17:1–25:55, The need for holy living
- Leviticus 23:15–21, Feast of Weeks
- Leviticus 23:33–43, Feast of Tabernacles or Booths
- Numbers 3–4, On the priesthood and the tabernacle
- Numbers 5, Trial of jealousy for women
- Numbers 6, Law of the Nazarite
- Numbers 7, Dedication of the tabernacle
- Numbers 8, Consecration of Levites
- Numbers 9, Law of Passover, notes on the tabernacle
- Numbers 10, Ark of covenant accompanies Israel's march
- Numbers 15, Sacrificial offerings
- Numbers 18, Laws pertaining to the priesthood
- Numbers 19, Sacrifice of the red heifer, water of separation
- Numbers 28–29, Law of sacrifice
- Deuteronomy 31:24–29;

---

3. The Hebrew uses two different words for the two occurrences of "hands" in this verse.

- 32:45–47, Depositing the law into the ark
- Ruth 3, Washing, anointing, clothing for marriage
- 1 Kings 5–7, Building of Solomon's temple
- 1 Kings 8, Dedicatory Prayer for Solomon's temple
- Ezra 1, 3–7, Rebuilding the temple
- Psalm 11:1–7, The Lord is in His holy temple
- Psalms 15, 24, Metaphoric/poetic temple recommends
- Psalms 20, 21, 89, 110, 132, Royal songs
- Psalm 26, Temple entrance hymns
- Psalm 27:1–14, Desire to dwell in the Lord's house
- Psalms 29, 95, 100, 150, Psalms of praise
- Psalm 30, Psalm of the temple dedication
- Psalm 43:1–5, God's light and truth lead us to the temple
- Psalms 46, 48, 76, 84, 87, 122, Songs of Zion
- Psalms 47, 93, 96–99, Kingship and enthronement psalms
- Psalm 50, Regarding covenants and sacrifices
- Psalm 66:13–15, Offer sacrifices in the temple
- Psalm 68, God dwells in the mountain (temple)
- Psalm 79:1–13, Heathens destroy the temple
- Psalm 84, Liturgical hymn; blessed are they who dwell in God's temple
- Psalm 96:1–13, Strength is in God's temple
- Psalm 99:1–9, Worship God at His holy hill
- Psalm 116:17–19, Worship in God's temple
- Psalm 118, Thanksgiving hymn
- Psalms 120–134, Ascension hymns
- Psalm 122:1–9, Go to the Lord's house
- Psalm 132:1–18, Worship the Lord in His temple
- Psalm 134:1–3, Lift your hands in God's temple
- Psalm 138 1–8, David worships toward the temple
- Psalm 150:1–6, Praise God in His sanctuary
- Isaiah 1:10–15, Condemnation against Israel's apostate temple practices
- Isaiah 2:1–5, The mountain (temple) of the Lord
- Isaiah 6, Isaiah's vision in the heavenly temple

- Isaiah 8:11–15, Jesus is like a temple to the righteous
- Isaiah 22:15–25, Shebna and Eliakim
- Isaiah 33:14–17, The righteous dwell in everlasting burnings
- Isaiah 58:1–8, Righteous receive a name in the temple
- Lamentations 1–4, Lamentations for the destruction of Jerusalem and her temple
- Ezekiel 4:10–35, The name of the city is "The Lord is there"
- Ezekiel 16, Washing, anointing, clothing for marriage
- Ezekiel 40–46, Ezekiel's vision of the future temple of Jerusalem
- Ezekiel 47, Water will flow from under the temple and heal the Dead Sea
- Daniel 5, Belshazzar drinks from the vessels of the temple
- Daniel 12:5–13, Angel in sacred vestments gives a sacred gesture
- Joel 3:17–21, The Lord dwells in Zion, the holy mountain
- Micah 4, Latter-day temples
- Habakkuk 2:14–20, Earth is filled with knowledge and glory of God
- Habakkuk 3:3–6, The Lord's glory
- Haggai 1, Haggai exhorts the people to build a temple
- Zechariah 3, The investiture and clothing of Joshua
- Zechariah 4, Temple of Zerubbabel
- Matthew 17, Mount of Transfiguration
- JST John 13, Washing of feet
- Hebrews 8–10, Paul's teachings on the temple in heaven
- Revelation 1, John's vision of Christ in the temple
- Revelation 2–3, Seven "he who overcometh" statements about the temple
- Revelation 4–5, Description of the temple in heaven
- Revelation 21–22, Description of the temple in heaven
- 1 Nephi 11, Nephi is caught away in spirit to a mountain
- 1 Nephi 17, Nephi speaks with the Lord
- 3 Nephi 11–18, Sermon at the temple (also contains ritual elements)
- Ether 2–3, Brother of Jared's temple experience
- D&C 36:7–8, The Lord will suddenly come to His temple
- D&C 38:7–9, Christ is in the midst of the Saints and they will soon see Him
- D&C 45:17–21, Temple of Jerusalem, destruction

- D&C 84:1–5, The temple in Missouri
- D&C 88:119–126, Saints are to establish a house of prayer
- D&C 88:127–141, Order of the School of the Prophets
- D&C 95, Saints are to build temples
- D&C 97:10–19, Purpose of the temple is set forth
- D&C 105:31–36, Elders are to receive endowment
- D&C 107:53–57, Adam-ondi-Ahman
- D&C 109, Dedication of the Kirtland Temple
- D&C 110, Visions of Joseph Smith and Oliver Cowdery in Kirtland Temple
- D&C 115:7–16, Saints commanded to build a temple in Far West
- D&C 116, Adam-ondi-Ahman
- D&C 124:49–51, Saints excused from building Jackson County temple
- D&C 124:22–28, Saints commanded to build a temple in Nauvoo
- D&C 124:29–36, Baptisms for the dead
- D&C 124:37–44, The Lord's people always build temples
- D&C 127:5–12, What is bound on earth is bound in heaven
- D&C 128:1–4, What is bound on earth is bound in heaven
- D&C 130, Celestialized earth
- D&C 131:1–4, Celestial marriage
- D&C 131:5–6, Eternal life
- D&C 132, Celestial marriage, Joseph Smith given power to seal on earth and in heaven
- D&C 137, Joseph Smith's vision (while in the Kirtland Temple) of the heavenly temple
- Abraham Facsimile 2, A hypocephalus with temple notes
- Moses 7:3–4, Enoch sees the Lord

THREE TIMES A YEAR

God established several Israelite festivals through His prophet Moses; men, women, and children participated in these festivals. These festivals were called "feasts of the Lord, even holy convocations" (Lev. 23:4). Some of the festivals serve as prophecies of future events, including events that pertain to Jesus Christ, His atoning sacrifice, Resurrection, and His dealings with humankind. For instance, Passover featured a number of symbols that pointed to Jesus's atoning sacrifice; the Day of Atonement focused on Jesus's Atonement; and Firstfruits anticipated Jesus's Resurrection, wherein He was the firstfruits of the Resurrection.

Furthermore, the Mosaic law required Israelite males to present themselves at the tabernacle or temple ("appear before the Lord God") at least three times a year. "Three times in a year shall all thy males appear before the Lord thy God in the place which he shall choose; in the feast of unleavened bread [Passover], and in the feast of weeks, and in the feast of tabernacles" (Deut. 16:16; see also Ex. 23:14, 23; 34:23). Three times was the minimum; some Israelites visited the temple more frequently. Wives and children also visited the temple with their husbands and fathers.

With regard to temple attendance in our day, President Russell M. Nelson spoke to men and women, "Our need to be in the temple on a regular basis has never been greater. . . . If you have reasonable access to a temple, I urge you to find a way to make an appointment regularly with the Lord—to be in His holy house—then keep that appointment with exactness and joy. I promise you that the Lord will bring the miracles He knows you need as you make sacrifices to serve and worship in His temples."[1]

THRONE

The significance and status of the Lord's throne in the temple setting cannot be overstated. In the tabernacle, the throne was located in the Holy of Holies, called the mercy seat, or "the throne of grace" (Heb. 4:16). This throne was a focal point of the Atonement. On either side of the mercy seat was a cherub; thus Isaiah wrote, "O Lord of hosts, God of Israel, that dwellest [or, sits] between the cherubims" (Isa. 37:16; see also 2 Sam. 6:2).

---

1. Nelson, "Becoming Exemplary Latter-day Saints," 114.

God's throne is also located in the temple of heaven. God possesses and sits upon the throne, which is at the center of activity in the temple in heaven (see Rev. 3:21; 4:2–3, 9–10; 5:7, 13; 6:16; 7:10; 12:5; 19:4; 22:1, 3). The throne is the source of lightnings, thunderings, and voices (see Rev. 4:5).[1] Isaiah's vision of "the Lord sitting upon a throne, high and lifted up, and his train filled the temple" (Isa. 6:1) was a vision of the temple in heaven. Similarly, Joseph Smith wrote of God's "blazing throne" in the celestial kingdom, "whereon was seated the Father and the Son" (D&C 137:1, 3).

Exalted Saints are granted the privilege of sitting with Jesus Christ on His throne: "To him that overcometh will I grant to sit with me in my throne, even as I also overcame, and am set down with my Father in his throne" (Rev. 3:21). Compare what Enoch said to God: "Thou hast made me, and given unto me a right to thy throne, and not of myself, but through thine own grace" (Moses 7:59). Joseph Smith referred to "the throne of eternal power" when he wrote that the righteous are "to inherit the same power, the same glory and the same exaltation, until you arrive at the station of a God, and ascend the throne of eternal power, the same as those who have gone before."[2]

TOWERS

Several temples feature one or more towers. For example, the Cochabamba Bolivia, Oakland California, and Provo City Center Temples feature four corner towers together with a prominent central tower; the Salt Lake Temple has six towers; and the Manti and Logan Utah Temples each have two chief towers. Towers have multiple symbolic significances:

(1) With regard to the six towers of the Salt Lake Temple, President

---

1. Adapted from Parry and Parry, *Understanding the Book of Revelation*, 57–58.
2. *Teachings of Presidents of the Church: Joseph Smith*, 222.

Brigham Young explained, "There will be three towers on the east, representing the President and his two Counselors; also three similar towers on the west representing the Presiding Bishop and his two Counselors; the towers on the east the Melchisedek priesthood, those on the west the Aaronic priesthood. The center towers will be higher than those on the sides, and the west towers a little lower than those on the east end."[3]

Six towers of the Salt Lake Temple; the three to the east are higher than the three to the west.

Similar to those of the Salt Lake Temple, the east tower of both the Logan (170 feet) and Manti (179 feet) temples are more prominent in height than the west towers (Logan 165 feet, Manti 169 feet).[4] And once again, the east towers of these two temples signify the Melchizedek Priesthood and the west the Aaronic Priesthood.

(2) Metaphorically, God Himself is our "high tower" (2 Sam. 22:3; Ps. 144:2)! He is "a strong tower from the enemy" (Ps. 61:3; see also Prov. 18:10); and "the name of the Lord is a strong tower" (Prov. 18:10; see also D&C 97:20). As a mighty tower, He has an exalted vantage point and perfect view of the happenings below; He also has the power to protect us from all categories of armies and marauders, whether they be evil spirits or mortal enemies. Like the towers of old that stood high above cities, villages, and castles—God (as a high tower) protects Zion's inhabitants from evil and other destructive powers.

---

3. Young, cited in Ward, "Who Designed the Temple?" 578–79; spelling in original.
4. Olsen, *Logan Temple*, 122.

TRUMPETS AND TRUMPET STONES

Anciently, the blowing of ram's horns announced holy days and convocations associated with temples and temple worship (see Lev. 23:23–25; Num. 29:1–6). Correspondingly, the Lord commanded Moses to make two special silver trumpets, which were sounded at various sacred events that took place at the temple (see Num. 10:3, 10).

In the latter days, images of trumpets are featured on various temples, including the Nauvoo Illinois Temple, which has two trumpets situated above each of the sunstone images on the temple's exterior. The first Nauvoo Temple featured a weather vane with an angel blowing a trump. This image, perhaps, is reminiscent of the most iconic trumpet image affiliated with latter-day temples—the one held by Moroni, which is represented with the statue that stands atop temples.

In the scriptures, a trumpet signals the declaration of an important event (see Alma 29:1; Rev. 1:10; D&C 88:105–6). The trumpets of latter-day temples sound the coming forth of the gospel; additionally, the trumpets call us to attend the temple.

UNIVERSITY OF THE LORD

Each temple constitutes the Lord's university. Ezra Taft Benson taught that the laws and ordinances "were given by revelation and are comprehended by revelation. It is for this reason that one of the Brethren has referred to the temple as the 'university of the Lord.'"[1]

VEIL OF THE TEMPLE

This entry will refer to the veils of the tabernacle and Herod's temple. *Tabernacle's two sacred veils.* The tabernacle featured two veils (see

---

1. *The Teachings of Ezra Taft Benson*, 252.

Ex. 26:31–37), both of which consisted of elaborate and fine fabrics and featured the colors blue, purple, and scarlet. The aesthetic beauty of the veils must have been magnificent. Expert spinners, artisans, embroiderers, and weavers—those "filled with wisdom of heart"—made these veils and other appurtenances of the temple (Ex. 35: 35; see also v. 25).

The "first" veil (Heb. 9:2), visible to women and men who were worshipping in the tabernacle's courtyard, separated the holy place from the courtyard. The "second veil" (Heb. 9:3) separated the Holy of Holies from the holy place (Ex. 26:33) and was visible only to priests and high priests. This veil was more elaborate than the first veil

(top) First (or outer) veil of the tabernacle of Moses, with laver.
(bottom) Holy place of tabernacle of Moses showing veil with two cherubs. Also showing is lampstand, table of shewbread, altar of incense, and high priest (mannequin).

and featured woven figures of cherubim (see Ex. 26:31; 36:35). While priests were permitted to enter the first veil, only the high priest could enter the second veil. If he entered at other times, he would die (see Lev. 16:2). Both veils served to conceal singularly sacred space from unauthorized eyes.

The second veil conveyed symbolism of great import, for the veil

Sacred scene, with a veil (with sacred geometric symbols on it), a hand (God's) reaching through the veil, an altar (with Melchizedek officiating), and other sacred symbols. Sant Apollinare Church, Ravenna, Italy.

signifies the flesh of Jesus Christ. The Apostle Paul wrote, "Having therefore, brethren, boldness to enter into the holiest [referring to the Holy of Holies] by the blood of Jesus [a reference to the atonement], by a new and living way, which he hath consecrated for us, through the veil, that is to say, his flesh" (Heb. 10:19–20). This image is extremely powerful! Inasmuch as the Holy of Holies represents the celestial kingdom, entering through the veil shows that the crucified Lord (the veil) stands between individuals and the presence of God (the celestial kingdom). Or, in other words, it is only through Christ and His atoning blood that one can enter into heaven.

The rending of Herod's temple veil. At the time of Jesus Christ's death, the veil of Herod's temple was torn into two pieces. "Jesus, when he had cried again with a loud voice, yielded up the ghost. And, behold, the veil of the temple was rent in twain from the top to the bottom" (Matt. 27:50–51; see also Mark 15:37–38). The rending of the veil points to three items:

(1) For about 1,300 years, only certain males from the family of Levi could enter the temple building itself (the holy place and the Holy of

Holies). No females and no males from the other eleven tribes were permitted to enter, but the veil's rending signified that all—females and males from all twelve tribes—could now have full access to the temple and its blessings.

(2) The veil's rending also indicated that the law of Moses, with all of its rites and regulations, had been fulfilled. The law of Christ was now in effect, together with the blessings, ordinances, and power of the Melchizedek Priesthood (which had been removed because of wickedness; see D&C 84:19–27).

(3) The torn veil, in a very impactful manner, signified Jesus Christ's flesh, pierced and torn during the Crucifixion. His torn flesh (i.e., His Atonement), signaled that each of us (depending on our worthiness) can enter the Holy of Holies, which represents heaven.

VESSELS

Anciently, temple officiants employed scores and hundreds of vessels as they served God in the tabernacle and temple (see Ezra 1:7–11). These "holy vessels" (2 Chr. 5:5) were anointed with oil and sanctified (see Ex. 40:9). In one sacred ceremony, Moses "sprinkled" blood on "all the vessels of the ministry" (Heb. 9:21).

Symbolically, a holy vessel of the temple might be interpreted to represent a righteous woman or man. Mary, the mother of Jesus, is called "a precious and chosen vessel" (Alma 7:10). The Lord designated Paul "a chosen vessel" (Acts 9:15). Paul would later write that whosoever would "purge himself . . . shall be a vessel unto honour, sanctified, and meet for the master's use, and prepared unto every good work" (2 Tim. 2:21). Ministering angels declare "the word of Christ unto the chosen vessels of the Lord" (Moroni 7:31). And Moroni wrote, speaking of individuals, "Now I would that ye should remember that God has said that the inward vessel shall be cleansed first, and then shall the outer vessel be cleansed also" (Alma

60:23). Based on this last passage of scripture, President Ezra Taft Benson gave an important talk titled "Cleansing the Inner Vessel."[1]

VESTMENTS, SACRED

The first mention of sacred clothing exists in the Garden of Eden, where the Lord God made Adam and Eve (archetypes of all humankind) "coats of skins" and then He "clothed them" (Gen. 3:21). Three biblical passages, found mostly in Exodus and Leviticus and numbering a total of seventy-nine verses, refer to priestly garments (see Ex. 28:1–43; 39:1–31; Lev. 8:5–9). Beyond these key passages, sacred vestments are referred to in various scriptures throughout the standard works.

The priest's vestments consisted of four parts—headpiece,[2] sash, tunic (robe), and linen breeches (underwear).[3] The high priest wore eight vestments—the four belonging to the priest, plus the ephod (or "special apron," Ex. 39:2, note *a*), robe, breastplate, and golden plate of the headpiece (see Ex. 28:2–4). All temple vestments were deemed to be holy (see Ex. 28:2–3). On the Day of Atonement, the high priest dressed in white (see Ex. 28:2–3).

Apart from the important fact that all sacred vestments were emblems of power and served to identify the

The high priest's sacred vestments consisted of eight pieces (on a mannequin).

---

1. Benson, "Cleansing the Inner Vessel," 4–7.
2. The headpiece was like a "turban, bound cap"; see Exodus 28:4, footnote d.
3. The linen breeches were "undergarments of plain linen." Durham, *Exodus*, 385.

wearer's place in the sacred precinct, the vestments served three distinct functions: (1) a pragmatic or practical function, such as to protect the priests from the elements and to provide a high degree of modesty (Ex. 28:42 refers to breeches, which provided modesty to the wearer); (2) a spiritual function, pointing the wearers towards divine actions and attributes through a variety of symbols; and (3) an aesthetic function, conveying beauty to those who were privileged to behold them in the setting of the temple precinct (Ex. 28:2 refers to making holy garments "for glory and for beauty"). Anciently, a man named Aristeas saw and described the exceptional beauty of the high priest's sacred vestments:

> It was an occasion of great amazement to us when we saw [the high priest] Eleazar engaged on his ministry, and all the glorious vestments. . . . [The vestments'] appearance makes one awe-struck and dumbfounded: A man would think he had come out of this world into another one. I emphatically assert that every man who comes near the spectacle of what I have described will experience astonishment and amazement beyond words, his very being transformed by the hallowed arrangement on every single detail. (Letter of Aristeas, 96–99)[4]

God holds a high regard for orderliness, and His temple is a house of order; therefore, He revealed the sequence of vesting the high priest. In a sacred ceremony, Moses clothed the high priest (Aaron) as follows: Moses put the white tunic over Aaron's undergarments; then Moses wrapped the white sash around the tunic at the waist; after this, Moses placed the blue robe over the tunic and sash. Moses then placed the apron (ephod) on Aaron and girded the elegant sash on him. And then Moses placed the breastplate on Aaron and put the Urim and Thummim in the breastplate; after this, Moses placed the headpiece on Aaron's head; and last of all he placed the "golden plate, the holy crown" on the headpiece (Lev. 8:7–9).

---

4. Letter of Aristeas, 96–99, in Charlesworth, *The Old Testament Pseudepigrapha*, 2:19.

In ancient Israelite temples, God required temple priests to wear certain sacred vestments according to the specific temple zone wherein they were serving. That is to say, as temple officiants moved from profane to holy (temple) space, and again moved to a greater gradient of sacred space, they would change their vestments. Biblical scholar Gary Anderson explains:

> The vestments of the priest matched exactly those particular areas of the Temple to which he had access. . . . Each time the high priest moved from one gradient of holiness to another, he had to remove one set of clothes and put on another to mark the change. . . . (a) Outside the Tabernacle priests wear ordinary clothes. (b) When on duty in the Tabernacle, they wear four pieces of clothing whose material and quality of workmanship match that of the fabrics found on the outer walls of the courtyard (Exodus 28). (c) The High Priest wears those four pieces plus four additional ones—these added garments match the fabric of the Holy Chamber where he must go daily to tend the incense altar.[1]

Women and men who worship in our temples, too, wear certain vestments according to the specific temple zone wherein they are serving.

VESTMENTS, SACRED, ANTICIPATE THE RESURRECTION

Sacred vestments anticipate the Resurrection, when men and women will be "clothed" with an immortal body. The Apostle Paul used language suggesting that at the Resurrection we will *put on* immortality, similar to *putting on* clothing: "So when this corruptible *shall have put on*

---

1. Anderson, *The Genesis of Perfection*, 122–23.

incorruption, and this mortal *shall have put on* immortality, then shall be brought to pass the saying that is written, Death is swallowed up in victory" (1 Cor. 15:54; emphasis added; see also 2 Cor. 5:1–4).

The theme of being clothed with a body at the Resurrection continues in Latter-day Saint scriptures: "Wherefore, it must needs be an infinite atonement—save it should be an infinite atonement this corruption could not *put on* incorruption" (2 Ne. 9:7; emphasis added). Enos concluded his book by stating, "I rejoice in the day when my mortal shall *put on* immortality" (Enos 1:27; emphasis added; see also 2 Ne. 9:13–14). A passage in the Doctrine and Covenants refers to human "bones, which were to be *clothed upon* with flesh, to come forth again in the resurrection of the dead" (D&C 138:43; emphasis added).

Latter-day Saint prophets also refer to *clothe* and *clothed* in reference to the Resurrection.[2] Joseph Smith declared that "we have a knowledge that those we bury here. God bring them up again. clothed upon, & quckend [quickened] by the spirit of the great god."[3] So also President Thomas S. Monson speaks of the resurrected Christ being "clothed with an immortal body of flesh and bones."[4]

VESTMENTS, SACRED, POINT TO JESUS CHRIST AND HIS ATONEMENT

Sacred priestly vestments point directly to Jesus Christ and His Atonement. All things testify of Christ (see Moses 6:63; 2 Ne. 11:4), and the sacred vestments are no exception, containing Christ-centered types

---

2. See also, Talmage, *Articles of Faith*, 344–45.
3. "Discourse, 16 April 1843, as Reported by Willard Richards," p. [146–147], The Joseph Smith Papers, accessed March 27, 2019, https://www.josephsmithpapers.org/paper-summary/discourse-16-april-1843-as-reported-by-willard-richards/8. See also "History, 1838–1856, volume D-1 [1 August 1842–1 July 1843]," p. 1535, The Joseph Smith Papers, accessed March 27, 2019, https://www.josephsmithpapers.org/paper-summary/history-1838-1856-volume-d-1-1-august-1842-1-july-1843/178, and Lee, "Easter Morning," 7–8.
4. Monson, "An Invitation to Exaltation," 73.

Golden crown of high priest with words "Holiness to the Lord."

and symbols. Here are three examples—the high priest's crown, breastplate, and washing the blood from the clothing.

(1) Anciently, the high priest wore a pure gold "holy crown" on his forehead that read "Holiness to the Lord" (but written in Hebrew; see Ex. 39:30). The high priest wore this crown for two reasons: it served as a visual reminder that the Lord and His temple are most holy, and the crown "shall be upon Aaron's forehead, that Aaron may bear the iniquity of the holy things, which the children of Israel shall hallow in all their holy gifts; and it shall be always upon his forehead" (Ex. 28:38). This high priest's holy crown foreshadowed the divine mission of Jesus Christ, who would become the ultimate High Priest.

(2) The linen breastplate, attached to the high priest's ephod, bore twelve precious stones (see Ex. 28:15–30); the stones were attached to the face of the breastplate, each set in gold. The breastplate itself was an artistic work consisting of "fine twined linen," made of the colors scarlet, gold, blue, and purple. These colors together with the twelve precious stones presented a magnificently beautiful article. Isaiah identified the breastplate with righteousness, "For [the Lord] put on righteousness as a breastplate" (Isa. 59:17).

The names of the twelve tribes of Israel were inscribed on the stones, each name on an individual stone. Each of the stones, therefore, signifies one of the twelve tribes of Israel. Exodus 28:29 states, "Aaron shall bear the names of the children of Israel in the breastplate of judgment upon his heart, when he goeth in unto the holy place."

The high priest represents Jesus Christ, who symbolically carried the twelve tribes of Israel on His heart, the seat of emotion and love, into the temple and there made atonement for the tribes. The fact that the stones were precious indicates that the tribes were treasured unto the Lord. These things have direct application to each of us, especially when we learn of our tribal identification when we receive our patriarchal blessing.

(3) The washing of the blood of the vestments also speaks concerning Jesus and His Atonement. Sacrificing animals in the temple precinct was a bloody event, and blood often stained the priests' vestments. The stained garments and subsequent cleansing signifies our repenting, coming unto Christ, and washing our own garments "white through the blood of the Lamb" (Alma 13:11; see also Rev. 7:14). So how does

High priest's breastplate, featuring twelve precious stones with names of tribes (on a mannequin).

Onyx stone on left shoulder of high priest's vestment; six names of tribes of Israel were inscribed on each stone.

one wash his or her garments in Christ's blood? "No unclean thing can enter his kingdom . . . save it be those who have washed their garments in my blood, because of their faith, and the repentance of all their sins, and their faithfulness unto the end" (3 Ne. 27:19).

VESTMENTS, SACRED, SYMBOLISM OF

There are a number of symbols associated with sacred vestments (belonging to both ancient and modern temples).[1] As President Boyd K. Packer explained, "[The clothing worn inside the temple] . . . has great symbolic meaning."[2] Each piece of clothing points to divine actions and attributes through a variety of symbols, which can be broadly classified into several groups, four of which are dealt with here:

(1) The investiture of special vestments signifies one of the gestures of approach. When we approach sacred space, we change from our daily, ordinary clothing into special, set-apart, and sacred vestments. Such a change makes us new persons and puts us on a higher spiritual level.

(2) The act of putting on sacred vestments is related to putting on Christ and His holiness. The physical act of putting on sacred clothing is symbolically related to the spiritual act of *putting on* Christ and His holiness. This idea is underscored through translations of "put on" in both the Old and New Testaments. In the book of Leviticus, the Hebrew verb *lbsh* ("to put on") is used with various articles of sacred clothing, including linen garments, linen breeches, and the linen coat or tunic. For example, "The priest shall put on [*lbsh*] his linen garment, and his linen breeches shall he put upon [*lbsh*] his flesh" (Lev. 6:10; see also 16:4; 16:23–24, 32; 21:10).

For each of the passages of Leviticus listed above, the Greek

---

1. For various symbols associated with ancient temple vestments, see Nibley, *Temple and Cosmos*, 91–138, and Parry, "Ancient Sacred Vestments: Scriptural Symbols and Meanings," 219–39.
2. Packer, *The Holy Temple*, 72.

Septuagint translates the Hebrew *lbsh* with Greek inflections of *enduo* (from whence comes the temple-related term "endow"). Paul used this same verb in several New Testament passages that pertain to Jesus Christ and His Atonement, baptism, God's armor, and more.

- "Put ye on [*enduo*] the Lord Jesus Christ" (Rom. 13:14).
- "For as many of you as have been baptized into Christ have put on [*enduo*] Christ" (Gal. 3:27).
- "Ye have put off the old man . . . and have put on [*enduo*] the new man" (Col. 3:9–10).
- "Let us put on [*enduo*] the armour of light" (Rom. 13:12).
- "Put on [*enduo*] the whole armour of God" (Eph. 6:11).
- "That ye put on [*enduo*] the new man, which after God is created in righteousness and true holiness" (Eph. 4:24).

Evidently, the act of putting on sacred vestments is related to putting on Christ and His holiness.

(3) Sacred vestments are associated with salvation, righteousness, glory, and strength. While putting on sacred vestments calls to mind putting on Christ and accepting His Atonement, being clothed in sacred vestments also has other symbols attached to it. In the following passages, note how *salvation, righteousness, glory,* and *strength* are positioned with the words *clothed, linen,* and *garments*:

- *Salvation.* "He hath clothed me with the garments of salvation" (Isa. 61:10); "I will also clothe her priests with salvation" (Ps. 132:16).
- *Righteousness.* "Let thy priests be clothed with righteousness" (Ps. 132:9); "Righteousness shall be the girdle of his loins, and faithfulness the girdle of his reins" (Isa. 11:5); "For he put on righteousness as a breastplate" (Isa. 59:17); "He hath covered me with the robe of righteousness" (Isa. 61:10); "I put on righteousness, and it clothed me: my judgment was as a robe and a diadem" (Job 29:14); "the fine linen is the righteousness of saints" (Rev. 19:8).
1. *Glory.* "Thou shalt make holy garments for Aaron thy brother for

glory and for beauty" (Ex. 28:2; see also Ex. 28:40); "I was clothed upon with glory; And I saw the Lord" (Moses 7:3–4); "They shall see me . . . clothed with power and great glory" (D&C 45:44); "Clothed in the brightness of his glory" (D&C 65:5).

2. *Strength.* "Awake, awake! Clothe yourself with strength, O Zion; clothe yourself with your beautiful garments, O Jerusalem, the holy city" (Isa. 52:1, translation by author).

Men and women who worship in the temple who are clothed in sacred vestments are in actuality dressing themselves in *salvation, righteousness, glory,* and *strength.* Or, stated more forcefully, God gives *salvation, righteousness, glory,* and *strength* to those who wear sacred vestments.

Here are two examples of specific vestments that have symbolic values:

(a) *The Sash ("Girdle")*: God commanded priests and high priests when serving in the temple to wear sacred vestments, which included a sash (Hebrew: *'avnet*; KJV "girdle"). The priest's sash was white; the high priest's sash was embroidered or woven, a colorful sash of blue, purple, and scarlet (see Ex. 38:29).

The Lord's angels are sometimes depicted as wearing sashes. For

Representation of the high priest's sash.

example, the seven angels in the temple in heaven were "clothed in pure and white linen, and having their breasts girded with golden girdles [sashes]" (Rev. 15:6). The high rank of the angels is deduced from the golden girdles (or sashes) they wear, which are like that worn by Jesus Christ Himself (see Rev. 1:13). In addition, Daniel saw a heavenly being, a "man clothed in linen, whose loins were girded with fine gold of Uphaz" (Dan. 10:5).

The temple sash is associated with strength, referring to spiritual rather than physical strength. One passage states, "I will clothe him with thy robe, and strengthen him with thy girdle [sash]" (Isa. 22:21). And Psalm 18:32 reads, "It is God that girdeth me with strength" (see also Ps. 18:39; Prov. 31:17).

(b) *Robes*: Priestly officiants who served in the tabernacle and Solomon's temple wore robes, which were designated "holy" and which were part of the assemblage of sacred vestments (Ex. 28:4). Also, those who dwell in the temple in heaven will be dressed in white robes, which are made white through the Lamb's blood (see Rev. 7:9, 13, 14; see also 1 Ne. 12:10–11; Alma 5:21; Morm. 9:6).

The priestly robe could be interpreted to signify righteousness, or, more specifically, the righteousness of the person who wears it. Various scriptures refer to the "robe of righteousness." Jacob spoke of the righteous "being clothed with purity, yea, even with the robe of righteousness" (2 Ne. 9:14). Isaiah rejoiced, saying, "God . . . hath clothed me with the garments of salvation, he hath covered me with the robe of righteousness" (Isa. 61:10); also, "That our garments may be pure, that we may be clothed upon with robes of righteousness" (D&C 109:76).

(4) Vestments and clothing sometimes symbolize the person who wears them. A number of scriptural passages contain symbolic implications that sacred vestments represent the wearer of the vestments or clothing. For example, the expression "keep your garments spotless" (Alma 7:25) suggests "keep yourself spotless," and one who is "clothed with purity" and wears "the robe of righteousness" (2 Ne. 9:14) is one who is both pure and

righteous. The term *garments* in the following passage symbolically refers to the person who wears them: "For there can no man be saved except his garments are washed white; yea, his garments must be purified until they are cleansed from all stain, through the blood of him of whom it has been spoken by our fathers, who should come to redeem his people from their sins" (Alma 5:21). In other words, the redeemed person has to be washed, purified, and cleansed from all stain by the accepting the atoning blood of Jesus Christ.

The following account of Joseph F. Smith reinforces the idea that the garments represent the person that wears them. While serving as a young missionary, Joseph F. Smith had a vision that provided him with great confidence. He wrote, "I was hurrying as fast as I could. . . . I turned aside quickly and went into the bath and washed myself clean. I opened up this little bundle that I had, and there was a pair of white, clean garments, . . . I put them on. Then I rushed to what appeared to be a great opening, or door. I knocked and the door opened, and the man who stood there was the Prophet Joseph Smith. He looked at me a little reprovingly, and the first words he said: 'Joseph, you are late.' Yet I took confidence and said:

"'Yes, but I am clean—I am clean!'

"He clasped my hand and drew me in, then closed the great door."[1]

There is a direct correlation in this account of Joseph F. Smith washing himself clean, putting on clean, white garments, and then informing the Prophet, "I am clean—I am clean!"

During a severe illness, Lorenzo Snow had a singular experience that pertains to being clothed at the Resurrection. He related the following vision: "My spirit seems to have left the world and introduced into that of [the temple of heaven]. I heard a voice calling me by name saying 'he is worthy, he is worthy, take away his filthy garments.' My cloths [clothes] were then taken off piece by piece and a voice said 'let him be clothed, let

---

1. Smith, *Life of Joseph F. Smith*, 445–47.

him be clothed.' Immediately I found a celestial body gradually growing upon me untill [until] at length I found myself crowned with all its glory and power."[2]

VESTMENTS, SACRED, WORN BY GOD, ANGELS, AND REDEEMED SOULS

When priestly officiants wore sacred vestments, they emulated celestial persons—God, angels, and redeemed souls—who wear sacred vestments. A number of scriptural passages convey the concept that the resurrected Jesus Christ wears sacred vestments, as do angels and redeemed souls. In this manner, the priestly officiants served as types and shadows of heavenly beings; they wore sacred vestments in anticipation of the time when they would reside in the temple of heaven wearing similar eternal vestments.

The Lord: When John the Revelator envisioned Jesus Christ in the setting of the temple of heaven, Jesus was clothed in sacred vestments (see Rev. 1:13; see also D&C 76:108). In this vision, the resurrected Lord dons the vestments of a priest, with a robe and sash (girdle) (see Ex. 28:4; 39:29).

Angels: There are scriptural accounts that portray the Lord's angels wearing sacred vestments, including robes, linen, girdles (sashes), or crowns. For example, the seven angels who will come out of the temple in heaven will be "clothed in pure and white linen, and having their breasts girded with golden girdles" (Rev. 15:6). The angels' golden girdles (sashes) recall the golden girdle (sash) of Jesus Christ, as described in Revelation 1:13; see also the statements by Brigham Young, Wilford Woodruff, and George Q. Cannon,[3] and Daniel (Dan 10:5; 12:6–7).

Exalted Saints: The scriptures provide several details regarding the

---
2. Beecher, "The Iowa Journal of Lorenzo Snow," 269; spelling has been modernized.
3. Recorded in Wilford Woodruff, January 2, 1854, Journals and Papers, 1828–1898; Wilford Woodruff, *The Deseret Weekly* 38 (March 23, 1889): 390; and Cannon, "Reports Concerning the Saints," *JD* 22:289.

sacred apparel of those who dwell in the temple of heaven. They are "arrayed in white robes" (Rev. 7:13; see also Rev. 3:5; 7:13); they are "clothed in white raiment; and they had on their heads crowns of gold" (Rev. 4:4). Other celestial beings will also wear white linen, robes, or other sacred clothing (see Rev. 19:8, 14; D&C 109:75–76). Latter-day Saint prophets and apostles have provided several accounts that pertain to the dress of celestial persons.

VICARIOUS WORK FOR THE DEAD

Vicarious work for the dead, which is directly linked to our temples, constitutes a grand and prodigious undertaking. In fact, President Boyd K. Packer provides us with a glimpse as to the greatness of this endeavor: "We can build those thousands of temples and we can redeem our dead by the thousands and tens of thousands and millions and billions and tens of billions. We have not yet moved to the edge of the light."[1] Our prophets and apostles have made several doctrinal statements regarding the great and eternal significance of vicarious work for the dead. A few of the teachings are as follows:

(1) *Work for the dead started after Jesus's death and Resurrection.* This means that work on behalf of the dead was not conducted in the tabernacle, Solomon's temple, or any other temple before the death of Jesus Christ. Several authorities have discussed this matter, including Joseph Fielding Smith, who stated, "Until the Son of God had finished his preparations for the salvation of man and to bring to pass the resurrection of the dead, there could be no ordinance or labor of any kind pertaining to the resurrection and redemption of mankind that could be performed for the dead."[2]

(2) *Vicarious work testifies of Jesus Christ and His Atonement.* Elder D. Todd Christofferson elucidates the manner in which work for the dead

---

1. Tate, *Boyd K. Packer: A Watchman on the Tower*, 203.
2. Smith, *Answers to Gospel Questions*, 5:94–95.

The Manti Utah Temple.

"constitutes as powerful a statement as we can make concerning [Jesus Christ's] divine character and mission." He stated, work for the dead "testifies, first, of Christ's Resurrection; second, of the infinite reach of His Atonement; third, that He is the sole source of salvation; fourth, that He has established the conditions for salvation; and, fifth, that He will come again. . . . By identifying our ancestors and performing for them the saving ordinances they could not themselves perform, we are testifying of the infinite reach of the Atonement of Jesus Christ. Christ 'died for all.'"[3]

(3) *Those doing vicarious work for the dead become "Saviors on Mount Zion"* (Obadiah 21). Many Church authorities have spoken on this topic. Joseph Smith taught, "But how are they to become Saviors on Mount Zion by building their temples erecting their Baptismal fonts & going forth & receiving all the ordinances, Baptisms, Confirmations, washings anointings ordinations, & sealing powers upon our heads, in behalf of all our progenitors who are *dead* & redeem them . . . & herein is the chain that

---

3. Christofferson, "The Redemption of the Dead and the Testimony of Jesus," 10.

binds the hearts of the fathers to the Children, & the Children to the Fathers."¹

(4) *Vicarious work "approaches" the vicarious sacrifice of Jesus.* Vicarious work that is conducted in temples is a form of sacrifice itself—a sacrifice of both time and means. As President Gordon B. Hinckley expressed: "I think that vicarious work for the dead more nearly approaches the vicarious sacrifice of the Savior Himself than any other work of which I know. It is given with love, without hope of compensation, or repayment or anything of the kind. What a glorious principle."²

(5) *Temple work is our "greatest responsibility."* In 1844, the Prophet Joseph Smith made this solemn declaration: "The greatest responsibility in this world that God has laid upon us, is to seek after our dead. The Apostle says, 'they without us cannot be made perfect' [see Hebrews 11:40]."³

(6) *It is a manifestation of Jesus's perfect grace, love, and mercy.* The temple is the quintessential place of grace—the grace that is perfected and available because of Jesus Christ's Atonement. The temple is also a manifestation of His matchless love and mercy, which extends to all of God's children, not just those who have the privilege and opportunity of learning about the plan of salvation during mortality.

(7) *"For we have been commanded."* President Boyd K. Packer wrote the following dialogue (regarding work for the dead) between two anonymous individuals: "'Strange,' one may say. It *is* passing strange. It is transcendent and supernal. The very nature of the work [for the dead] testifies that He is our Lord, that baptism is essential, that He taught the truth.

---

1. "Discourse, 21 January 1844, as Reported by Wilford Woodruff," p. [182], The Joseph Smith Papers, accessed March 27, 2019, https://www.josephsmithpapers.org/paper-summary /discourse-21-january-1844-as-reported-by-wilford-woodruff/2.
2. "Excerpts from Recent Addresses of President Gordon B. Hinckley," 73.
3. "History, 1838–1856, volume E-1 [1 July 1843–30 April 1844]," p. 1975, The Joseph Smith Papers, accessed March 27, 2019, https://www.josephsmithpapers.org/paper-summary /history-1838-1856-volume-e-1-1-july-1843-30-april-1844/347.

"And so the question may be asked, 'You mean you are out to provide baptism for all who have ever lived?'

"And the answer is simply, 'Yes.' For we have been commanded to do so.

"'You mean for the entire human family? Why, that is impossible. If the preaching of the gospel to all who are living is a formidable challenge, then the vicarious work for all who have ever lived is impossible indeed.'

"To that we say, 'Perhaps, but we shall do it anyway.'"[4]

VIOLATING SACRED SPACE

Ancient temples were most holy to the Lord; therefore, He revealed strict rules regarding approaching and accessing them. For instance, non-Levite Israelites were forbidden to come near to the tabernacle structure itself, "lest they bear sin, and die" (Num. 18:22). Also, the Lord commanded, "Thus shall ye separate the children of Israel from their uncleanness; that they die not in their uncleanness, when they defile my tabernacle that is among them" (Lev. 15:31).

And again, when the priests came to the tabernacle's altar, "They shall wash their hands and their feet, that they die not" (Ex. 30:21). When the sons of Kohath packed up and carried the tabernacle, they were commanded, "They shall not touch any holy thing, lest they die" (Num. 4:15).

The scriptures offer multiple examples of individuals who violated sacred space or overstepped divine directives regarding things that were holy:

(1) *Uzzah*: When oxen shook the ark of the covenant, Uzzah attempted to steady it, so "God smote him . . . and there he died by the ark of God" (2 Sam. 6:6–7; see also 1 Chr. 13:9–10).

(2) *Hophni and Phinehas*: Hophni and Phinehas disgraced the priestly office; first, they committed an extremely gross sin, in that "they lay with

---
4. Packer, "The Redemption of the Dead," 97.

the women that assembled at the door of the tabernacle of the congregation" (1 Sam. 2:22); and second, they inappropriately partook of the sacrificial meat in the tabernacle (see 1 Sam. 2:13–17). In the end, they were killed in a battle against the Philistines, in fulfillment of prophecy (see 1 Sam. 2:27–34; 4:11).

(3) *Men who gazed inside the ark*: The Lord "smote the men of Beth-shemesh, because they had looked into the ark of the Lord, even he smote of the people fifty thousand and threescore and ten men" (1 Sam. 6:19).

(4) *The Philistines*: A series of disasters came upon the Philistines because they stole the ark of the covenant—"the hand of the Lord was against the city with a very great destruction" (1 Sam. 5:6–12).

(5) *King of Tyre*: The king of Tyre desecrated sacred space, so the Lord destroyed him by the flaming sword of the cherubim (such is the implication; see Ezek. 28:11–19).

(6) *Nadab and Abihu*: Aaron and Elisheba's two oldest sons were slain for making an unauthorized offering ("strange fire") in the temple (Lev. 10:1–2).

(7) *King Uzziah*: God smote Uzziah with leprosy for his unlawful trespass into Solomon's temple (see 2 Chr. 26:17–20). Uzziah remained a leper and was forced to live in a place reserved for lepers until his death.

(8) *Lucifer*: When Lucifer violated sacred space, he was halted by the cherubs' flaming, revolving sword: "How art thou *cut down* to the ground" (Isa. 14:13–19).

WASHING WITH WATER, FOR SACRIFICIAL ANIMALS

Priests washed the "inwards and the legs" of certain sacrificial animals with water in order to cleanse the animal for the sacrifice (Lev. 1:9, 13; 8:21). This act of washing with water brings to mind the ceremonial washings of individuals.

WASHING WITH WATER

The Doctrine and Covenants refers to ceremonial "washings." The Lord stated, "Therefore, verily I say unto you, that your anointings, and your washings, and your baptisms for the dead . . . are ordained by the ordinance of my holy house" (D&C 124:39; see also 124:37; 138:58–59). The Bible, too, presents several references to ceremonial washings with water. "When they go into the tabernacle of the congregation, they shall wash with water, that they die not" (Ex. 30:20; see also 40:12). The book of Hebrews mentions "divers washings" (Heb. 9:10) and "our bodies washed with pure water" (Heb. 10:22).

Ceremonial washings with water took place in the tabernacle courtyard.

Washings are attached to multiple symbolisms; as President Boyd K. Packer stated, "Associated with the endowment are washings and anointings—mostly symbolic in nature, but promising definite, immediate blessings as well as future blessings."[1] Washings denote the cleansing of the soul from sin and filth by the power of the Atonement. The Psalmist wrote, "Wash me throughly from mine iniquity, and cleanse me from my sin" (Ps. 51:2). As President Gordon B. Hinckley summarized, "Temple blessings include our washings and anointings that we may be clean before the Lord."[2] Ancient priests used water for their washings, but the water symbolized Jesus's blood; thus John the Revelator wrote, Jesus Christ has "washed us from

---

1. Packer, *The Holy Temple*, 154.
2. As cited in Nelson, "Personal Preparation for Temple Blessings," 34.

Certain temples give prominence to water features on the temple grounds, such as this water feature belonging to the Oakland California Temple.

our sins in his own blood" (Rev. 1:5). Jesus, then, is the one who conducts the washing, and He does so through the power of the Atonement.

WATER

Water serves a multitude of ceremonial purposes in the temple environment:

- The tabernacle laver contained water, which was used for ceremonial washings of the priests (Ex. 40:12).
- The large molten sea of the temple of Solomon, which stood on the backs of twelve oxen, served temple officiants (1 Kgs. 7:23–25).
- Members of the priesthood washed certain portions of select sacrificial animals (Lev. 8:21; see also Lev. 1:9, 13).
- Priests used water to wash blood that had splattered on their garments.
- In the New Testament period, priesthood officiants conducted baptisms for the dead (1 Cor. 15:29).
- "Living water" was utilized in a number of temple ceremonies; "for an unclean person they shall take of the ashes of the burnt heifer of purification for sin, and running water [the Hebrew reads, "living water"] shall be put thereto in a vessel" (Num. 19:17; see also Lev. 14:5, 6, 50–52; 15:13).
- Ezekiel 47 prophesies that water will issue from Jerusalem's future temple and heal the waters of the Dead Sea (Ezek. 47:1, 8, 12).

Perhaps most significantly, water symbolically cleanses individuals from sin. The symbolic value of the water points to Jesus Christ, who is "the fountain of living waters" (Jer. 17:13; see also 2:13). Compare also Jesus's teachings in the New Testament, where He employed the expression "living water" (John 4:10–11; 7:38).

WOMEN AND THE ANCIENT TEMPLE

During the many centuries that the Mosaic Law prevailed in ancient Israel, only Aaron and his male progeny were authorized to enter ancient Israelite temples. Although women and men from the other eleven tribes could not enter the temple itself, they had other sacred privileges. With regard to Israelite women during this time period:

(1) Women had access to the temple court area.

(2) Women donated jewelry (earrings, rings, bracelets, jewels of gold) for the maintenance of the temple and for the purchase of items to make the holy garments (see Ex. 35:21, 29).

(3) Women donated their mirrors, which were set in frames of brass, to the temple; the brass was utilized to build the laver of brass (see Ex. 38:8).

(4) Women spun textiles of blue, purple, scarlet and linen (see Ex. 35:25–26) for the priestly vestments as well as the curtains and veils.[1]

(5) A female could become a Nazarite, one who made sacred vows and was consecrated (Hebrew: *Nazarite*, "consecrated one") before the Lord (see Num. 6:1–21). A Nazarite vow permitted non-priests to become consecrated and to have a role that is somewhat similar to that of a priest. At the conclusion of the period of the vow, the Nazarite was presented at the tabernacle, where she or he offered burnt, sin, and peace offerings (under the direction of a priest) together with a basket of unleavened bread and other items. The Nazarite then shaved her or his head at the door of the tabernacle, and burned the hair in the sacrificial fire.

(6) A mother could vow to make her child a Nazarite (see 1 Sam. 1:11–28).

(7) A woman could bring sacrifices to the temple (see 1 Sam. 1:24;

---

1. Ariel, *The Holy Temple in Jerusalem*, 209.

Luke 2:24); and according to Rabbi Yisrael Ariel, women were "even obligated to slaughter the Passover offering, unless a family member does it instead. The women would accompany their sacrifices with prayer, confession, repentance, prostration and thanks to God for His kindnesses."[2]

(8) Women made vows at the temple (see 1 Sam. 1:11).

(9) Women prayed at the temple (see 1 Sam. 1:10–13). On one solemn occasion many men of Judah, "with their little ones, their wives, and their children" (2 Chr. 20:1–13) gathered to the temple court to pray.

(10) According to ancient, non-scriptural sources, women sometimes entered the court of Herod's temple to console others who were mourning, downtrodden, or seeking comfort at the temple.[3]

(11) Women, as well as men, brought firstfruits to the temple, presented them to a priest, and then worshipped the Lord (see Deut. 26:5–10;[4] see also entry "Hannah, Anna, and Mary").

(12) It was a matter of dispute whether or not women could lay their hands on the heads of sacrificial animals (see entry "Hands, Laying on of, on Sacrificial Animals"). Some early rabbinic authorities argued on their behalf while others ruled that they could not do so.[5]

(13) Women participated in the Passover, including going to the temple as well as partaking of the Passover offering.

WOMEN THEN, WOMEN NOW

From Moses to John the Baptist (for more than a millennium), only a relatively few Israelites were authorized to enter the temple, with its

---

2. Ariel, *The Holy Temple in Jerusalem*, 201.
3. Ariel, *The Holy Temple in Jerusalem*, 203.
4. Ariel, *The Holy Temple in Jerusalem*, 211.
5. Ariel, *The Holy Temple in Jerusalem*, 205.

holy place and Holy of Holies. In fact, only males, of a certain age, of a single family (Aaron and his male descendants), of a single tribe of Israel (Levites), could enter the temple. In total, a very small percentage of ancient Israel were permitted to enter the temple during this period of time. Furthermore, only those same relatively few Israelites were permitted to participate in various temple rituals, such as washings, anointings, and wearing the sacred vestments. Members of the other eleven tribes—both males and females—were not permitted to enter the temple, nor were they permitted to participate in temple rituals or wear sacred vestments. Males and females of the other tribes were restricted to the temple court.

Why such restrictions on who was permitted to enter the temple and participate in temple rituals? After the Lord brought ancient Israel out of Egypt with great power and many miracles, He declared, "ye shall be unto me a kingdom of priests, and an holy nation" (Ex. 19:6). *Kingdom* here deals with kings *and* queens and *priests* pertains to priesthood. Note that Hebrew masculine plural nouns may also pertain to females (sometimes, the masculine plural is used when both males and females are present). Thus the plural *priests* (Hebrew: *kohanim*) is also relevant to females. But Israel rejected the eternal blessing of becoming a "kingdom of priests"; rather, "they hardened their hearts and could not endure [God's] presence.... Therefore, [the Lord in his wrath] took Moses out of their midst, and the Holy [Melchizedek] Priesthood also; And the lesser [Aaronic] priesthood continued . . . which the Lord in his wrath caused to continue with the house of Aaron among the children of Israel until John" (D&C 84:24–27).

Things changed after John the Baptist, and again with the Restoration of the gospel through the Prophet Joseph Smith. Now, in our dispensation, all worthy women and men are authorized to enter the temple equally! Also, women and men engage in rituals such as washings and anointings, and they wear sacred vestments. Both men and women have priestly roles, pray at the altar, and enter various holy places in the temple.

Women, together with men, now participate fully in the rituals, covenants, and ordinances. When they do so, they are exercising priesthood power, as President Russell M. Nelson clarified while speaking to the women of the Church: "When you are set apart to serve in a calling under the direction of one who holds priesthood keys—such as your bishop or stake president—you are given priesthood authority to function in that calling. Similarly, in the holy temple you are authorized to perform and officiate in priesthood ordinances every time you attend. Your temple endowment prepares you to do so."[1]

In our dispensation, the Lord's desire that His covenant people become a "kingdom of priests" is in full effect. John's statement, the Lamb "hast made us unto our God kings and priests: and we shall reign on the earth" (Rev. 5:10; see also Rev. 1:6; 20:6), also applies to us, as does Peter's: "Ye are a chosen generation, a royal priesthood, an holy nation" (1 Pet. 2:9). Joseph Smith's words speak to women and men: "Those holding the fullness of the Melchizedek Priesthood are kings and priests of the Most High God, holding the keys of power and blessings."[2] And also, "men may receive their endowments and be made kings and priests unto the Most High God."[3]

---

1. Nelson, "Spiritual Treasures," 78.
2. Joseph Smith, *HC* 5:555.
3. Joseph Smith, *Teachings of Presidents of the Church: Joseph Smith*, 418.

BIBLIOGRAPHY

Anderson, Gary A. *The Genesis of Perfection: Adam and Eve in Jewish and Christian Imagination*. London: John Knox Press, 2001.

Anderson, James H. "The Salt Lake Temple." *Contributor* 14 (April 1893): 243–303.

Angell, Truman O. *Autobiography of Truman Osborn Angell, Sr.* 1884.

———. "The Salt Lake City Temple." *Millennial Star* 36, no. 18 (May 5, 1874): 273–275.

Apple Dictionary Version 2.2.1 (143.1) © 2005–2011 Apple Inc. All Rights Reserved.

Ariel, Yisrael. *The Holy Temple of Jerusalem*. Jerusalem: Maggid Books, 2018.

Arrington, Leonard J. "Oliver Cowdery's Kirtland, Ohio, 'Sketch Book.'" *BYU Studies* 12, no. 4 (Summer 1972): 410–426.

Asay, Carlos E. "The Temple Garment: 'An Outward Expression of an Inward Commitment.'" *Ensign* 27 (August 1997): 18–23.

Ballard, M. Russell. "The Law of Sacrifice." *Ensign* 28 (October 1998): 6–13.

———. "Men and Women and Priesthood Power," *Ensign* 44 (September 2014): 28–33.

———. "Let Us Think Straight," Devotional, BYU Speeches (August 20, 2013), speeches.byu.edu.

Bednar, David A. "The Hearts of the Children Shall Turn." *Ensign* 41 (November 2011): 24–27.

———. "Honorably Hold a Name and Standing." *Ensign* 39 (May 2009): 97–100.

———. "Prepared to Obtain Every Needful Thing." *Ensign* 49 (May 2019): 101–04.

———. "Two Apostles Lead a Virtual Tour of the Rome Italy Temple: Elder Bednar and Elder Rasband explain a temple's purpose and promise." (Rome, Italy: The Church of Jesus Christ of Latter-day Saints, 2019), news release, 11 min.

Beecher, Maureen Ursenbach, ed. "The Iowa Journal of Lorenzo Snow." *BYU Studies* 24, no. 3 (Summer 1984): 261–73.

Benson, Ezra Taft. "Cleansing the Inner Vessel." *Ensign* 16 (May 1986): 4–7.

———. *The Teachings of Ezra Taft Benson*. Salt Lake City: Bookcraft, 1988.

———. "What I Hope You Will Teach Your Children about the Temple," *Ensign* 15 (August 1985): 6–10.

Benson, Ezra Taft, Gordon B. Hinckley, Thomas S. Monson, First Presidency Letter, 10 Oct. 1988, cited in Asay, Carlos E. "The Temple Garment: 'An Outward Expression of an Inward Commitment.'" *Ensign* 27 (August 1997): 18–23.

Bingham, Jean B. "The Temple Gives Us Higher Vision." *Ensign* 48 (January 2018): 34–39.

Brandt, Edward J. "Why are oxen used in the design of our temples' baptismal fonts?" *Ensign* 23 (March 1993): 54–55.

Brazil de Souza, Elias. *Toward a Theology of the Heavenly Sanctuary in the Hebrew Bible*. Verlag: VDM Verlag Dr. Müller, 2008.

Brinkerhoff, Val. "The Symbolism of the Beehive in the Latter-day Saint Tradition." *BYU Studies* 52, no. 2 (2013): 140–150.

Brown, Francis. S. R. Driver, and Charles A. Briggs. *A Hebrew and English Lexicon of the Old Testament*. Translated by Edward Robinson. Oxford: Clarendon Press, 1977.

Brown, Matthew B. "The Handclasp, the Temple, and the King." In *Temple Insights: Proceedings of the Interpreter Matthew B. Brown Memorial Conference,"The Temple on Mount Zion," 22 September 2012*. Edited by William J. Hamblin and David R. Seely, 5–9. Salt Lake City, UT: Eborn Books, 2014.

Brown, Matthew B. and Paul Thomas Smith. *Symbols in Stone: Symbolism on the Early Temples of the Restoration.* American Fork, UT: Covenant Communications, 1997.

Brown, William. *The Tabernacle: Its Priests and Its Services.* Peabody, MA: Hendrickson, 1996.

Calabro, David. "The Divine Handclasp in the Hebrew Bible and in Near Eastern Iconography." In *Temple Insights: Proceedings of the Interpreter Matthew B. Brown Memorial Conference, "The Temple on Mount Zion," 22 September 2012.* Edited by William J. Hamblin and David R. Seely, 83–97. Salt Lake City, UT: Eborn Books, 2014.

Calabro, David M. "Gestures of Praise: Lifting and Spreading the Hands in Biblical Prayer." In *Ascending the Mountain of the Lord: Temple, Praise, and Worship in the Old Testament* (2013 Sperry Symposium). Edited by Jeffrey R. Chadwick, Matthew J. Grey, and David Rolph Seely, 105–21. Provo, UT: Religious Studies Center, Brigham Young University; Salt Lake City: Deseret Book, 2013.

Cannon, George Q. "The Angels Who Visit Us." *Juvenile Instructor* 26, no. 2 (1891): 53–54.

———. *Gospel Truth: Discourses and Writings of President George Q. Cannon.* 2 vols. Edited by Jerreld L. Newquist. Salt Lake City: Deseret Book, 1974.

———. "The Logan Temple." *Millennial Star* (Nov. 12, 1877): 743.

Chadwick, Jeffrey R. "The Great Jerusalem Temple Prophecy: Latter-day Context and Likening unto Us." In *Ascending the Mountain of the Lord: Temple, Praise, and Worship in the Old Testament* (2013 Sperry Symposium). Edited by Jeffrey R. Chadwick, Matthew J. Grey, and David Rolph Seely, 367–83. Provo, UT: Religious Studies Center, Brigham Young University; Salt Lake City: Deseret Book, 2013.

Charlesworth, James H. ed. *The Old Testament Pseudepigrapha.* 2 vols. Garden City, NY: Doubleday, 1985.

Christofferson, D. Todd. "The Redemption of the Dead and the Testimony of Jesus." *Ensign* 40 (November 2000): 9–12.

Clarke, J. Richard. "The Temple—What It Means to You," *New Era* 23 (April 1993): 4–7.

Clawson, Clara L. "Pioneer Stake," *Woman's Exponent* 34, Nos. 2–3 (July and Aug. 1905): 14.

Compton, Todd M. "The Handclasp and Embrace as Tokens of Recognition." In vol. 1 of *By Study and Also by Faith: Essays in Honor of Hugh W. Nibley on the Occasion of His Eightieth Birthday.* Edited by John M. Lundquist and Stephen D. Ricks, 611–42. Salt Lake City: Deseret Book, 1990.

Cook, Quentin L. "See Yourself in the Temple." *Ensign* 46 (May 2016): 97–100.

"Coronation of the Czar." *New York Times* (April 5, 1896).

Cowan, Richard O. "Joseph Smith and the Restoration of Temple Service." In *Joseph Smith and the Doctrinal Restoration: The 34th Annual Sidney B. Sperry Symposium,* 109–22. Provo, UT: Religious Studies Center; Salt Lake City: Deseret Book, 2005.

———. "Latter-day Saint Temples as Symbols." *Journal of the Book of Mormon and Other Restoration Scripture* 21, no. 1 (2012): 2–11.

———. *Temples to Dot the Earth.* Salt Lake City: Bookcraft, 1989; paperback edition Springville, UT: Cedar Fort Inc., 1997; revised and enlarged Springville, UT: Cedar Fort, 2011.

———. "What Old Testament Temples Can Teach Us About Our Own Temple Activity." In *Ascending the Mountain of the Lord: Temple, Praise, and Worship in the Old Testament.* Edited by David R. Seely, Jeffry R. Chadwick, and Matthew J. Grey, 385–402. Salt Lake City: Deseret Book, 2013.

Cowley, Matthew. "The Sacred Triangle." *Improvement Era* 55 (December 1952): 916–917.

Cowley, Matthias F. *Wilford Woodruff.* Salt Lake City: Bookcraft, 1964.

Dalton, Elaine S. "Now Is the Time to Arise and Shine!" *Ensign* 42 (May 2012): 123–126.

Davies, J. G. "Architecture." In *The Encyclopedia of Religion.* Edited by Mircea Eliade, 1:382–392. 16 vols. New York, NY: Macmillan, 1993.

Dew, Sheri. "Are We Not All Mothers?" *Ensign* 31 (Nov. 2001): 96–98.

———. *Women and the Priesthood: What One Mormon Woman Believes.* Deseret Book: Salt Lake City, 2013.

Douglas, Mary. "Atonement in Leviticus." *Jewish Studies Quarterly* 1, no. 2 (1993–94): 109–30.

Draper, Richard D. and Donald W. Parry. "Seven Promises to Those Who Overcome: Aspects of Genesis 2–3 in the Seven Letters." In *The Temple in Time and Eternity*. Edited by Donald W. Parry and Stephen D. Ricks, 121–42. Provo, UT: Foundation for Ancient Research and Mormon Studies, 1999.

Durham, John I. *Word Biblical Commentary. Exodus*. Waco, TX: Word Books, 1982.

Eliade, Mircea. *Symbolism, the Sacred, and the Arts*. Edited by Diane Apostolos-Cappadona. New York: Crossroad, 1985.

England, Kathy. "The Washington D.C. Temple." *Ensign* 7 (October 1977): 88.

Faust, James E. "Who Shall Ascend into the Hill of the Lord?" *Ensign* 31 (August 2001): 2–5.

Featherstone, Vaughn J. *The Incomparable Christ: Our Master and Model*. Salt Lake City: Deseret Book, 1995.

Fetzer, Emil B. "Could you tell me a little about the history of our temple baptismal fonts?" *New Era* (March 1976): 26–28.

Freedman, R. David. "Woman, A Power Equal to Man: Translation of Woman as a 'Fit Helpmate' for Man is Questioned." *Biblical Archaeology Review* 9, no. 1 (Jan.–Feb. 1983): 56–58.

Gardner, Barbara M. "Connecting Daughters of God with His Priesthood Power." *Ensign* 49 (March 2019): 30–37.

Gaskill, Alonzo L. *Sacred Symbols: Finding Meaning in Rites, Rituals, and Ordinances*. Springville, UT: Bonneville Books, 2011.

Gong, Gerrit W. "Temple Mirrors of Eternity: A Testimony of Family." *Ensign* 40 (November 2010): 36–38.

Haight, David B. "Come to the House of the Lord." *Ensign* 22 (May 1992): 15–17.

———. "The Keys of the Kingdom." *Ensign* 10 (November 1980): 73–75.

———. "Symbol of Sacrifice, Monument to Life." *Ensign* 23 (October 1993): 9–11.

Hales, Robert D. "Blessings of the Priesthood." *Ensign* 25 (November 1995): 32–34.

Hamilton, C. Mark. *Nineteenth-Century Mormon Architecture and City Planning.* Oxford: Oxford University Press, 1995.

Haran, Menahem. *Temples and Temple-Service in Ancient Israel.* Winona Lake, IN: Eisenbrauns, 1985.

Hinckley, Gordon B. "Closing Remarks." *Ensign* 34 (November 2004): 104–5.

———. "The Cornerstones of Our Faith." *Ensign* 14 (November 1984): 50–53.

———. Dedicatory Prayer of the Johannesburg South Africa Temple, August 24, 1985.

———. "Excerpts from Recent Addresses of President Gordon B. Hinckley." *Ensign* 28 (January 1998): 72–73.

———. "'An Humble and a Contrite Heart.'" *Ensign* 30 (November 2000): 88–89.

———. "Of Missions, Temples, and Stewardship." *Ensign* 25 (November 1995): 51–54.

———. "'O That I Were an Angel, and Could Have the Wish of Mine Heart.'" *Ensign* 32 (November 2002): 4–6.

———. "Reverence and Morality." *Ensign* 17 (May 1987): 45–48.

———. "The Salt Lake Temple." *Ensign* 23 (March 1993): 2–6.

———. "Stay the Course—Keep the Faith." *Ensign* 25 (November 1995): 70–72.

———. *Teachings of Gordon B. Hinckley.* Salt Lake City: Deseret Book, 1997.

———. "This Great Millennial Year." *Ensign* 30 (November 2000): 67–71.

———. "We Look to Christ." *Ensign* 32 (May 2002): 90–92.

Holland, Jeffrey R. *Christ and the New Covenant: The Messianic Message of the Book of Mormon.* Salt Lake City: Deseret Book, 2006.

———. "Lessons from Liberty Jail." Devotional, BYU Speeches (September 7, 2008), 1–10.

———. "The Message, the Meaning, and the Multitude," *Ensign,* November 2019.

———. "President Thomas S. Monson: Man of Action, Man of Faith, Always 'on the Lord's Errand.'" *Ensign* 16 (February 1986): 10–17.

Holzapfel, Richard Neitzel, "Every Window, Every Spire 'Speaks of the Things of God.'" *Ensign* 23 (March 1993): 7–21.

Hunter, Howard W. *The Teachings of Howard W. Hunter*. Salt Lake City: Bookcraft, 1997.

Jenson, Andrew. *The Historical Record*. Salt Lake, Utah.

Journal of Discourses. 26 vols. London: Latter-day Saints' Book Depot, 1854–86.

Kikawada, Isaac M. "Two Notes on Eve." *Journal of Biblical Literature* 91, no. 1 (March 1972): 33–37.

Kimball, Heber C. "Address to My Children," In *Encyclopedia of Mormonism*. Edited by Daniel H. Ludlow, 4:1444. 5 vols. New York, NY: Macmillan, 1992.

Kimball, J. Golden. Conference Report (April 1915): 78–80.

Kimball, Spencer W. "Jesus of Nazareth." *Ensign* 14 (December 1984): 2–7.

———. "The Lord Expects His Saints to Follow the Commandments." *Ensign* 7 (May 1977): 4–7.

———. "Remarks and Dedication of the Fayette, New York, Buildings." *Ensign* 10 (May 1980): 54–59.

———. *The Teachings of Spencer W. Kimball*. Edited by Edward L. Kimball. Salt Lake City: Bookcraft, 1982.

———. "Things of Eternity–Stand We in Jeopardy?" *Ensign* 7 (January 1977): 3–7.

Koehler, Ludwig, and Walter Baumgartner. *The Hebrew and Aramaic Lexicon of the Old Testament*. Koninklijke Brill NV, Leiden, Cologne, New York 2000.

Korsak, Mary Phil. *At the Start: Genesis Made New: A Translation of the Hebrew Text*. New York, NY: Doubleday, 1993.

Kvam, Kristen E., Linda S. Schearing, and Valarie H. Ziegler, eds. *Eve and Adam: Jewish, Christian, and Muslim Readings on Genesis and Gender*. Bloomington, IN: Indiana University Press, 1999.

LDS Bible Dictionary.

Lee, Harold B. "Easter Morning—A Newness of Life," Deseret News, *Church News Section,* 19 April 1941, 7–8.

———. "Strengthen the Stakes of Zion." *Ensign* 3 (July 1973): 2–6.

Lundquist, John M. "C. G. Jung and the Temple: Symbols of Wholeness." In *C. G. Jung and the Humanities: Toward a Hermeneutics of Culture*. Edited by Karin Barnaby and Pellegrino D'Acierno, 113–23. Princeton, NJ: Princeton University Press, 1990.

———. *The Temple: Meeting Place of Heaven and Earth*. London: Thames and Hudson, 1993.

———. "What is a Temple? A Preliminary Typology." In *Temples of the Ancient World: Ritual and Symbolism*. Edited by Donald W. Parry, 83–117. Salt Lake City: Deseret Book, 1994.

Lyon, Jack M. *Understanding Temple Symbols Through Scripture, History, and Art*. Salt Lake City: Deseret Book, 2016.

Macfarlane, Roger. Professor in Classical Studies, Brigham Young University. Personal correspondence (May 18, 2016).

Marshall, Evelyn T. "Garments." In *Encyclopedia of Mormonism*. Edited by Daniel H. Ludlow, 2:534–35. 5 vols. New York, NY: Macmillan, 1992.

McConkie, Bruce R. *Doctrinal New Testament Commentary*. 3 vols. Salt Lake City: Bookcraft, 1965–73.

———. *Mormon Doctrine*. Salt Lake City, UT: Bookcraft, 1958.

———. *The Promised Messiah: The First Coming of Christ*. Salt Lake City: Deseret Book, 1978.

———. "The Promises Made to the Fathers (Genesis 12–36)." In *Studies in Scripture Vol. 3: The Old Testament: Genesis to 2 Samuel*. Edited by Kent P. Jackson and Robert L. Millet, 47–62. Salt Lake City, UT: Randall Book, 1985

———. "The Purifying Power of Gethsemane." *Ensign* 15 (May 1985): 9–11.

———. "The Three Pillars of Eternity." In *Brigham Young University 1981 Fireside and Devotional Speeches, 1981,* 27–32. Provo, UT: BYU Press, 1981.

McConkie, Joseph Fielding and Donald W. Parry. *A Guide to Scriptural Symbols*. Salt Lake City, UT: Bookcraft, 1990.

Monson, Thomas S. "The Holy Temple—a Beacon to the World." *Ensign* 41 (May 2011): 90–93.

———. "An Invitation to Exaltation." *Ensign* 18 (May 1988): 53–56.

———. "The Temple of the Lord." *Ensign* 23 (May 1993): 4–5.

Mulvay, Jill C. "Eliza R. Snow and The Woman Question," *BYU Studies* Vol. 16, Issue 2 (1976): 250–264.

Nebenzahl, Kenneth. *Maps of the Holy Land. Images of Terra Sancta through Two Millennia*. New York: Abbeville Press, 1986.

Nelson, Russell M. "The Atonement." 26 *Ensign* (November 1996): 33–36.

———. "Becoming Exemplary Latter-day Saints." *Ensign* 48 (November 2018): 113–114.

———. "'Come, Follow Me.'" *Ensign* 49 (May 2019): 88–91.

———. "Personal Preparation for Temple Blessings." *Ensign* 31 (May 2001): 32–35.

———. "Prepare for Blessings of the Temple." *Ensign* 32 (March 2002): 16–23.

———. "Spiritual Treasures." *Ensign* 49 (May 2019): 76–79.

———. *Teachings of Russell M. Nelson*. Salt Lake City: Deseret Book, 2018.

Nelson, Russell M. and Wendy W. Nelson. "Hope of Israel." Worldwide Youth Devotional (June 2018).

Neuenschwander, Dennis B. "Ordinances and Covenants." *Ensign* 31 (August 2001): 20–26.

Nibley, Hugh W. "Abraham's Temple Drama," in *The Temple in Time and Eternity*. Edited by Donald W. Parry and Stephen D. Ricks, 1–42. Provo: Foundation for Ancient Research and Mormon Studies, 1999.

———. *Eloquent Witness: Nibley on Himself, Others, and the Temple*. Edited by Stephen D. Ricks. Collected Works of Hugh Nibley Vol. 17. Salt Lake City: Deseret Book, 2008.

———. "A House of Glory." In *Temples of the Ancient World: Ritual and Symbolism*. Edited by Donald W. Parry, 29–47. Salt Lake City: Deseret Book, 1994.

———. "Looking Backward." In *The Temple in Antiquity: Ancient Records and Modern Perspectives*. Edited by Truman G. Madsen, 39–51. Provo: BYU Religious Studies Center, 1984.

———. "On the Sacred and the Symbolic." In *Temples of the Ancient World: Ritual and Symbolism*. Edited by Donald W. Parry, 535–621. Salt Lake City: Deseret Book, 1994.

———. "Meanings and Functions of Temples." In *Encyclopedia of Mormonism*. Edited by Daniel H. Ludlow, 4:1458–63. 5 vols. New York: Macmillan, 1992.

———. *Mormonism and Early Christianity*. Edited by Todd M. Compton and Stephen D. Ricks. Collected Works of Hugh Nibley 4. Salt Lake City: Deseret Book, 1987.

———. *Temple and Cosmos: Beyond This Ignorant Present*. Edited by Don E. Norton. Collected Works of Hugh Nibley 12. Salt Lake City: Deseret Book, 1992.

———. "Temples Everywhere," presentation given at the Temples through the Ages conference held at Brigham Young University, December 4, 1999.

Oaks, Dallin H. "Healing the Sick." *Ensign* 40 (May 2010): 47–50.

———. "The Keys and Authority of the Priesthood," *Ensign* 44 (May 2014): 49–52.

———. "Taking upon Us the Name of Jesus Christ." *Ensign* 15 (May 1985): 80–83.

Olsen, Nolan P. *Logan Temple: The First 100 Years*. Logan, UT: Olsen, 1978.

Oman, Richard G. "Exterior Symbolism of the Salt Lake Temple: Reflecting the Faith That Called the Place into Being." *BYU Studies* 36 (1996–97): 6–68.

———. "Sculpting an LDS Tradition." *Ensign* 20 (October 1990): 38–43.

Oscarson, Bonnie L. "Rise Up in Strength, Sisters in Zion." *Ensign* 46 (November 2016): 12–15.

Packer, Boyd K. "The Aaronic Priesthood." *Ensign* 11 (November 1981): 30–33.

———. "Temples Received with Thanks." *Church News* (January 26, 1986): 3, 6.

———. "Come to the Temple." *Ensign* 37 (October 2007): 18–22.

———. *The Holy Temple*. Salt Lake City: Bookcraft, 1980.

———. "The Redemption of the Dead." *Ensign* 5 (November 1975): 97–99.

Parry, Donald W. "Ancient Sacred Vestments: Scriptural Symbols and Meanings." In *Temple Insights: Proceedings of the Matthew B. Brown Memorial Symposium, "The Temple on Mount Zion," 22 September 2012*. Edited by William J. Hamblin and David R. Seely, 219–239. Salt Lake City: Eborn Books, 2014.

———. "The Cherubim, the Flaming Sword, the Path, and the Tree of Life." In

The Tree of Life: From Eden to Eternity, 1–24. Salt Lake City: Deseret Book; Provo, UT: Neal A. Maxwell Institute, 2011.

———. "Eve's Role as a 'Help' ('Ezer) Revisited," forthcoming.

———. "Garden of Eden: Prototype Sanctuary." In *Temples of the Ancient World: Ritual and Symbolism*. Edited by Donald W. Parry, 126–151. Salt Lake City: Deseret Book, 1994.

———. "The Meaning of the Temple." In *Temples of the Ancient World: Ritual and Symbolism*. Edited by Donald W. Parry, xi–xxiv. Salt Lake City: Deseret Book, 1994.

———. "Sinai as Sanctuary and Mountain of God." In *By Study and Also By Faith: Essays in Honor of Hugh W. Nibley on the Occasion of his Eightieth Birthday*. Edited by John M. Lundquist and Stephen D. Ricks, 1: 482–500. 2 vols. Salt Lake City: Deseret Book, 1990.

———., ed. *Temples of the Ancient World: Ritual and Symbolism*. Salt Lake City: Deseret Book, 1994.

———. "Who Shall Ascend into the Mountain of the Lord? Three Biblical Temple Entrance Hymns." In *Reason, Revelation, and Faith: Essays in Honor of Truman G. Madsen*. Edited with Daniel C. Peterson and Stephen D. Ricks, 729–742. Provo: Foundation for Ancient Research and Mormon Studies, 2002.

Parry, Donald W. and Jay A. Parry. *Symbols and Shadows: Unlocking A Deeper Understanding of the Atonement*. Salt Lake City: Deseret Book, 2009.

Parry, Donald W., and Stephen D. Ricks. *The Temple: Ancient and Restored: Proceedings of the Interpreter Matthew B. Brown Memorial Conference—Temple on Mount Zion. 25 October 2014*. Orem, UT: The Interpreter Foundation/Salt Lake City: Eborn Books, 2016.

Parry, Donald W. and Stephen D. Ricks, eds. *The Temple in Time and Eternity*. Provo, UT: Foundation for Ancient Research and Mormon Studies, 1999.

Parry, Jay A., and Donald W. Parry. "The Temple in Heaven: Its Description and Significance." In *Temples of the Ancient World*. Edited by Donald W. Parry, 515–32. Salt Lake City, UT: Deseret Book, 1994.

Parry, Donald W. and Jay A. Parry and Tina M. Peterson. *Understanding Isaiah.* Salt Lake City: Deseret Book, 1998.

Parry, Jay A. and Donald W. Parry. *Understanding the Book of Revelation.* Salt Lake City: Deseret Book, 1998.

Patai, Raphael. *The Hebrew Goddess.* Detroit: Wayne State University Press, 1990.

———. *Man and Temple in Ancient Jewish Myth and Ritual.* London: Thomas Nelson and Sons, 1947.

Pike, Dana M. "Seals and Sealing Among Ancient and Latter-day Israelites." In *Thy People Shall Be My People and Thy God My God.* Edited by Paul Y. Hoskisson, 101–17. Salt Lake City: Deseret Book, 1994.

Porter, Bruce H. and Stephen D. Ricks, "Names in Antiquity: Old, New, and Hidden." In *By Study and Also by Faith: Essays in Honor of Hugh W. Nibley on the Occasion of His Eightieth Birthday.* Edited by John M. Lundquist and Stephen D. Ricks, 501–22. Salt Lake City: Deseret Book, 1990.

Pratt, Parley P. *Autobiography of Parley P. Pratt.* Salt Lake City: Deseret Book, 1985.

Pratte, Paul Alfred. "Temple of Refuge in the Pacific." *Improvement Era* 72, no. 12 (December 1969): 26–27.

Rasmussen, Victor J. *The Manti Temple.* Manti: Manti Temple Centennial Committee, 1988.

Renlund, Dale G. "Our Good Shepherd." *Ensign* 47 (May 2017): 29–32.

Ricks, Stephen D. "*Dexiosis* and *Dextrarum Iunctio:* The Sacred Handclasp in the Classical and Early Christian World." *The Farms Review* 18, no. 1 (2006): 431–36.

———. "Liturgy and Cosmogony: The Ritual Use of Creation Accounts in the Ancient Near East." In *Temples of the Ancient World: Ritual and Symbolism.* Edited by Donald W. Parry, 118–25. Salt Lake City: Deseret Book, 1994.

———. "The Sacred Embrace and the Sacred Handclasp in Ancient Mediterranean Religions." In *Ancient Temple Worship: Proceedings of the Expound Symposium 14 May 2011.* Edited by Matthew B. Brown, Jeffrey M. Bradshaw, Stephen D. Ricks, and John S. Thompson, 159–69. Temple on

Mount Zion Series 1. Orem, UT: Interpreter Foundation; Salt Lake City, UT: Eborn Books, 2014.

Ricks, Stephen D., and John J. Sroka. "King, Coronation, and Temple: Enthronement Ceremonies in History." In *Temples of the Ancient World: Ritual and Symbolism.* Edited by Donald W. Parry, 236–71. Salt Lake City: Deseret Book, 1994.

Roberts, Brigham H. *A Comprehensive History of The Church of Jesus Christ of Latter-day Saints.* 6 vols., Provo, UT: Brigham Young University Press, 1965.

Romney, Marion G. "The House of the Lord." *Improvement Era* 68 (February 1965): 119–120.

———. "Temples–The Gates to Heaven." *Ensign* 1 (March 1971): 12–16.

Rooke, Deborah W. "Breeches of the Covenant: Gender, Garments and the Priesthood." In *Embroidered Garments: Priests and Gender in Biblical Israel.* Edited by Deborah W. Rooke, 19–37. Sheffield: Sheffield Phoenix Press, 2009.

Rubin, Rehav. *Image and Reality: Jerusalem through Maps and Views.* Jerusalem: Hebrew University Magnes Press, 1999.

Scott, Richard G. "Receive the Temple Blessings." *Ensign* 29 no. 5 (May 1999): 25–27.

Seely, David Rolph. "The Raised Hand of God as an Oath Gesture." In *Fortunate the Eyes that See.* Edited by Astrid B. Beck, A. H. Bartlet, P. R. Rabbe, and C. A. Franke, 411–21. Grand Rapids, MI: Eerdmans, 1995.

Skinner, Andrew C. "Seeing God in His Temple: A Significant Theme in Israel's Psalms." In *Ascending the Mountain of the Lord: Temple, Praise, and Worship in the Old Testament.* (2013 Sperry Symposium). Edited by Jeffrey R. Chadwick, Matthew J. Grey, and David Rolph Seely, 270–90. Provo, UT: Religious Studies Center, Brigham Young University; Salt Lake City: Deseret Book, 2013.

Smith, George A. "Description of the Temple." *Millennial Star* 16 (October 7, 1854): 635–36.

Smith, George Albert. *Sharing the Gospel with Others: Excerpts from the Sermons of President Smith.* Salt Lake City: Deseret News Press, 1948.

Smith, Joseph. *Encyclopedia of Joseph Smith's Teachings.* Edited by Larry E. Dahl and Donald Q. Cannon. Salt Lake City: Bookcraft, 1997.

———. *History of the Church of Jesus Christ of Latter-day Saints.* 2nd ed. Edited by B. H. Roberts. Salt Lake City: Deseret Book, 1957.

———. *Teachings of Presidents of the Church: Joseph Smith.* Salt Lake City: The Church of Jesus Christ of Latter-day Saints, 2007.

Smith, Joseph F. Conference Report (October 1913): 1–10.

Smith, Joseph Fielding. *Answers to Gospel Questions.* 5 vols. Salt Lake City: Deseret Book, 1963.

———. *Doctrines of Salvation,* compiled by Bruce R. McConkie. 3 vols. Salt Lake City: Bookcraft, 1954–66.

———. *Life of Joseph F. Smith.* Salt Lake City: Deseret News Press, 1938.

———. "Magnifying Our Callings in the Priesthood." *Improvement Era* 73, no. 6 (June 1970): 65–66.

———. "The Mission of the Kirtland Temple." *Improvement Era* 39, no. 4 (April 1936): 204–8.

———. "Privileges concerning Temple and Other Ordinances." *Improvement Era* 30 (June 1927): 736–738.

———. "Relief Society—An Aid to the Priesthood." *Relief Society Magazine* (Jan. 1959): 4–6.

Snow, Eliza R. "The Temple." *Contributor* 14 (April 1893): 254; also published in *Deseret News,* April 16, 1853.

Snow, Lorenzo. *Teachings of Presidents of The Church: Lorenzo Snow.* Salt Lake City: The Church of Jesus Christ of Latter-day Saints, 2012.

———. *The Teachings of Lorenzo Snow.* Edited by Clyde J. Williams. Salt Lake City, UT: Bookcraft, 1998.

———. "A Visit from the Savior," *Ensign* 45 (September 2015): 80.

Stuy, Brian H. ed. *Collected Discourses.* Burbank, CA: BHS Publishing, 1992.

Talmage, James E. *Articles of Faith.* Salt Lake City, Utah: Deseret Book, 1977.

———. *The House of the Lord.* Salt Lake City: Deseret Book, 1976.

———. *Jesus the Christ*. Salt Lake City: Deseret Book, 1982.

Talmon, Shemaryahu. "Synonymous Readings in the Textual Traditions of the Old Testament." *Scripta hierosolymitana* 8 (1961): 335–83.

Tanner, N. Eldon. "The Administration of the Church." *Ensign* 9 (November 1979): 42–48.

Tate, Lucile C. *Boyd K. Packer: A Watchman on the Tower*. Salt Lake City: Bookcraft, 1995.

Taylor, John. *The Gospel Kingdom: Writings and Discourses of John Taylor*. Salt Lake City: Bookcraft, 1943.

———. *The Mediation and Atonement*. Salt Lake City: Deseret News, 1882.

Terrien, Samuel. "The Omphalos Myth and Hebrew Religion." *Vetus Testamentum* 20 (1970): 315–338.

Tvedtnes, John A. "Olive Oil: Symbol of the Holy Ghost." In *The Allegory of the Olive Tree,* edited by Stephen D. Ricks and John W. Welch, 427–59. Salt Lake City: Deseret Book, 1994.

Uchtdorf, Dieter F. "Hold on a Little Longer." *Ensign* 40 (January 2010): 5–8.

Ward, William. "Who Designed the Temple?" *Deseret News* (April 23, 1892): 578–79.

Welch, John W. "The Temple in the Book of Mormon: The Temples at the Cities of Nephi, Zarahemla, and Bountiful." In *Temples of the Ancient World: Ritual and Symbolism*. Edited by Donald W. Parry, 297–387. Salt Lake City: Deseret Book, 1994.

Welch, John W. and Claire Foley, "Gammadia on Early Jewish and Christian Garments." *BYU Studies* 36, no. 3 (1996–97): 253–58.

Welch, John W. and Donald W. Parry, "Introduction." In *The Tree of Life: From Eden to Eternity*. Edited by John W. Welch and Donald W. Parry, xiii–xvi. Salt Lake City: Deseret Book; Provo, UT: Neal A. Maxwell Institute, 2011.

Wells, Junius F. "Logan Temple." *Contributor* 5 (June 1884): 354–57.

Wenham, Gordon J. "Sanctuary Symbolism in the Garden of Eden Story." In *Proceedings of the Ninth World Congress of Jewish Studies,* 19–25. Jerusalem: World Union of Jewish Studies, 1986.

Whitney, Orson F. "Latter-day Saint Ideals and Institutions." *Improvement Era* 30 (August 1927): 861.

Widtsoe, John A. *Gospel Interpretations*. Salt Lake City: Bookcraft, 1947.

———. "Looking toward the Temple." *Improvement Era* 65 (October 1962): 706–11, 765. Reprinted in *Ensign* 2 (January 1972): 56–58.

———. "Symbolism in the Temples," in *Saviors on Mount Zion*. Edited by Archibald F. Bennett, 163–68. Salt Lake City: Deseret Sunday School Union Board, 1950.

———. "Temple Worship." *Utah Genealogical and Historical Magazine* 12 (April 1921): 49–64.

———. "What Is the Need of Ordinances?" *Improvement Era* 51 no. 2 (February 1948): 97, 117.

Woodger, Mary Jane. "Recollections of David O. McKay's Educational Practices," *Religious Educator* 4, no. 2 (2003): 25–39.

Woodruff, Wilford. *The Deseret Weekly* 38 (March 23, 1889): 390.

———. *The Deseret Weekly* 53 (November 7, 1896): 642–43.

———. Journals and Papers, 1828–1898. Church History Library, Salt Lake City, UT.

Young, Brigham. *Discourses of Brigham Young,* comp. by John A. Widtsoe. Salt Lake City: Deseret Book, 1977.

———. *Teachings of Presidents of the Church: Brigham Young.* Salt Lake City; Church of Jesus Christ of Latter-day Saints, 1997.

Zohar, translated by Harry Sperling and Maurice Simon. London: The Soncino Press, 1984.

INDEX

Aaron: rod of, 57; sacred vestments put on, 255
Aaronic Priesthood, 173–75, 206, 207–8, 249, 276
Abihu, 270
Abrahamic covenant, 27–28
Adam: as archetype of all righteous men, 33; as *ancient of days*, 38; apron of, 45; creation of, 106, 107; and Eve's creation, 107–8; and fig leaves, 111–12; Fall of, 119; sacrifices offered by, 215. *See also* Garden of Eden
Alah, 58
Albuquerque New Mexico Temple, 46, 84
All-seeing eye, 111
Almond tree, 57, 169, 170
Alpha and Omega, 33
Altars, 34–36; of incense, 34–36, 128, 156, 161; horns of the two, 155–56; sacrificial, 155–56, 171; significance of, 231
Anchorage Alaska Temple, 46
Ancient of days, 38
Ancient order of things, 37–39
Ancient temples: studying, 22–25; Joseph Smith as restorer of, 163–65; remnants of, found "everywhere," 238–39; women and, 274–76. *See also* Herod, temple of; Solomon's Temple; Tabernacle of Moses
Anderson, Gary, 256
Anderson, James H., 102
Angelic weather vane, 39
Angell, Truman O., 26, 67, 102, 138, 226
Angels: communication with, 36–40; attend Salt Lake Temple cornerstone laying, 91–92; as sentinels, 124, 136–38; linen clothing worn by, 177; sacred vestments worn by, 263, 265–66. *See also* Cherubim; Moroni statue
Animal sacrifice, 40–42; rituals and ceremonies involving, 27; altars and, 34, 35–36; and sprinkling of blood, 36, 68; blemishes and, 68; of red heifer, 90, 150; and Day of Atonement, 97; flaying, 114–15; laying on of hands on, 128, 145–46; offered by Mary, 149; under law of Moses, 216–17; and washing blood from vestments, 259–60; and washing with water, 270
Anna, 147, 148–49
Anointing, 42–44, 128, 189, 271

Apostles, gaining understanding of temple through words of, 6–8
Approach, gestures of, 127–30, 260
Apron, 44–45
Architecture of temples: features, 45–53, 84, 99–100, 176, 179–82, 226, 248–49; safeguards, 53–55
Ariel, Yisrael, 113, 275
Aristeas, 255
Ark of the covenant, 56–58, 178, 269, 270
Asay, Carlos E., 122, 123
Ascension, 58–59, 228
Atonement: temple focuses on, 60; cleansing through, 90; scope of, 95–96; cities of refuge point to, 150–51; plagues and, 198–99; as typified by sacrifice, 215–16; sin and, 224–25; sacred vestments point to, 257–60; vicarious work for dead testifies of, 267, 268. *See also* Day of Atonement; Gethsemane, temple symbolism in; Mercy seat
Atonement money, 59

Ballard, M. Russell, 19–20, 114
Baptism, symbols attached to ordinance of, 3
Baptismal font, 7, 63–64, 83, 194–95, 218–19
Baptismal prayer, 62
Baptism for the dead, 62–63
Bednar, David A., 2–3, 6–7, 130, 188, 193–94
Beehives, 64
Bells of gold, 64–65
Benson, Ezra Taft, 11–12, 122, 123, 250

Benson, Sarah Dunkley, 11–12
Bethel, 123, 162
Big Dipper (Ursa Major), 65–67
Bingham, Jean B., 211
Bishops, as sentinels, 137
Blemishes: priests and high priests with, 67, 70; sacrificial animals with, 68
Blood: rituals and ceremonies involving, 27; sprinkling of, 36, 68, 128, 216; meaning of, 68–69; applied to ear, thumb, and toe, 101; and entering Holy of Holies, 154; pomegranate juice as symbolic of, 200; washing, from vestments, 259–60
Blue, 86–87
Bnh, 106–7
Boaz, 198
Bodily conditions, 70–71. *See also* Blemishes
"Born again," 63
Brass, laver of, 132, 170–71
Breastplate, 258–59
Brother of Jared, 86
Buenos Aires Argentina Temple, 46
Bünting, Heinrich, map of, 79
Burnt offering, flaying, 114–15

Candlestick, 169–70
Cannon, George Q., 14, 16
Cardinal directions, 71–73, 195
Carr, Julie, 24
Celestial bodies, 73–75
Celestial kingdom: gold in, 88; fire associated with, 112–13; temple ordinances as concerned with, 191
Celestial room, 75
Center place, temple as, 75–78

Ceremony, sacred, 213–14
Cherubim, 80–83. *See also* Angels
Childbirth, ritual uncleanliness following, 70
Children, teaching, about temple, 9–10
Christofferson, D. Todd, 267
Church leaders, gaining understanding of temple through words of, 6–8
Church of Jesus Christ of Latter-day Saints, The, fundamental principles of, 17
Circle, 83–84; squared, 227–28. *See also* Prayer circle
Circumcision, 27–28
Cities of refuge, 150–51
Clasped hands, 142–44
Cleanliness, 70–71, 90, 263–65
Clothing: white, 63, 90, 222, 231, 264; atonement for, 70; temple, 90, 260; stripped, 114; linen, 177. *See also* Sacred vestments / clothing
Clouds and Cloudstones, 84–86
Colors, 86–90
Columbus Ohio Temple, 46–47
Concepción Chile Temple, 47
Consecrate, 140
Cook, Quentin L., 90, 178–79, 211
Copenhagen Denmark Temple, 47
Cornerstones, 91–92, 176
Coronation, 167–69
Covenants, 92–94; antiquity of, 37; hands and, 138–40; connection between ordinances and, 192
Cowan, Richard, 72–73, 134, 230
Cowdery, Oliver, 85, 221
Cowley, Matthew, 214–15
Cowley, Matthias F., 105–6

Creation narrative, 94–96, 176
Crimson, 89–90
Crown, 258
Cultural understanding, 9

Dalton, Elaine S., 181
Daniel, 202
David, King, 88, 199, 233
Davies, J. G., 195
Day of Atonement, 35–36, 97–98, 156, 177
Deacons, 173–75
Dead, vicarious work for, 266–69
Dedication of temple, 98–99
Dew, Sheri, 19, 110
Directional prayer, 201–2
Directions, cardinal, 71–73, 195
Disease, 70–71, 172
Doctrine(s), focused on Jesus Christ, 16–18
Domes, 99–100
Douglas, Mary, 71
Drama, ritual, 100–101
Draper Utah Temple, 47, 99

Ear, 101
Earth: and Creation narrative, 95–96; obedience of, to laws, 96
Earthstones, 73–74, 102
East, 72–73
Edmonton Alberta Temple, 47
Eliade, Mircea, 77–78
Endowment, 102–5; and priesthood power, 19, 277; and equality in temple, 20–21; as "order pertaining to the ancient of days," 38; as ascension, 58; and Creation narrative, 94; meaning

of, 104–5; and conditions in Garden of Eden, 119; and angels as sentinels, 138; as source of light, 175; of Peter, James, an John, 184–85

Endowment House, 105–6

Enthronement, 167–69

Ephod (apron), 44–45

Equality, in temple, 20–21

Eternity, 83, 178–79, 191–92, 193; pillars of, 96

Eve: as archetype of all righteous women, 33; apron of, 45; creation of, 106–8; as help, 108–9; as life-giver, 109; as life, 109–10; as mother, 110; and fig leaves, 111–12; sacrifices offered by, 215. *See also* Garden of Eden

Exalted Saints, sacred vestments worn by, 266

Eye, all-seeing, 111

Ezekiel, Temple of, 233

'Ezer, 108–9

Faith, in ordinances, 191

Fall of Adam, 119

Far West Temple, 234–35

Faust, James E., 21

Featherstone, Vaughn J., 137

Fedorovna, Empress Alexandra, 168–69

Female animals, as sacrifices, 40–42

Festivals, Israelite, 246–47

Fetzer, Emil B., 48

Fetzer, John Sr., 47

Fig leaves, 111–12

Fire, 112–13; pillar of, 175–76; devouring, 209

Firstborn son, 113, 173; redemption money for, 59

Firstfruits, 113–14

Flaying the burnt offering, 114–15

"Flight of steps," 162

Flowers, 115–17

Font, baptismal, 7, 63–64, 83, 194–95, 218–19

Fort Lauderdale Florida Temple, 47

Fortress, temple as, 117–18

Foundation, temple, 118

Future temples, 239–40

Gabriel, 161

Garden of Eden: cherubim in, 81; temple symbolism in, 118–20; sacred clothing in, 254. *See also* Adam; Eve

Gardner, Barbara, 19

Garments, 121–23

Gate, the tabernacle, 124–25

Gatekeepers, 124, 136–38

Gate of heaven, 123

Gathering of Israel, 125–26, 240

Geometry, sacred, 126–27

Gestures of approach, 127–30, 260

Gethsemane, temple symbolism in, 130–32

Girdle, 262–63, 265

Glory, sacred vestments associated with, 262

God: knowledge and comprehension of, 8; ascension to, 58–59; heavenly bodies point to, 74–75; and symbolism of clouds, 84–86; as source of endowment, 103; eyes of, 111; fire and glory of, 112–13; as fortress, 117–18; as Geometer, 126–27; light of presence of, 175; knowing, through ordinances, 192; ordinances and our relationship with, 193; seeing, in temple, 220–21; presence of, 224–25; temples built by, 237; throne of, 247–48; as "high tower," 249; sacred vestments worn by, 265

Gold, 87–88

Golden altar, incense at, 161

Golden lampstand, 169–70

Gong, Gerrit W., 178

Gradations of holiness, 131–36

Guards, temple, 124, 136–38

Hair, shaving and burning, 27, 274

Hand(s): filling of priest's, 128, 140–41; laying on of, 128, 139, 144–46, 216; prayer with uplifted, 128, 146–47; and covenants, 138–40; right, 139–40; raised in oath, 141–42; clasped, 142–44; ordinances and gestures of, 191

Hannah, 147–48

Haran, Menahem, 44, 240, 241

Hartford Connecticut Temple, 47

Healing, through laying on of hands, 139

Heaven: temple in, 83, 124–25, 138, 209–10, 235–36, 248; gate of, 123

Heifer, red, 90, 150

Help, Eve as, 108–9

Herod, temple of: gradations of holiness in, 133–34; rending of veil in, 252–53

Hidden manna, 222

High priest(s), 206–7; with blemishes, 67, 70; undergarments of, 121–22; cities of refuge and death of, 151; crown of, 152; and burning of incense at golden altar, 161; linen clothing worn by, 177; and tabernacle veil, 251; vestments of, 254, 255, 258–59, 262

Hill, holy, 209

Hinckley, Gordon B.: on celestial room, 75; on Jesus Christ as cornerstone, 91; on covenants, 94; on dedication of Salt Lake Temple, 98; on temple garment, 122; on Hosanna Shout, 157; on Moroni, 180–81, 182; on temple ordinances, 190; on temple as place of refuge, 211; on temple as place of revelation, 213; on proper behavior in temple, 224; on North Star, 229–30; on vicarious work for dead, 268; on washings and anointings, 271

Holiness, gradations of, 131–36

Holiness to the Lord, 152

Holland, Jeffrey R., 7, 17, 171–72, 200, 206–7

Holy Ghost: gaining understanding of temple through, 6; understanding spiritual things through, 28–29; olive oil as symbol of, 44, 189

Holy of Holies, 84, 86–87, 152–54, 251–52

Holy Spirit of Promise, sealing by, 220

Holzapfel, Richard, 73–74

Hong Kong China Temple, 47

Hophni, 269–70

Horn of oil, 189–90

Horn of Salvation, 44

Horns of the two altars, 155–56

Hosanna Shout, 157–58

House, atonement for, 70–71

House of Life, temple as, 158

House of prayer, temple as, 158–59

House of the Lord, temple as, 160

Hunter, Howard W., 14

Hyssop, 160–61

Idaho Falls Idaho Temple, 47

Immersion, 62

Immortality, putting on, 256–57

Incense: altar of, 34–36, 156; offering of, 128; and filling of priest's hand, 141; at golden altar, 161

Independence, Missouri, 77

Israel: gathering of, 125–26, 240; twelve oxen and tribes of, 195; protected from plagues, 198–99

Israelite festivals, 246–47

Israelite temples: gradations of holiness in, 132–34; gatekeepers of, 136–37; pathway of progression in, 195; and temple in heaven, 235–36; sacred vestments in, 256

Jachin, 198

Jacob, 123

Jacob's ladder, 162

Jerusalem, centrality of, 76, 78–80

Jesus Christ: temples testify of, 4; symbols in teachings of, 5; recognition of, 8; doctrines focused on, 16–18; presence of, in temple, 26, 221; as Alpha and Omega, 33; sacrifices point to, 34, 41–42, 114–15, 150; anointed priests as types and shadows of, 43–44; anointing of, 44; rod of Aaron points to, 57; manna as type and shadow of, 57–58; temple focuses on Atonement of, 60; baptism as centered on, 62–63; and meaning of blood, 68–69; stands on platform of gold, 88; as cornerstone, 91; and Creation, 94; endowment received by, 104; firstborn males as symbols of, 113; as firstfruits, 114; and gate of tabernacle, 124; laying on of hands on sacrificial animals points to, 145–46; cities of refuge point to, 150–51; as focal point of garden temples, 158; as focus of temple, 162; symbols of, in tabernacle of Moses, 162–63; symbolized in menorah, 170; music and praising, 187; temples built unto name of, 187–88; new name of, 188; ordinances done in name of, 190; correspondences between Passover and death of, 196–97; as high priest, 206; priests as type of, 207; seeing, in temple, 220–21; stars as symbols of, 229; sunstones as reminders of, 230–31; tabernacle as symbol of, 232–33; throne of, 248; rending of temple veil as symbol of, 252–53; sacred vestments point to, 257–60; putting on holiness and, 260–61; vicarious work for dead testifies of, 267; temple as manifestation of love and mercy of, 268; water points to, 273

Johnson, Rick, 23–25

Kansas City Missouri Temple, 47

Kapporet, 178

Keys, 166–67, 185

Kikawada, Isaac, 110

Kimball, Heber C., 104, 185, 193

Kimball, J. Golden, 4, 98

Kimball, Spencer W., 114, 122, 200, 205

Kingdoms, many, 222

Kings / Kingship, 167–69, 200, 205

Kirtland Temple: dedicatory prayer for, 5–6, 146, 157, 159; angelic

INDEX | 301

communication in, 40; clouds and, 85; dedication of, 98; pillar of fire at, 112–13; Holy of Holies of, 155; pulpits in, 207–8; revelation in, 212; Lord appears in, 221; solemn assembly at, 225; revelation of design of, 233–34
Kotter, Jason, 22–23

Laie Hawaii Temple, 47–48, 211
Lampstand, golden, 169–70
Las Vegas Nevada Temple, 48, 230
Laver of brass, 132, 170–71
Law of Moses, 171–72; testifies of Jesus Christ, 18; temple garment and, 121; Mary's compliance with, 149; and cities of refuge, 150–51; rituals under, 213; sacrifices under, 215–17; sins under, 224; temple attendance under, 247; fulfillment of, 253; women's temple attendance under, 274–76
Laying on of hands, 128, 139, 144–46, 216
Lbsh, 260–61
Learning: through temple symbols, 1, 3–4, 5; through temple worship, 4, 92–93; through ritual drama, 101
Lee, Harold B., 25–26
Lepers / Leprosy, 70–71, 172
Levites, 173–75, 177
Liberty Jail, 207
Life, Eve as, 109–10
Light, temple as quintessential place of, 175–76
Linen, 177
Living water, 273
Logan Utah Temple, 48, 134, 249
Lubbock Texas Temple, 48

Lucifer, 270
Lundquist, John, 71–72, 100–101, 214

Macfarlane, Roger, 104
Male, firstborn, 59, 113
Manhattan New York Temple, 48
Manna, 57–58, 222
Manti Utah Temple, 48, 92, 134, 228, 249
Marriage: and clasped hands, 144; as sacred triangle, 214–15; and sealing ordinances, 219–20
Mary, 147, 149, 253
McConkie, Bruce R., 18, 96, 97–98, 132
McKay, David O., 4, 58
Melchizedek Priesthood, 167–68, 206, 207–8, 249, 276
Men, Adam as type and shadow of, 33
Menorah, 169–70
Mercy seat, 177–78
Meridian Idaho Temple, 48
Mesa Arizona Temple, 48, 126
Mexico City Mexico Temple, 48
Milgrom, Jacob, 185–86
Millennium, 152, 239–40
Mirrors, 178–79
Molten sea, 218–19
Money, atonement and redemption, 59
Monson, Thomas S., 13, 122, 257
Moonstones, 73–74, 179–80
Morning stars, 229
Moroni statue, 13, 180–82
Mother, Eve as, 110
Mountain: temple as, 182–84; revelations received on, 211–12
Mount of Transfiguration, 184–85
Mount Sinai, 85, 185–86

Mount Zion, Saviors on, 267–68
Music, 187

Nadab, 270
Nakedness, 111–12
Name(s), 187–88; new, 188, 222
Nauvoo Illinois Temple: angelic weather vane of, 39; architectural features of, 49, 84; moonstones on, 179, 230; Moroni statue on, 182; starstones on, 230; sunstones on, 230; trumpets on, 250
Nauvoo Temple, 179, 234, 250
Navel of the earth, temple as, 77–78
Nazarites, 27, 274
Nelson, Russell M.: on learning through temple symbols, 1, 5; on scripture study and understanding temples, 7, 26; on teaching children about temple, 11; on importance of temple, 13, 17; on equality in temple, 20–21; on temple ordinances, 37, 38–39, 60, 192; on white clothing, 90; on covenants, signs, and tokens, 92–93, 94; on Atonement, 96; on endowment, 102–3; on temple garment, 121; on gathering of Israel, 125; on phrase "Holiness to the Lord," 152; on temple as House of the Lord, 160; on pathway of progression, 195–96; on temple recommends, 208–9; on sealing ordinances, 220; on temple symbols, 231; on temple attendance, 247; on women and priesthood, 277
Neuenschwander, Dennis, 192
New name, 188, 222
Nibley, Hugh: on temple as house of learning, 6; on boundaries and openings, 55; on centrality of Salt Lake Temple, 77; on ritual drama, 100; on gestures of approach, 129; on filling of priest's hand, 141; on Joseph Smith and restoration of temple ordinances, 164; on prayer circle, 200–201; on remnants of ancient temples, 238
Nicholas II, Emperor, 168–69
North Star, 65–66, 67, 229–30

Oakland California Temple, 49
Oaks, Dallin H., 20, 43, 187–88
Oath, hand raised in, 141–42
Olive oil, 42–44, 128, 141, 169–70, 189–90
"One eternal round," 83
Ordinances: testify of Jesus Christ, 17; understanding, 190–93; sealing, 219–20. *See also* Temple ordinances
Ornan, 199
Orton, Roger, 137
Ovals, 193–94
Oxen, twelve, 194–95, 228

Packer, Boyd K.: on learning through temple symbols, 3–4; on importance of temple, 14; on washings and anointings, 42, 189, 271; on temple garment, 121; on Holy of Holies, 154; on temple as place of light, 175; on temple ordinances, 190; on sacrifice and sacrament, 217; on temple clothing, 260; on vicarious work for dead, 266, 268–69
Palmyra New York Temple, 49

Paris France Temple, 50–51
Partridge, Edward, 139
Passover, 196–97, 275
Pathway of progression, 195–96
Paul, 253
Peter, James, and John: clouds and, 86; endowment received by, 184–85
Philadelphia Pennsylvania Temple, 51
Philistines, 270
Phinehas, 199, 212, 269–70
Pidyon haben, 59
Pillar of fire, 112–13, 175–76
Pillars of eternity, 96
Pillars of temples, 198, 222
Pinnacles, 226
Plagues, and Atonement, 198–99
Planets, people on other, 96
Pomegranate, 199–200
Portland Oregon Temple, 211
Pratt, Orson, 233–34
Pratt, Parley P., 39, 92, 212–13
Prayer: altar as place of, 34; baptismal, 62; with uplifted hands, 128, 146–47; temple as house of, 158–59; directional (toward temple), 201–2
Prayer circle, 83–84, 200–201
Prayer roll, 202–3
Presentism, 9
Priestesses, 203–5
Priesthood: Melchizedek, 167–68, 206, 207–8, 249, 276; Aaronic, 173–75, 206, 207–8, 249, 276
Priesthood authority: women and, 20; for temple ordinances, 191
Priesthood keys, 166–67, 185, 219–20
Priesthood power, 19–20, 277
Priest(s), 206–7; with blemishes, 67, 70; undergarments of, 121–22; filling of hand of, 128, 140–41; kings versus, 205; and tabernacle veil, 251; vestments of, 254, 256, 262, 263; and women's involvement in temple worship, 276. *See also* High priest(s)
Prison-temple, 207
Procreation, 111–12
Profane items, removal of, 127
Progression, pathway of, 195–96
Prophet(s): gaining understanding of temple through words of, 6–8; testify of Jesus Christ, 17–18; Joseph Smith as, 21
Pulpits, 207–8
Purity, 90, 263–65

Queens, 167–69, 200

Rashi, 80
Rebirth, 63
Recommends, temple, 208–9
Red, 89–90
Redeemed souls, sacred vestments worn by, 266
Redemption: through Christ's blood, 69; of dead, 266–69
Redemption money, 59
Red heifer, 90, 150
Refuge: cities of, 150–51; temple as place of, 210–11
Renlund, Dale G., 71
Reproductive powers, 111–12
Resurrection, 256–57, 266
Revelation: in temple, 211–13; of temple designs, 233–35
Rexburg Idaho Temple, 51

Rib, Eve created from, 107
Ricks, Stephen, 94, 144, 168
Rigdon, Sidney, 139, 157
Righteous, to inherit earth, 96
Righteousness, sacred vestments associated with, 261
Right hand, 139–40
Ritual cleanliness and uncleanliness, 70–71
Rituals, 213–14
Robes, 263
Rod of Aaron, 57
Rome Italy Temple, 51, 193
Romney, Marion G., 123, 185
Rooke, Deborah, 121–22

Sacrament, 217
Sacred ceremonies, 213–14
Sacred geometry, 126–27
Sacred space, violating, 269–70
Sacred triangle, 214–15
Sacred vestments / clothing, 254–56; and gestures of approach, 128; and temple symbolism in Gethsemane, 131; anticipate Resurrection, 256–57; point to Jesus Christ and Atonement, 257–60; symbolism of, 260–65; worn by God, angels, and redeemed souls, 265–66
Sacrifice(s): altar of, 36; law of, 128; as symbols of Atonement, 215–16; under law of Moses, 215–17; offered by women, 274–75. *See also* Animal sacrifice
Sacrificial altar, 155–56, 171
Sacrificial meals, 217
Salt Lake Temple: testifies of Jesus Christ, 4; announcement of, 15; symbols in, 26; architectural features of, 51; Beehives in, 64; as center point, 77; cloudstones on, 86; cornerstones of, 91–92; dedication of, 98, 202; earthstones on, 102; all-seeing eye on, 111; gradations of holiness in, 134; Holy of Holies of, 154, 155; and Hosanna Shout, 157–58; moonstones on, 179–80; Moroni statue on, 182; Lord appears in, 221; pinnacles on, 226; stairs in, 228; sunstones on, 230; revelation of design of, 235; towers on, 248–49
Salvation, sacred vestments associated with, 261. *See also* Redemption
Samuel, 148
Sanctification, through anointing, 43
San Salvador El Salvador Temple, 51
Santiago Chile Temple, 51
Sapporo Japan Temple, 52
Sashes, 262–63, 265
Saviors on Mount Zion, 267–68
Scapegoat, 97, 145, 218
Scarlet, 89–90, 200
Schedel, H., 79–80
Scott, Richard C., 4
Scourging, 114–15
Scripture(s): gaining understanding of temple through studying, 7–8, 26; information regarding temples in, 25, 26
Sea, molten, 218–19
Sealing ordinance, 219–20
Seely, David, 141, 143
Sentinels, 124, 136–38
Seoul Korea Temple, 52

Seven promises "to him that overcometh," 221–22
Sha-ked, 57
Shewbread, 222–23
Shoe removal, 224
Side, Eve created from, 107
Signs, 92–94, 167
Silver, 88–89
Sin: disease as metaphor for, 71; intentional and unintentional, 224–25
Skin diseases, 70–71, 172
Sleep, deep, of Adam, 107–8
Smith, Bathsheba W., 203–4
Smith, George A., 73–74
Smith, George Albert, 64
Smith, Joseph: Kirtland Temple dedication prayer of, 6, 146, 157, 159; on importance of temple, 14; on fundamental principles of Church, 17; as prophet and seer, 21; and Ancient order of things, 38; on angelic communication in Kirtland Temple, 40; on baptism for the dead, 62; and centrality of temple, 76–77; vision of celestial kingdom given to, 88; and endowment, 103, 175; on endowment of Jesus Christ, 104; on gate of temple in heaven, 124–25; on gathering of Israel, 125; on angels as sentinels, 137; on Millennium, 152; as restorer of ancient temple, 163–65; and keys of kingdom, 166–67; connects temple with concept of kingship, 167–68; on temple ordinances, 191–92, 193; on Daniel's custom of prayer, 202; and priestesses, 203–4; imprisoned in Liberty Jail, 207; on glory in temple, 209; on sacrifices, 215; sees Lord in Kirtland Temple, 221; and design of Kirtland and Nauvoo Temples, 233–34; on temples and gathering, 240; on Lord's throne, 248; on Resurrection, 257; Joseph F. Smith's vision of, 264; on vicarious work for dead, 267–68; on Melchizedek Priesthood, 277

Smith, Joseph F., 220, 264
Smith, Joseph Fielding: on other earths, 96; on endowment of Peter, James, and John, 184; on Mount Sinai, 185; on temple ordinances, 191, 192–93; on priests and priestesses, 205; on large basin of water, 219; on vicarious work for dead, 266
Snow, Eliza R., 176, 203, 213
Snow, Lorenzo, 14, 92, 137, 157–58, 221, 264–65
Snowflake Arizona Temple, 52
Solemn assembly, 225
Solomon's Temple: cherubim in, 81; clouds and, 85; gold in, 88; dedication of, 98, 201; Holy of Holies of, 154–55; correspondences between modern temples and, 165–66; squares in, 227; revelation of design of, 233
Son, firstborn, 59, 113, 173
Spires, 226
Squared circle, 227–28
Squares, 227
Sroka, John J., 168
Stairs / Staircases, 228
Stake presidents, as sentinels, 137
Stars, 65–67, 73, 228–30
Starstones, 228–30
Steeples, 226

St. George Temple, 16
St. Louis Missouri Temple, 84, 179, 195–96
Stone, white, 188, 222
Strength, sacred vestments associated with, 262
Sun images, 230–31
Sunstones, 73–74, 230–31
Symbols, diverse, 231. *See also* Temple symbols

Tabernacle of Moses: studying, 22–25; as geographical center of Israelite tribes, 75–76; cherubim in, 81; gold in, 87–88; silver in, 88–89; red in, 89–90; and overcoming effects of Fall, 119–20; gate of, 124–25; Holy of Holies of, 154; symbols of Jesus Christ in, 162–63; correspondences between modern temples and, 165–66; menorah in, 169–70; Levites' service in, 173; mercy seat in, 177–78; Mount Sinai as archetype of, 186; pillars of, 198; squares in, 227; symbolism of, 232–33; revelation of design of, 233; sacred veils in, 250–52; violation of, 269–70
Taipei Taiwan Temple, 52
Talmage, James E.: on Holy of Holies, 84, 86–87, 155; on endowment, 94; on Garden of Eden, 118, 119; on clasped hands, 142
Tanner, N. Eldon, 34, 200
Taylor, John, 18, 205
Teachers, 173–75
Template, 77
Temple attendance, 9–11, 247

Temple ceremonies, as "foolishness" to world, 27–29
Temple clothing, 90, 260
Temple covenants, antiquity of, 37
Temple garment, 121
Temple guards, 124, 136–38
Temple in heaven, 83, 124–25, 138, 209–10, 235–36, 248
Temple of Ezekiel, 233
Temple ordinances: antiquity of, 37–39; teach of power of Atonement, 60; and divine inspiration of Joseph Smith, 163–64; and Jesus's name, 188; understanding, 190–93; sealing, 219–20
Temple recommends, 208–9
Temple(s): discussing, 2–3; learning in, 4, 92–93; understanding meaning of, 5–11, 16–18; teaching children about, 9–10; importance of, 13–16, 17; opposition to, 15; truths regarding women and, 18–21; equality in, 20–21; studying ancient, 22–25; scriptural information regarding, 25, 26, 242–46; Jesus Christ's presence in, 26; as place of divine communication, 36–40; architectural features of, 45–53, 84, 99–100, 176, 179–82, 226, 248–49; architectural safeguards of, 53–55; as center place, 75–78; as navel of the earth, 77–78; at center of map, 78–80; cornerstones of, 91–92, 176; dedication of, 98–99; as fortress, 117–18; foundation of, 118; as gate of heaven, 123; as House of Life, 158; as house of prayer, 158–59; as House of the Lord, 160; as Jesus Christ-focused,

162; Joseph Smith as restorer of ancient, 163–65; correspondences between ancient and modern, 165–66; as quintessential place of light, 175–76; as mountain, 182–84; pillars of, 198, 222; prayer toward, 201–2; as place of refuge, 210–11; revelation in, 211–13; sealing, 219–20; seeing Lord in, 220–21; proper behavior in, 224; design of, as revealed by God, 233–35; categories of, 237; future, 239–40; God's people commanded to build, 240–42; as Lord's university, 250

Temple symbols: learning through, 1, 3–4, 5; in Salt Lake Temple, 4; understanding, 5–11; significance of, 12–13; purpose of, 231

Temple texts, 25, 26, 242–46

Temple walls, 53–54

Ten Commandments, 58

Thompson, Mercy R., 175

Three times a year, 246–47

Threshold rituals, 127–30

Throne of Atonement, 177–78, 247–48

Thumb, 101

Tijuana Mexico Temple, 52

Toe, 101

Tokens, 92–94

Towers, 248–49

Tree of life, eating of, 221–22

Triangle, sacred, 214–15

Trumpets and trumpet stones, 250

Truths: taught through temple symbols, 5; regarding women and temple, 18–21

Tsela, 107

Tucson Arizona Temple, 52

Twelve, 223

Twelve oxen, 194–95, 228

Twin Falls Idaho Temple, 52, 53

Tyre, king of, 270

Understanding: leaning on our own, 8–9; superimposition of cultural, 9; teaching children proper, 11–12

University of the Lord, 250

Urim and Thummim, 45

Ursa Major (Big Dipper), 65–67

Uzzah, 269

Uzziah, King, 270

Veil of the temple, 250–53; of tabernacle, 124; entering, 128

Vessels, 253–54

Vicarious work for dead, 266–69

Violating sacred space, 269–70

Walls, 53–54

Washings: and endowment, 42, 189; and gestures of approach, 128; kingship and, 167–68; and laver of brass, 170–71; of Levites, 173; with water, 270–73

Washington D.C. Temple, 52–53, 84

Water, 63, 270–73

Weather vane, angelic, 39

Weeks, William, 234

Western Wall, 202

White, 90

White clothing, 63, 90, 222, 231, 264

White stone, 188, 222

Whitney, Orson F., 3

Wickedness, overcoming, 221–22

Widtsoe, John A.: on temple symbols, 13;

on ancient temples, 119, 238–39; on temple as House of the Lord, 160; on temple ordinances, 163–64, 191; on temples in all ages, 241

Winter Quarters Nebraska Temple, 53

Women: vital truths regarding temple and, 18–21; and priesthood power, 19–20, 277; Eve as type and shadow of, 33; as queens, 167–69, 200; as priestesses, 203–5; temples built by, 237; and ancient temple, 274–76; and modern-day temple worship, 275–77

Woodruff, Wilford, 104, 157, 235, 239–40

World, overcoming, 221–22

Yad, 139

Young, Brigham: on importance of temple, 14–15; and St. George Temple dedication, 16; and symbols in Salt Lake Temple, 26; and laying of Salt Lake Temple cornerstones, 91; on endowment, 103–4, 138; on all-seeing eye, 111; on laying on of hands, 139; on temple ordinances, 192; and design of Salt Lake Temple, 235; on future temples, 239; on Salt Lake Temple towers, 248–49

Zacharias, 161

IMAGE CREDITS

p. x: © Robert Boyd, used by permission

p. 32: Everett - Art/Shutterstock.com

p. 33: Photo courtesy of Val Brinkerhoff

p. 34: Photo courtesy of Daniel Smith

p. 35: Photo courtesy of Daniel Smith

p. 36: Photo courtesy of Daniel Smith

p. 37: Photo courtesy of Daniel Smith

p. 39: Wikimedia Commons

p. 41: Wikimedia Commons

p. 43: Photo courtesy of Daniel Smith

p. 46: Courtney K. Johnson/Shutterstock.com

p. 49: Photo courtesy of Val Brinkerhoff

p. 50: © Robert Boyd, used by permission

p. 52: © Robert Boyd, used by permission

p. 53: Photo courtesy of Val Brinkerhoff

p. 54: Photo courtesy of Daniel Smith

p. 55: Adri Johari/Shutterstock.com

p. 56: Photo courtesy of Daniel Smith

p. 57: Photo courtesy of Daniel Smith

p. 61: © By Intellectual Reserve, Inc.

p. 64: Photo courtesy of Val Brinkerhoff

p. 65: Photo courtesy of Daniel Smith

p. 66 (top and bottom): Photos courtesy of Val Brinkerhoff

p. 68: Photo courtesy of Daniel Smith

p. 69: Photo courtesy of Daniel Smith

p. 73: Photo courtesy of Val Brinkerhoff

p. 74: Photo courtesy of Val Brinkerhoff

p. 76–77: Illustrations created by Normandy Poulter

p. 79 (top): Wikimedia Commons

p. 79 (bottom): Wikimedia Commons

p. 81 (top): Photo courtesy of Daniel Smith

p. 81 (bottom): Photo courtesy of Daniel Smith

p. 82: Photo courtesy of Val Brinkerhoff

p. 85: Photo courtesy of Val Brinkerhoff

p. 86: Photo courtesy of Daniel Smith

p. 87: Image courtesy of Brian Olson

p. 88: Image courtesy of Daniel Smith

p. 89: Image courtesy of Daniel Smith

p. 95: buradaki/Shutterstock.com

p. 97: Image courtesy of Daniel Smith

p. 101: Image courtesy of Braden Olsen

p. 102: Photo courtesy of Val Brinkerhoff

p. 105: Used by permission, Utah State Historical Society

p. 111: Photo courtesy of Val Brinkerhoff

p. 116: Photo courtesy of Val Brinkerhoff

p. 117: Photo courtesy of Val Brinkerhoff

p. 119: Illustration courtesy of Michael P. Lyon

p. 124: Image courtesy of Daniel Smith

p. 125: Photo courtesy of Val Brinkerhoff

p. 126: © Robert Boyd, used by permission

p. 129: Illustration courtesy of Michael P. Lyon

310 | IMAGE CREDITS

p. 131: kavram/Shutterstock.com
p. 133: Image courtesy of Normandy Poulter
p. 143: Photo courtesy of Val Brinkerhoff
p. 144: Photo courtesy of Daniel Smith
p. 145: Image courtesy of Normandy Poulter
p. 148: Wikimedia Commons
p. 149: Wikimedia Commons
p. 150: Wikimedia Commons
p. 153: Photo courtesy of Val Brinkerhoff
p. 154: Photo courtesy of Daniel Smith
p. 156: Photo courtesy of Daniel Smith
p. 160: Photo courtesy of Val Brinkerhoff
p. 161 (top): Photo courtesy of Daniel Smith
p. 161 (bottom): Photo courtesy of Daniel Smith
p. 163: © By Intellectual Reserve, Inc.
p. 170: Photo courtesy of Daniel Smith
p. 171: Photo courtesy of Daniel Smith
p. 174: © Robert Boyd, used by permission
p. 179: Image courtesy of Michael P. Lyon
p. 180: Photo courtesy of Val Brinkerhoff
p. 181: Photo courtesy of Val Brinkerhoff
p. 183: © Robert Boyd, used by permission
p. 186: Mountains Hunter/Shutterstock.com
p. 189: Photo courtesy of Daniel Smith
p. 194: Image courtesy of Brian Olson
p. 196: Shnarf/Shutterstock.com
p. 198: Image courtesy of Brian Olson
p. 199: Photo courtesy of Daniel Smith
p. 200: Photo courtesy of Daniel Smith
p. 203: Wikimedia Commons
p. 204: Wikimedia Commons
p. 206: Photo courtesy of Daniel Smith
p. 207: Wikimedia Commons

p. 208: Photo courtesy of Val Brinkerhoff
p. 217: Photo courtesy of Daniel Smith
p. 218: Photo courtesy of Daniel Smith
p. 219: Wikimedia Commons
p. 223: Photo courtesy of Daniel Smith
p. 226 (top): Photo courtesy of Val Brinkerhoff
p. 226 (bottom): © Robert Boyd, used by permission
p. 227: Image courtesy of Normandy Poulter
p. 228: Photo courtesy of Val Brinkerhoff
p. 229 (all): Photos courtesy of Val Brinkerhoff
p. 230 (left): Photo courtesy of Val Brinkerhoff
p. 230 (middle): Photo courtesy of Val Brinkerhoff
p. 230 (right): © Robert Boyd, used by permission
p. 231: MR.WUTTISAK PROMCHOO/Getty Images
p. 232: Photo courtesy of Daniel Smith
p. 234: Everett Historical/Shutterstock.com
p. 241: © Robert Boyd, used by permission
p. 249: Photo courtesy of Val Brinkerhoff
p. 251 (all): Photos courtesy of Daniel Smith
p. 252: Wikimedia Commons
p. 254: Photo courtesy of Daniel Smith
p. 258: Photo courtesy of Daniel Smith
p. 259 (all): Photos courtesy of Daniel Smith
p. 262: Photo courtesy of Daniel Smith
p. 267: Photo courtesy of Val Brinkerhoff
p. 271: Photo courtesy of Braden Olsen
p. 272: Photo courtesy of Val Brinkerhoff